Beginning iOS Game Center and Game Kit: For iPhone, iPad, and iPod touch

Kyle Richter

Apress®

Beginning iOS Game Center and Game Kit: For iPhone, iPad, and iPod touch

ISBN-13 (pbk): 978-1-4302-3527-9

ISBN-13 (electronic): 978-1-4302-35286

President and Publisher: Paul Manning
Lead Editor: Michelle Lowman
Development Editors: Matthew Moodie and Douglas Pundick
Technical Reviewer: Marcus Zarra
Editorial Board: Steve Anglin, Mark Beckner, Ewan Buckingham, Gary Cornell, Jonathan Gennick, Jonathan Hassell, Michelle Lowman, James Markham, Matthew Moodie, Jeff Olson, Jeffrey Pepper, Frank Pohlmann, Douglas Pundick, Ben Renow-Clarke, Dominic Shakeshaft, Matt Wade, Tom Welsh
Coordinating Editor: Jennifer L. Blackwell
Copy Editor: Ralph Moore
Compositor: MacPS, LLC
Indexers: BIM Indexing & Proofreading Services
Artist: SPi Global
Cover Designer: Anna Ishchenko

Distributed to the book trade worldwide by Springer Science+Business Media, LLC., 233 Spring Street, 6th Floor, New York, NY 10013. Phone 1-800-SPRINGER, fax (201) 348-4505, e-mail orders-ny@springer-sbm.com, or visit www.springeronline.com.

For information on translations, please e-mail rights@apress.com, or visit www.apress.com.

Apress and friends of ED books may be purchased in bulk for academic, corporate, or promotional use. eBook versions and licenses are also available for most titles. For more information, reference our Special Bulk Sales–eBook Licensing web page at www.apress.com/bulk-sales.

The source code for this book is available to readers at www.apress.com.

A12005 746765

This book is dedicated to my mentor and friend Ian Baird,
without whom I never would have followed the path that led me to here.

— Kyle

Contents at a Glance

Contents

About the Author

 **Kyle Richter** started writing code in the early 90's on the Commodore 64, and soon after progressed to a Mac SE. Since then he has been dedicated to working exclusively with Apple products. In 2004 Kyle Richter founded Dragon Forged Software to release a new shareware title. Since that time Dragon Forged has grown into a much larger entity which now provides custom software and training. Dragon Forged was behind the release of the first iOS trivia game, as well as the first game to support true non-local multiplayer. He also worked on other popular iOS titles such as Handshake and Transactions. Kyle has devoted the last couple of years to managing Dragon Forged Software and writing custom software for corporations and startups. He is also a frequent speaker on software development and entrepreneurship at technology conferences and other events across the globe. Kyle is an outspoken supporter of the indie development community and spends a considerable amount of time moderating and contributing to various software development forums. In his spare time he enjoys traveling, nature, and sport shooting. He can be found on twitter @kylerichter.

About the Technical Reviewer

Marcus Zarra is the owner of Zarra Studios, where he builds Mac, iPhone, and iPad software for a wide variety of clients and customers. Outside of Apple, there are very few people with a better understanding of Core Data. He has not only written the book on Core Data—*Core Data: Apple's API for Persisting Data on Mac OS X* (Pragmatic Bookshelf, 2009)—he has also been doing iPhone, and now iPad, development as long as it has been possible to do so, and Mac programming for even longer. With Matt Long, Marcus is the co-author of the popular programming blog *Cocoa Is My Girlfriend*. Marcus is also a co-author (with Matt Long) of *Core Animation: Simplified Animation Techniques for Mac and iPhone Development* (Addison-Wesley Professional, 2009).

Acknowledgments

Writing this book would not have been possible without the support and help of many people. Looking at the acknowledgments for any technical book shows that, while there may only be one author, there are dozens of people needed to ship a technical book such as this. First, I would like to thank Jordan Langille of One Toad Design for taking time out of his busy schedule to provide the graphics for the sample program contained within.

I would also like to thank Dave Wiskus for convincing me that I should write a book in the first place; without his counseling I may of never taken the first steps necessary. In addition, I would like to thank all the people along with Dave who offered support and feedback over the course of writing. Without all of their persistence, nagging, and support, this book would have never seen the light of day.

Joe Keeley also deserves a spot of recognition. Joe took a lot off my plate with Dragon Forged Software to allow me the time required to write this book. If it had not been for Joe, I would not have been able to take myself away from my day-to-day work to be able to get even a single chapter written.

Additionally I would also like to thank Marcus Zarra, who put his life on hold more often then I care to admit in writing to offer his expertise with technically reviewing this book. Marcus, an experienced writer himself, knows how much work goes into a technical book and without hesitation offered to review my work. In addition, I would like to thank Brent Simmons for taking time out of his schedule—during a product release, no less—to write the foreword.

Last but not least I would like to thank the community in whole. Never before in my life have I met such a supportive, outstanding group of people. From Cocoaheads and NSCoders, to conferences and forums, everyone has always been of the highest caliber. It is often said of the Apple development community that two competing developers can be friends and share code and secrets amongst each other. Whenever I got stuck on a seemingly unsurmountable problem, there has always been someone there to help me through it. Throughout all my years of development and my travels across the globe, I have never met another group of people as awesome as the Apple development community, without whom I may have never shipped my first app.

Foreword: The Legend of Kyle, Game Hero

by Brent Simmons for Kyle Richter's book on writing games

You picked up the right book. You're awesome! You're awesome and you want to write games. Cool. If I wanted to learn to write games, what I'd do is park myself at Kyle Richter's house and make him teach me. But then we'd get distracted, and some friends would be in town, and we'd end up going out and I'd learn nothing. Lucky us, lucky you and me both—we have this book. Whew.

Let me tell you a bit about the author. Folks in the developer community will tell you that "Kyle Richter" is of course a pseudonym. You may recognize the name from one of Tom Clancy's novels: "Kyle Richter" is a highly trained, highly experienced covert ops agent who retired from service before turning 30 and who then made millions by creating simulations—games—out of the tangles he encountered in various undeclared theaters around the world and in low-earth orbit.

It's obvious, if you think about it—the name "Kyle Richter" is a transparent fiction. "Kyle" sounds like "Guile," and "Richter" is obviously a reference to earthquakes. A perfect name for a perfect game hero: smart, cunning, and dangerous. However, in the interest of comprehensiveness, I should point out that a small minority of people claim that "Kyle Richter" is actually an elite group of ninja Valley Girl programmers. This claim has been investigated, and not a single shred of evidence has been found. Nothing. Our top people have looked, I assure you.

"Which proves the point," some say. "If they weren't ninjas, there'd be some evidence. Ergo, they're ninjas." (I should also point out that this theory and this faulty logic come from designers, not programmers. As Kyle would say: "I know, right?")

Since I know Kyle personally, I can clear this up. Let's take the superficial qualities first: Kyle is built like Thor, but has a decided height advantage. His cherry-red hair is so radiant you can tell when he's coming around the corner. Children, squirrels, and vegetarians often mistake his face for the sun.

And then there's the laugh, that laugh, which is, well, pleasant enough, I guess.

Anyway, what's important is his mind, how he thinks, how he communicates. In a recent conversation with him, he recounted how he handles firing employees and contractors. "The second I realize things aren't working out, then it's over," he says. (Kyle drags a hand across the throat here. I recoil in horror until he assures me he's just letting them seek their bliss elsewhere.) "No point in dragging it out," he says.

What that tells me is that he has no patience for nonsense, that he's highly practical, and that he has Vulcan-like emotional control. All of which are superb characteristics in a teacher, especially for technical topics. In other words, you want to learn how to write games without having to wade through a bunch of fluff and nonsense. That's where this book comes in. (Fluff and nonsense are strictly relegated to this Foreword. The rest of the book is information-packed and well-written.)

Not that Kyle is trigger-happy to fire people. He isn't. Quite the opposite. This industry is very short on talent, and Kyle, like everybody else, works hard to find good iOS developers. There aren't enough of them—so please learn what's in this book and help us all out!

At the same time, Kyle's knowledge and the contents of this book go beyond the merely technical. Kyle knows the history of games and what makes some successful and others not.

You have questions. ("Longevity. Morphology. Incept dates.") The book has answers.

- Does your game need a leaderboard? See Chapter 3.

- How awesome is it to add a multiplayer element to your game? Find out in Chapter 5.

But the book is a technical book, and it has the goods. And the code and the explanations—even for the newest APIs. Chapter 9, for instance, talks about turn-based gaming via GameCenter. Not a ton of people are expert at this yet, much less expert enough to write about it. Kyle is, though, and it's in the book.

If, in the end, it turns out that Kyle is "just this guy, you know?"—and a good sport who's fun to tease, and not actually Thor-like—it doesn't matter, because this book is a gold mine. And I'm proud of him.

In the eternal words of George Clinton: "Nothing is good unless you play with it." By which I mean: read, learn, and play. The book is technical, but the things you make will be for play, and making those things should be like playing. Have fun!

In the immortal, sunny words of Kyle Richter (or "Kyle Richter"): "I know, right?"

Introduction

As the iOS platform begins to become more popular, developers are looking for ways to add additional polish and functionality to their software. Game Center and Game Kit provide an easy path for adding advanced functionality to your software with only a fraction of the work in the past.

Prerequisites

This book assumes that you have the basic skills and understanding required to create an iOS app. The book also assumes that you have the background necessary to work with Xcode 4.2. There will be no primer on how to define methods and variables, install and launch Xcode, or create and work with new classes. There are many excellent books on those topics. When you feel that you are ready to begin working with some of the more advanced Cocoa technologies such as Game Center and Game Kit, we assume that you have the basics mastered to a degree that allows you to move through this book without consulting other texts for help.

In addition to the basic requirements, Game Center also heavily leverages blocks, which are a fairly new programming concept to Objective-C. If you haven't yet worked with blocks, we recommend that you read Apple's guide to them, which you can find by searching for *blocks* at `http://developer.apple.com`. You should also feel comfortable working with all the features that were introduced with the Objective-C 2.0 release.

How This Book Is Organized

As you begin working through this book, you will notice that is it broken down into standalone chapters. Every effort has been made so that each chapter can be read independently of the others. If you have no experience with Game Center or Game Kit yet, it is highly recommended that you read the first two chapters before skipping around, as they will provide you with the basic information on how to get Game Center and Game Kit up and running in your development environment.

Each chapter follows along with a simple sample iOS game that is introduced in Chapter 1. Following along with the book from start to finish will walk you through the process of creating a fully functional Game Center and Game Kit–leveraged iOS game. In addition, each chapter will build onto a Game Center Manager class that is designed to be reusable across all of your projects.

If you already have a background in Game Center and Game Kit and are looking for help on a specific technology, each chapter is designed to walk you through its covered technology, as well as provide samples on how to apply the technology to your software.

Required Software, Materials, and Equipment

To develop iOS software—and more specifically, Game Center and Game Kit–based iOS software—you will first need an Intel-based Mac computer running OSX 10.6 (Snow Leopard) or newer. While you can develop on 10.5, it will not support the most up-to-date release of Xcode. You will also need a copy of Xcode, which you can download for free from the Mac App Store or at `http://developer.apple.com`. This book has been targeted to work with iOS 5; since it is being released at the time when users will be migrating from iOS 4 to iOS 5, it is also written to support iOS 4. Unless otherwise noted within the text, all code is iOS 4–compatible.

In addition to the software and hardware requirements, you will also need an iOS developer account provided by Apple. This account lets you build and test software on devices, as well as ship your finished product to the App Store. The software developer account is available for $99 USD a year and you can purchase yours at `http://developer.apple.com/iPhone`.

Getting Started with Game Kit and Game Center

Welcome to *Beginning iOS Game Kit and Game Center Development*! This book is designed to walk you through the process of adding Game Kit and Game Center functionality into your iOS apps and games. It is centered around a sample game that you will be introduced to later in this chapter. However, if you have an existing app or game that you want to add Game Kit or Game Center functionality to, you may use that project instead. This book is written as a reference and resource tool to aid you in the process of adding social functions into your iOS app. While I recommend you read it from beginning to end to gain the most knowledge of the covered technologies, it is not a requirement. Every chapter stands on its own. You can skip ahead to the chapters that are relevant to your project needs and quickly implement them into your software.

When Apple announced Game Kit on March 17, 2009, it was presented as an answer to easy networking on iOS devices, which until this point, had been challenging. Game Kit added support for Bluetooth and LAN as well as voice chat services. Shortly after, Apple announced the Game Center addition to Game Kit as part of iOS 4.0. With the newly announced SDK version, Apple brought a wealth of new features—the Game Center being the most important to the scope of this book.

Developers in the community have a tendency to think of Game Center as a whole new set of Application Programming Interfaces (APIs). This is a fallacy. Game Center is a new and integral part of Game Kit. The two complement one another and work hand in hand. You will see much evidence of this in the following pages. For the purpose of this book, we are going to address both of these technologies together as Game Kit; however, we may still refer to Game Center–specific functionality by its proper name.

> **NOTE:** Despite their names, Game Kit and Game Center are not designed for just games. Recently Apple has begun cracking down on Game Center technology being used in non-games. Some developers have received the following type of rejection email from Apple.
>
> "The intended use of Game Center is to complement game apps or game functionality within an app. However, we noticed that your app does not contain any game play or game features."
>
> These rejections seem to apply mainly towards the use of leaderboards and achievements in non-gaming apps. The argument can easily be made that adding a leaderboard or achievement system to your app adds a gameplay element. If you happen to receive this rejection you still have the option of appealing it. There haven't been any instances of rejection for using Game Kit networking in any app that I have observed.

Game Kit: An Overview

Game Kit can be broken up into three individual sections: networking, Game Center, and voice chat. Though all of these services work together to create one seamless environment, it can be helpful to look at each individually. While there might be overlap between sections, such as networking and Game Center, each section of Game Kit can be broken down into a primary category. While these sections are not differentiated in the API, it is useful to keep them separate while learning Game Kit development.

Networking

Networking in Game Kit allows you to send and receive data between peers. Game Kit networking also provides a connection protocol to connect to local clients that are found on your Wi-Fi network, or locally using Bluetooth.

Game Kit supports creating an ad-hoc Bluetooth or local wireless network between two iOS devices. With the introduction of iOS 4.0, Game Kit now supports networking on the world area network supporting up to 16 players at once. Game Kit networking is covered in Chapters 6, 7, and 8. Game Center matchmaking is covered in Chapter 5.

Game Center

Game Center itself handles authentication, friends, leaderboards, achievements, and invitations. In a sense, Game Center is providing us with the server services that are related to social interaction. It can also be argued that Game Center contains its own networking system. While this is true, we will be grouping that topic in the preceding section on networking, which is covered extensively in Chapter 5. Game Center technologies, such as leaderboards and achievements, are covered in Chapters 3 and 4.

> **NOTE:** Game Center, in various articles of print and reference documentation, sometimes refers to the collective set of Game Center APIs as well as to the Game Center.app itself.

Voice Chat

"Game Voice," as Apple refers to it, allows any app (not just games) to provide voice communication over a network connection. The APIs handle the entire recording and playback of audio feeds for the user and provide services to handle connections, communications, errors, and disconnections. This technology is discussed in Chapter 10.

Sample Game: UFOs

In my experience, most developers are "experience-type" learners. This means that they learn best by doing, not by watching or listening. When I first started to learn how to program, I would copy source code out of code magazines line by line into a Commodore 64. The experience of physically typing in each line of code is what made the information stick. Listening to a lecture or watching someone else write code prevented me from retaining a good deal of the information. I can't imagine I would have stayed with this career path if lectures and demonstrations were my only ways of learning. This book is designed in the spirit of experience-type learners.

The first thing we cover, before moving into Game Kit itself, is working with the supplied sample game. The game, which we call "UFOs," is designed not to be an award-winning, addictive game, but rather to be simple enough that it can be thought of as any generic project. I have made every effort to reduce the amount of code to less than 300 lines. Although the game itself is simple, I feel that it is vital that every reader understands the code as if they wrote it themselves. This will allow you, as the reader, to detach yourself from the project itself and focus on the Game Kit–specific information. We start by playing the game, then looking at the source code.

> **NOTE:** The source code for all the chapters, as well as the sample project, is available at (www.apress.com).

UFOs: Understanding the Game

The first thing you need to do is open the base project that you downloaded from apress.com. Figure 1–1 shows the file structure for the project. We'll quickly run the game to see what it's like.

Name		Date Modified
▶ 📁 Art Assets		Today, 2:57 PM
▶ 📁 build		Today, 2:57 PM
▶ 📁 Classes		Today, 2:56 PM
🅜 main.m		Today, 2:56 PM
🛠 MainWindow		Today, 2:58 PM
🅗 UFOs_Prefix.pch		Today, 2:56 PM
🗒 UFOs-Info.plist		Today, 2:59 PM
🛠 UFOs.xcodeproj		Today, 2:59 PM

Figure 1–1. *The file structure for the UFO sample project, as seen by the Finder*

To play the game, select Build and Run from Build Menu Bar. The game will launch to a generic screen with one button labeled "Play." Go ahead and select the Play button. You will be taken to the game screen, as seen in Figure 1–2.

The objective of the game is typical; tilt the device up/down or left/right to move your ship around the screen. Once you are positioned over a cow, tap anywhere on the screen and hold until the cow has been abducted. You are awarded one point for every cow you abduct. There is no ending to the game. Every time you abduct a cow, a new one will be spawned.

Figure 1–2. *A look at the gameplay view from the UFOs sample project*

Now that you understand how the gameplay fits together, you can take a look at the source code that makes everything happen.

UFOs: Examining the Source Code

In your group tree, you will see the three class files we will be working with,
UFOAppDelegate, UFOViewController, and UFOGameViewController. These files all have an
associated header (.h file) and implementation file (.m file). The group tree is shown in
Figure 1–3.

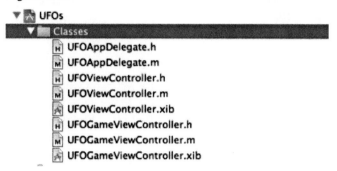

Figure 1–3. *A look at the group tree structure for the sample project from within Xcode*

First, take a look at the UFOAppDelegate.h and UFOAppDelegate.m files. These files should
look familiar to you from other iOS development work. They are nothing more than a
base UINavgiationController subclass. If you need to familiarize yourself with the code
found here, take a look at Apple's Sample Code for new projects.

The next group of files is also relatively simple; take a look at UFOViewController.h and
UFOViewController.m. These are the associated classes for the landing or home screen.
All that we have here right now is a play button, but we will be adding leaderboards,
achievement, and multiplayer controls to this view as we progress through this book.

Finally, we will be working with UFOGameViewController.m. This is the main class that will be
powering all gameplay, and where the majority of the Game Kit functionality will be added.

Setting Up the Accelerometer Delegate

We will start at the top of the source file you downloaded and work our way through it;
open the UFOAppDelegate file in Xcode. We have modified the init method of the App
Delegate to register for accelerometer feedback. Take a look at the following code
snippet, which is discussed in detail next.

```
- init
{
    if (self != [super init])
        return nil;

    [[UIAccelerometer sharedAccelerometer] setUpdateInterval:0.05];
    [[UIAccelerometer sharedAccelerometer] setDelegate:self];


    return self;
}
```

The first thing we need to do is override the `init` method and start listening for `UIAccelerometer` input. This will later allow us to listen for a delegate callback for accelerometer input. To do this, we call the `sharedAccelerometer` singleton and set an update frequency of 1/20 of a second. Then, we set the delegate to ourselves (an instance of `UFOGameViewController.m`).

Next, take a look at the `viewDidLoad` method. Let's break this down into sections to understand exactly what is going on here.

```
accelerometerDamp = 0.3f;
accelerometerOAngle = 0.6f;
movementSpeed = 15;
```

Here we set some class variables to hold onto some data that we will need when we begin to process the accelerometer input. We will be working with these variables again when we start to deal with ship movement. For now, you don't need to understand exactly what they are doing, just that they have been set.

Drawing the Player to the View

Next we need to create our "player."

```
CGRect playerFrame = CGRectMake(100, 70, 80, 34);
myPlayerImageView = [[UIImageView alloc] initWithFrame: playerFrame];
myPlayerImageView.animationDuration = 0.75;
myPlayerImageView.animationRepeatCount = 99999;
NSArray *imageArray = [NSArray arrayWithObjects: [UIImage imageNamed: @"Saucer1.png"],↵
  [UIImage imageNamed: @"Saucer2.png"], nil];
myPlayerImageView.animationImages = imageArray;
[myPlayerImageView startAnimating];
[self.view addSubview: myPlayerImageView];
```

To do this, we create a new `UIImageView` and initialize it with a predefined frame. The next four lines of code are a little-known, but very useful, part of `UIImageView`. We are setting an array of images that the `UIImageView` will cycle through. In this example, we are setting two images to be rotated through. We also specify how long we want the full animation to take (3/4 of a second for our purposes), and the number of times we want the animation to repeat. Once we have set up the animation details, we call `startAnimating` on the `UIImageView`. Then, all that is left for us to do is add the `UIImageView` to the main view. Now we have a player on the screen that is animating!

Setting Up Cows, Beams, and Scores

We have some objects to initialize and need to set up our score label.

```
cowArray = [[NSMutableArray alloc] init];
tractorBeamImageView = [[UIImageView alloc] initWithFrame: CGRectZero];
score = 0;
scoreLabel.text = [NSString stringWithFormat: @"SCORE %05.0f", score];
```

The score label itself has already been placed on the view using interface builder.

```
for(int x = 0; x < 5; x++)
{
        [self spawnCow];
}

[self updateCowPaths];
```

The last thing we need to do in our `viewDidLoad` method is create some cows for placement on the screen. I have created a helper method to spawn these cows. Every time it is called, it will create a new cow and place it on the screen. We will take a look at this a little later in this section. We also call another helper method to update the walking path for the cows. We will look at this method in more detail later.

Handling Rotation Events

The next method that appears in our code is the `shouldAutorotateToInterfaceOrientation` method.

```
(BOOL)shouldAutorotateToInterfaceOrientation:(UIInterfaceOrientation)↵
interfaceOrientation
{
        if(UIInterfaceOrientationIsLandscape(interfaceOrientation))
                return YES;

        return NO;
}
```

While it may appear to be a minor piece of code, it is important to make sure the game doesn't allow the user to rotate into portrait mode.

Adding Player Movements

That takes care of all our initialization and setup code. Now we can move into the more exciting parts of the game. First we look at user input and actions, and then the gameplay functionality.

```
- (void)accelerometer:(UIAccelerometer *)accelerometer didAccelerate:(UIAcceleration↵
  *)acceleration
{

        accel[0] = acceleration.x * accelerometerDamp + accel[0] * (1.0 -↵
accelerometerDamp);
        accel[1] = acceleration.y * accelerometerDamp + accel[1] * (1.0 -↵
accelerometerDamp);
        accel[2] = acceleration.z * accelerometerDamp + accel[2] * (1.0 -↵
accelerometerDamp);

        if(!tractorBeamOn)
                [self movePlayer:accel[0] :accel[1]];
}
```

The first method to look at is the accelerometer delegate method. We are taking the values of the accelerometer and applying a dampener to them to give a more realistic feel. We then perform a test to make sure that the tractor beam is off (we don't want to be able to move if it is on), and then pass the values to our movePlayer method, which is shown next.

```
-(void) movePlayer:(float)vertical :(float)horizontal;
{
        vertical += accelerometer0Angle;

        if(vertical > .50)
                vertical = .50;
        else if (vertical < -.50)
                vertical = -.50;

        if(horizontal > .50)
                horizontal = .50;
        else if (horizontal < -.50)
                horizontal = -.50;

        CGRect playerFrame = myPlayerImageView.frame;

        if ((vertical < 0 && playerFrame.origin.y < 120) || (vertical > 0 &&⏎
playerFrame.origin.y > 20))
                playerFrame.origin.y -= vertical*movementSpeed;

        if ((horizontal < 0 && playerFrame.origin.x < 440) || (horizontal > 0 &&⏎
playerFrame.origin.x > 0))
                playerFrame.origin.x -= horizontal*movementSpeed;


        myPlayerImageView.frame = playerFrame;
}
```

The preceding method is much more simple then first glance would imply. The first chunk of code sets our maximum speed. The next section of code ensures that the user cannot move their UFO off the screen. Once we have checked both of these safety nets, we update the player's frame and move the UFO.

Watching for Touch Events

The next aspect of the game that we need to worry about is touch events. We will be using a touch to initiate and control the tractor beam. The first step is overriding the touchesBegan event.

```
- (void)touchesBegan:(NSSet *)touches withEvent:(UIEvent *)event
{
        currentAbductee = nil;

        tractorBeamOn = YES;

tractorBeamImageView.frame = CGRectMake(myPlayerImageView.frame.origin.x+25,⏎
 myPlayerImageView.frame.origin.y+10, 28, 318);
        tractorBeamImageView.animationDuration = 0.5;
```

```
        tractorBeamImageView.animationRepeatCount = 99999;
NSArray *imageArray = [NSArray arrayWithObjects: [UIImage imageNamed:↵
 @"Tractor1.png"], [UIImage imageNamed: @"Tractor2.png"], nil];

        tractorBeamImageView.animationImages = imageArray;
        [tractorBeamImageView startAnimating];

        [self.view insertSubview:tractorBeamImageView atIndex:4];

        UIImageView *cowImageView = [self hitTest];

        if(cowImageView)
        {
                currentAbductee = cowImageView;
                [self abductCow: cowImageView];
        }

}
```

We first clear out the pointer to the current abducted cow. This value should be nil already, but it is best to be diligent. We then set a BOOL for whether the tractor beam is on to true/yes. At this point, we need to draw the tractor beam. To do this, we set the frame for our tractorBeamImageView to where the player's UFO is currently located. We will be using the same animation shortcut that was demoed earlier in this section to animate the tractor beam. We then add the tractor beam imageView to the main view; we use an insertSubview method here to make sure the tractor beam is below the cows but above the background. Then we call our hitTest method, which we will look at a little later in this chapter. If we get a result back from the hitTest, we call our abductCow method.

Before we can move on to the hitTest and abductCow methods, we must first finish handling our touch events. The only other touch event that we are concerned with at this point is the touchesEnded delegate call. When the user removes their finger from the screen, we want to remove the tractor beam from the view and let the user resume their movement.

```
- (void)touchesEnded:(NSSet *)touches withEvent:(UIEvent *)event
{
        tractorBeamOn = NO;

        [tractorBeamImageView removeFromSuperview];

        if(currentAbductee)
        {
                [UIView beginAnimations: @"dropCow" context:nil];
                [UIView setAnimationDuration: 1.0];
                [UIView setAnimationCurve:UIViewAnimationCurveEaseIn];
                [UIView setAnimationBeginsFromCurrentState: YES];

                CGRect frame = currentAbductee.frame;

                frame.origin.y = 260;
                frame.origin.x = myPlayerImageView.frame.origin.x +15;

                currentAbductee.frame = frame;
```

```
                [UIView commitAnimations];
        }

    currentAbductee = nil;
}
```

Set your state variable for the `tractorBeamOn` to NO. Then we can remove the tractor beam image from the view. The next section of code drops the cow back to the ground (if there was one midway in the air). To do this, we just begin a simple animation where we return the cow to ground level. The last thing we need to do is reset the `currentAbductee` pointer to `nil`.

Spawning and Moving Cows

We also have a convenience method to spawn a new cow. This is the method we call from `viewDidLoad` to give the player a base number of cows to try and abduct; we also call this whenever we are finished abducting a cow.

```
-(void)spawnCow;
{
UIImageView *cowImageView = [[UIImageView alloc] initWithFrame:CGRectMake↵
(arc4random()%480, 260, 64, 42)];
        cowImageView.image = [UIImage imageNamed: @"Cow1.png"];
        [self.view addSubview: cowImageView];
        [cowArray addObject: cowImageView];

        [cowImageView release];
}
```

> **TIP:** `Arc4Random()` will return a random number the same way that `rand()` or `random()` will, but will automatically seed itself if it is the first time it is being called.

We create a new `imageView` that will represent the cow. We then use an `arc4Random()` function to produce a random x position. We set the image that the cow will be using and add it to the main view. The last thing we need to do here is add the `imageView` to our `cowArray`. We will be using this for a hit test as well as updating the movement paths.

While UFOs is not designed to be an extremely challenging game, we do want to add at least some aspects of difficulty to the gameplay. The following method will cause our cows to randomly wander around the screen.

```
-(void)updateCowPaths
{
        for(int x = 0; x < [cowArray count]; x++)
        {
                UIImageView *tempCow = [cowArray objectAtIndex: x];

                if(tempCow != currentAbductee)
                {
```

```
                        continue;
                }

                [UIView beginAnimations:@"cowWalk" context:nil];
                [UIView setAnimationDuration: 3.0];
                [UIView setAnimationCurve:UIViewAnimationCurveLinear];

                float currentX = tempCow.frame.origin.x;
                float newX = currentX + arc4random()%100-50;

                if(newX > 480)
                        newX = 480;
                if(newX < 0)
                        newX = 0;

                if(tempCow != currentAbductee)
                        tempCow.frame = CGRectMake(newX, 260, 64, 42);

                [UIView commitAnimations];

                tempCow.animationDuration = 0.75;
                tempCow.animationRepeatCount = 99999;

                //flip cow
                if(newX < currentX)
{
        NSArray *flippedCowImageArray = [NSArray arrayWithObjects:↵
 [UIImage imageNamed: @"Cow1Reversed.png"], [UIImage imageNamed: @"Cow2Reversed.png"],↵
 [UIImage imageNamed: @"Cow3Reversed.png"], nil];
        tempCow.animationImages = flippedCowImageArray;
}

else
{
        NSArray *cowImageArray = [NSArray arrayWithObjects: [UIImage imageNamed:↵
 @"Cow1.png"], [UIImage imageNamed: @"Cow2.png"], [UIImage imageNamed: @"Cow3.png"],↵
 nil];
        tempCow.animationImages = cowImageArray;
}

                [tempCow startAnimating];
                }
        }

        //change the paths for the cows every 3 seconds
        [self performSelector:@selector(updateCowPaths) withObject:nil afterDelay:3.0];
}
```

We will need to cycle through our array of cow objects. We do this on the first line of the preceding method. We then randomize a new x position for the cow. A quick check ensures we are not instructing the cow to walk off the screen. Then we commit the animation. We also need to handle the direction change for the cow.

> **NOTE:** The code that we use to handle that event is not the most efficient manner of flipping an image, but it is the easiest to learn if you are new to this type of game.

As we had previously done with the tractor beam and the UFO images, we will add some animation frames so the cow walks more realistically. The last thing we do is call `performSelector` with a delay of three seconds. This will update the cow's path every three seconds, adding a more realistic appearance of random movement.

Performing a Hit Test with a UIImage

Before we worry about how to set up the cow abduction, there are preliminary steps for abducting the cow itself. For starters, we must implement our `hitTest` method that was being called from the `touchesBegan` event that was discussed earlier in this section.

```
-(UIImageView *)hitTest
{
        if(!tractorBeamOn)
                return nil;

        for(int x = 0; x < [cowArray count]; x++)
        {
                UIImageView *tempCow = [cowArray objectAtIndex: x];
                CALayer *cowLayer= [[tempCow layer] presentationLayer];
                CGRect cowFrame = [cowLayer frame];

                if (CGRectIntersectsRect(cowFrame, tractorBeamImageView.frame))
                {
                        tempCow.frame = cowLayer.frame;
                        [tempCow.layer removeAllAnimations];
                        return tempCow;
                }
        }

        return nil;
}
```

The first line is another sanity check to ensure that we are not calling the `hitTest` method when the `tractorBeam` is not on. Once we make sure we are supposed to be checking for the hit, we iterate through our array of cow objects. Since the cows are in the middle of an animation, we cannot rely on the data from the frame, as it will show where the cow will end up and not where the cow currently is.

To determine where the cow currently is, we ask for the `presentationLayer`. Core Graphics provides a useful method for testing whether two `GCRects` intersect, and that is what we will be using here. If we hit a cow, we return the object. If we get to the end of our loop without passing a hit test, we return `nil`.

> **TIP:** presentationLayer can be called on any CALayer to provide a best guess on the
> current values of a layer that is currently in the process of being animated.

Abducting a Cow

In our touchesBegan method, we tested to see if hitTest returned a cow. If it did, we call
abductCow with the object that was returned.

```
-(void)abductCow:(UIImageView *)cowImageView;
{
        [UIView beginAnimations: @"abduct" context:nil];
        [UIView setAnimationDuration: 4.0];
        [UIView setAnimationCurve:UIViewAnimationCurveEaseIn];
        [UIView setAnimationDelegate: self];
        [UIView setAnimationDidStopSelector: @selector(finishAbducting)];
        [UIView setAnimationBeginsFromCurrentState: YES];

        CGRect frame = cowImageView.frame;
        frame.origin.y = myPlayerImageView.frame.origin.y;
        cowImageView.frame = frame;

        [UIView commitAnimations];
}
```

We begin an animation event on our cow object (which is an imageView). We also set a
didStopSelector, which will be called once the animation has finished. We set the new y
axis coordinate for the cow to our UFO's current y coordinate and begin the animation.

Once the animation has stopped, we get a callback to finishAbducting. This allows us
to increase the score, clean up the abducting code, and spawn a new cow.

```
-(void)finishAbducting;
{
        if(!currentAbductee || !tractorBeamOn)
        {
                return;
        }

        [cowArray removeObjectIdenticalTo: currentAbductee];
        [tractorBeamImageView removeFromSuperview];

        tractorBeamOn = NO;

        score++;
        scoreLabel.text = [NSString stringWithFormat: @"SCORE %05.0f", score];

        [currentAbductee.layer removeAllAnimations];
        [currentAbductee removeFromSuperview];

        currentAbductee = nil;

        //make a new cow
        [self spawnCow];
}
```

At the beginning of the method, we check to see that the tractor beam is still on and that we have an abductee. Just as we did when the user released their touch from the screen, we also want to remove the tractor beam image from the view and correctly set the state variables. We award the user with a single point for abducting each cow and we update the scoreLabel accordingly. We clean up the old cow image and set it back to nil. Now we spawn a new cow to replace the abducted one.

Configuring iTunes Connect for Game Center

Before your iOS app or game can access any of the Game Center functionality, it will need to be configured in iTunes Connect. iTunes Connect predates the App Store and iPhone; it was introduced as the portal for musicians and media producers to upload their content to the iTunes Music Store. It has since been adapted to allow developers to upload their iOS software for sale on the App Store. iTunes Connect has evolved tremendously since being offered to iPhone developers in July of 2008. Apple has begun using it as a main source for app configuration. Such functionality as In App Purchase (IAP), iAds, and Game Center require iTunes Connect configuration.

> **NOTE:** You can still use any stand-alone Game Kit functionality without setting up Game Center for your app. See Chapters 6, 7, 8, and 10 for more information on Game Kit's stand-alone functionality.

Getting Started with iTunes Connect

If you have never uploaded an app to the App Store, you might be unfamiliar with the iTunes Connect Portal. However, if you have worked with iTunes Connect previously, you might want to skip to the next section, as this will be refresher for you.

iTunes Connect is a web portal, accessed from any web browser at http://itunesconnect.apple.com. You will use your existing AppleID, which you registered as a developer under, to gain access to the portal. This is the same web application that you will use when you want to upload new apps for sale on the App Store, as well as make any changes to them, such as price or description. A view of the landing page for iTunes Connect can be seen in Figure 1–4.

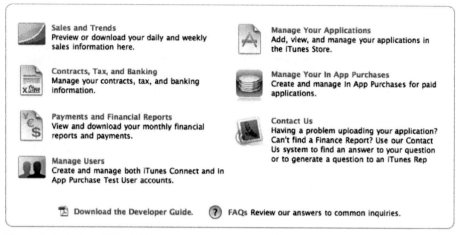

Figure 1–4. *A view of iTunes Connect taken December 2010*

When you log in to iTunes Connect, you will be presented with a wealth of options. The most important of these is setting up your contracts, tax, and banking information. While these requirements do not have anything to do with Game Center per se, it is good to get them out of the way.

It may take weeks for Apple to process this information, so submit it as soon as possible. Until this information is processed and approved, you will be unable to release software on the App Store. Once you have completed all the requested information under this section, you can focus on the app development itself.

> **NOTE:** If you plan on releasing only free iOS apps, you do not need to complete the paid apps contracts. However, if you plan on releasing any paid software in the future, these should be completed as soon as possible.

Before you can access any Game Center–specific information, you will need to create a new (or use an existing) iOS app. This is a straightforward process that you will be walked through in iTunes Connect. You begin under the Manage Your Applications section; there you will find an "Add New App" button. The rest should be fairly self-explanatory.

If you are not yet ready to upload an app, you can create placeholder data here to gain access to the Game Center portal. Once your app has been created in iTunes Connect, you can begin to configure the Game Center–specific information.

> **CAUTION:** If you create an app and fail to upload a release build within 90 days, Apple will delete the app information and restrict you from creating a new app with the same name in the future. This was introduced in late 2010 as an effort to prevent people from "Domain Squatting" app names.

Configuring Game Center in iTunes Connect

Once you have selected your app from within iTunes Connect, you will see a view similar to the screen capture in Figure 1–5, shown later in this section. If you direct your attention to the area in the upper right-hand side of the app screen, you will notice a Manage Game Center button.

If you are familiar with configuring iAds or In App Purchase in previous iOS apps, this area will seem very familiar to you. The process for configuring iAds and IAP are similar to working with Game Center.

When entering the Game Center portal for your app for the first time, you will be asked if you want to enable Game Center, as shown in Figure 1–5. Once enabled, you will be given an option to add a new leaderboard or achievement. We focus on these options more in later chapters (Chapter 3 covers leaderboards, and Chapter 4 covers achievements). For now, all we need to do is ensure that Game Center is enabled for our app.

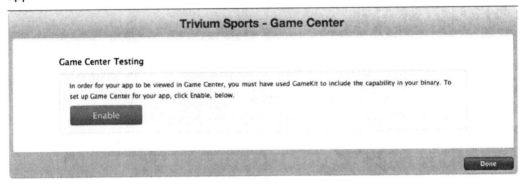

Figure 1–5. *The first view of the Game Center portal for a new App*

TIP: If you are having difficulty getting your app to acknowledge Game Center, the most likely culprit is one of two common issues. Make sure your app is using the same bundle ID that is shown in the App Info page (see Figure 1–6). The second issue may be that you have not let enough time pass. There can be up to a 30-minute delay between making changes in iTunes Connect to Game Center and having the iOS app notice those changes.

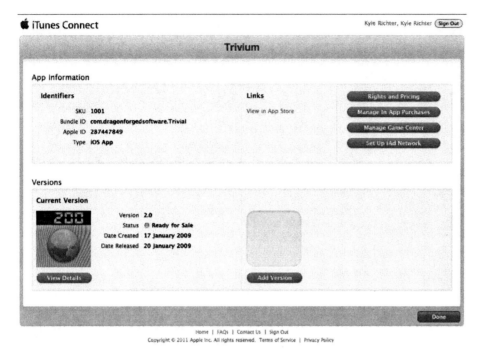

Figure 1–6. *An app-specific view, as seen in iTunes Connect. You can see the Manage Game Center button in the upper right of the image.*

Summary

You should now have a basic understanding of what Game Kit and Game Center have to offer, as well as an in-depth understanding of the sample project you will be working with throughout the course of this book. Additionally, you should now be comfortable setting up a new app in iTunes Connect for use with Game Center.

In the upcoming chapters, you will learn how to incorporate all the functionality of Game Center and Game Kit into an iOS app. The iOS-based device families are just starting to emerge from infancy, and Game Center is the first next-generation API that has been made available for developers. These new technologies are a glimpse at what the future holds for iOS developers. In the next chapter, you will learn how to get Game Center incorporated into a project.

Chapter 2

Game Center: Setting Up and Getting Started

In the last chapter, we learned how to configure Game Center in iTunes Connect and began working with the sample project, UFOs. In this chapter, we will discuss integrating Game Center into our app, and get our hands dirty with some code.

You will learn how to detect Game Center compatibility, explore the limitations of the sandbox, authenticate a local player, work with sessions, and retrieve a friends list. You will also create the Game Center Manager class that we will be working with throughout the rest of the book.

Testing for Game Center

Before any Game Center–specific code can be called, we need to perform a test to verify that the user has a version of iOS that supports Game Center. The first thing we need to do to perform this check is to create our new GameCenterManager class. We will use this class throughout the remainder of this book to keep our Game Center functionality in one easy-to-access class. This class will house all of our Game Center–specific code and callbacks, and can be easily shared across all of your apps.

First, create a new file in Xcode. You will want to select the Objective-C Subclass from the available templates. Make sure that you also select NSObject under the "Subclass of" pull-down menu. Name the new class GameCenterManager, as shown in Figure 2–1.

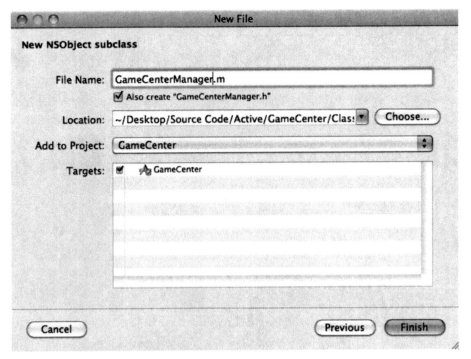

Figure 2–1. *Creating the GameCenterManager Class*

Add the following method to your GameCenterManager class.

```
+ (BOOL) isGameCenterAvailable
{
        Class gcClass = (NSClassFromString(@"GKLocalPlayer"));

        NSString *reqSysVer = @"4.1";
        NSString *currSysVer = [[UIDevice currentDevice] systemVersion];

BOOL osVersionSupported = ([currSysVer compare:reqSysVer options:NSNumericSearch] !=↵
 NSOrderedAscending);

        return (gcClass && osVersionSupported);
}
```

This method creates a new class object using the NSClassFromString function. If GKLocalPlayer exists in the API, gcClass will be non-nil. We also test against a minimum OS version. Since many of the Game Center classes were included in the API prior to availability, we need to perform two checks. The next three lines of code compare the current iOS version to a version string we set at 4.1. The method returns the results, which will be true if the device is set up to support Game Center.

> **NOTE:** You always want to make every effort available to allow users to interact with your app, regardless of whether they have a Game Center–enabled device. If a user does not have a Game Center–enabled device, you still want to make sure they are able to interact with the non-social features of your app.

> **TIP:** If you do want to limit your app to users who have Game Center–enabled devices, add a new key to your info.plist file called UIRequiredDeviceCapabilities. Then, set the value for that key to "gamekit." This will limit your app in the App Store to be purchased only by people who have Game Center–enabled devices.

You can now modify the UFOViewController.m file to perform the Game Center availability check. Create a new viewDidLoad method, as shown in this code snippet:

```
-(void)viewDidLoad
{
        [super viewDidLoad];

        if([GameCenterManager isGameCenterAvailable])
                NSLog(@"Game Center is available");

        else
                NSLog(@"Game Center not available");
}
```

> **CAUTION:** If you notice that the isGameCenterAvailable method is always returning NO even when Game Center should be available, the most likely culprit is forgetting to include the Game Kit framework in your target.

At this point, all the code will do is print whether Game Center is available to the console. We will be expanding on this code in the next section.

Authenticating with Game Center

Once your app has determined whether the device is Game Center–capable, you can authenticate the user. The user who is authenticated with Game Center will always be referred to as the local player and will be represented by the class GKLocalPlayer. Before any other Game Center functionality can be used, you must first authenticate a local player.

Apple recommends that you authenticate with Game Center as early as possible in your app. The primary reason to authenticate before the user needs to access any Game Center behavior is to ensure that the user is not waiting for the network callbacks to authenticate a user at a time when he or she wants to perform a Game Center action. Early authentication also makes sure that the user is not prompted for a login in the middle of gameplay. There are additional benefits that we will explore in upcoming chapters, such as resubmitting high scores that failed to submit earlier.

Modifying the GameCenterManager Class

Handling authentication requires additional code to the GameCenterManager class. Define a new protocol and add the following block of code above the @interface line in GameCenterManager.h. This will create a new optional delegate callback method named processGameCenterAuthentication.

```
@protocol GameCenterManagerDelegate <NSObject>
@optional
- (void)processGameCenterAuthentication:(NSError*)error;
@end
```

It is necessary to add a new method to the implementation of GameCenterManager. Create a new method that looks like the following code.

```
- (void) authenticateLocalUser
{
        if([GKLocalPlayer localPlayer].authenticated)
        {
                return;
        }

[[GKLocalPlayer localPlayer] authenticateWithCompletionHandler:^(NSError *error)
        {
[self callDelegateOnMainThread: @selector(processGameCenterAuthentication:) withArg:
 NULL error: error];
        }];
}
```

> **TIP:** Don't forget to import the <GameKit/GameKit.h> header and the associated Game Kit framework; otherwise, GKLocalPlayer will be undefined.

The preceding method will serve as a helper for authenticating with Game Center. The first line of code checks with the localPlayer singleton to see whether the user is already authenticated. If they are, the method is complete. If the user is not already authenticated, the authenticateWithCompletionHandler is called.

When authenticateWithCompletionHandler has finished executing, we call [self callDelegateOnMainThread: @selector(processGameCenterAuthentication:) withArg: NULL error: error]. In order to continue, we must implement this method.

> **NOTE:** Blocks can be slightly confusing if you have never worked with them before. Game Center relies heavily on blocks, and you will be seeing a lot of them throughout this book.
>
> The best way to approach blocks, in my experience, has been to view them as inline functions that are executed upon completion of the method that calls them. In the preceding example, after authenticateWithCompletionHandler finishes executing, it calls [self callDelegateOnMainThread: @selector(processGameCenterAuth:) withArg: NULL error: error];.
>
> It helps to have a solid background on blocks before proceeding. If you feel unsure about the use of blocks, I recommend you read the Apple Developer Connection article on blocks, located at http://developer.apple.com/library/mac/#documentation/Cocoa/ Conceptual/Blocks/Articles/bxUsing.html.

You will also need to add the following methods to GameKitManager.m. After you have added them, we will discuss what their exact functions are.

```
- (void) callDelegateOnMainThread: (SEL) selector withArg: (id) arg error:↵
 (NSError*) err
{
        dispatch_async(dispatch_get_main_queue(), ^(void)
        {
                [self callDelegate: selector withArg: arg error: err];
        });
}
```

All of our delegate callbacks need to be performed on the main thread; Game Center does not guarantee the callback blocks will be executed on the main thread, and may be run from a background thread if not forced onto the main thread. Since UIKit View Controllers can be safely accessed only on the main thread, calling a delegate on a background thread can cause crashes and other unexpected behavior. To avoid creating any threading-related bugs (which can be very hard to trace), we will pass everything back to the delegate on the main thread.

> **NOTE:** There are many different ways to force code to execute on the main thread or to otherwise ensure thread safety. For our purposes, we will use the preceding method. It will be easiest to comprehend for the reader who might not be very experienced with threading on the iOS platform.

The following method is called from within our callDelegateOnMathThread method after we ensure that we are operating on the main app thread. This method checks to make sure we are on the main thread, then calls our protocol method with the passed information.

```
- (void) callDelegate: (SEL) selector withArg: (id) arg error: (NSError*) err
{
        assert([NSThread isMainThread]);
        if([delegate respondsToSelector: selector])
        {
                if(arg != NULL)
                        [delegate performSelector: selector withObject:↵
 arg withObject: err];

                else
                        [delegate performSelector: selector withObject: err];
        }


        else
                NSLog(@"Missed Method");
}
```

If you have not implemented the delegate method, you will see an NSLog in the console for "Missed Method." This is solely here to assist in debugging, and will save you some head scratching in trying to debug the protocol methods.

The last thing that we need to do in our GameCenterManager class is to add the delegate property. Modify the relevant parts of the header file to look like the following code.

```
@interface GameCenterManager : NSObject <GameCenterManagerDelegate>
{
        id <GameCenterManagerDelegate, NSObject> delegate;
}

@property(nonatomic, retain) id <GameCenterManagerDelegate, NSObject> delegate;
```

In addition to these modifications, you also need to synthesize the delegate as well as release it in dealloc. This completes the required changes to the GameCenterManager class.

> **TIP:** If you are receiving warnings that GameCenterManager might not respond to any of the methods we have implemented, make sure that you are adding them to the interface file.

Authenticating from UFOViewController

Now that we have modified the GameCenterManager class to support authentication, we need to create a new object to represent the GameCenterManager in the UFOViewController class.

Import the header for GameCenterManager and create a new GameCenterManager object called gcManager. You also need to add the GameCenterManagerDelegate to the interface of UFOViewController.h. When you are done, UFOViewController.h should look like the following.

```
#import <UIKit/UIKit.h>
#import "GameCenterManager.h"

@interface UFOViewController : UIViewController <GameCenterManagerDelegate>
{
        GameCenterManager *gcManager;
}

-(IBAction)playButtonPressed;
@end
```

You will again be modifying the viewDidLoad method of UFOViewController. Make the necessary changes to the viewDidLoad method to match the following code snippet.

```
-(void)viewDidLoad
{
        [super viewDidLoad];

        if (![GameCenterManager isGameCenterAvailable])
return;

        gcManager = [[GameCenterManager alloc] init];
        gcManager.delegate = self;
        [gcManager authenticateLocalUser];
}
```

The first new line of code that we added initializes and allocates an instance of GameCenterManager. The next line sets self for the delegate to the UFOViewController class; this will allow us to get callbacks from the GameCenterManager.

Once we have completed these two steps, we can call our convenience method, authenticateLocalUser. Game Center handles the required login views and authentication as well as any account creation at this point. However, we do need to watch our delegate method processGameCenterAuthentication, in order to catch any errors encountered while authenticating.

> **CAUTION:** If you have cancelled a Game Center login three or more times from within an app, you will not be able to sign in from that app again until you have gone to the GameCenter.app and signed in. This is an undocumented behavior and can be a real pain to trace if you do not know what you are searching for. In addition, if you find you are unable to sign in even from Game Center.app, you can reset the simulator or restore the device to resolve these issues.

If you run the app again, you will see a console log stating "Missed Method." This is because we have not yet added the optional protocol method that is called when the authentication is completed. We need to add the following method to UFOViewController.m.

```
- (void)processGameCenterAuthentication:(NSError*)error;
{
        if (error != nil)
{
NSLog(@"An error occured during authentication: %@", [error localizedDescription]);
```

```
        }
else
{
                NSLog(@"Successfully authenticated");
}
}
```

Now when you log in, you should see "Successfully authenticated" printed to the console, as well as the image shown in Figure 2–2 (with your Game Center name instead).

> **CAUTION:** When logging in to Game Center for testing purposes, always create a new Apple ID. Never use an existing Apple ID to log in to Game Center from the Sandbox environment.

Figure 2–2. *The standard welcome back message the user will see when logging in to Game Center*

> **TIP:** If you are having trouble logging in, make sure your bundle ID in the info.plist matches a bundle ID that has Game Center enabled for it in iTunes Connect. See the Chapter 1 for more information on configuring Game Center in iTunes Connect.

The Sandbox

To help test your app before it goes live, Apple has provided a Sandbox environment for Game Center. The Sandbox functions exactly as the production version of Game Center, while keeping all activity hidden from normal users.

The Sandbox allows the developer to work on new Game Center functionality in secret, as well as not polluting the leaderboards and achievement systems with their test data. When logging in to a Sandbox environment, the login alert will state "*** Sandbox ***" at the top.

> **CAUTION:** At the time of writing, there is a bug that prevents the Sandbox message from
> showing up while in landscape orientation.

Once logged in, there is no way to determine whether you are currently logged in to the
Sandbox from within the app. However, if you open Game Center.app, you will see
whether you are in a Sandbox environment. The information in Table 2–1 will help you
determine what mode you are currently running in.

Table 2–1. *Determining the Sandbox Status on Various Types of Builds*

Type of Build	Sandbox Status
iOS Device Simulator	Sandbox Environment Only
Developer Provisioned Build	Sandbox Environment Only
Ad-Hoc Distributed Build	Sandbox Environment Only
Signed Distributed Build	Production Environment Only

Watching for Status Changes

Beginning with iOS 4.0, iOS devices gained the ability for multiple apps to run
simultaneously on a device. This can create some complex behavioral bugs when
dealing with state, especially if the user is accessing two different Game Center–enabled
apps at the same time. For example, the user may log out of Game Center, or even log
in as a different user, while your app is in the background. Therefore, it is vital that you
listen for changes to the local user through the NSNotification system.

Add the following snippet of code in viewDidLoad of UFOViewController.m, right after
the test is performed to verify whether Game Center is available.

```
[[NSNotificationCenter defaultCenter]
                    addObserver:self
                    selector:@selector(localUserAuthenticationChanged:)
                        name:GKPlayerAuthenticationDidChangeNotificationName
                    object:nil];
```

> **NOTE:** Don't forget to remove the NSNotification observers in viewDidUnload or you could
> experience crashes and other unintended behavior.

You also want to add a new method to UFOViewController. This method will be called
whenever player authentication status changes.

```
-(void)localUserAuthenticationChanged:(NSNotification *)notif;
{
        NSLog(@"Authenication Changed: %@", notif.object);
}
```

This new method will print the description for the new GKLocalPlayer when authentication changes. You will need to determine what special steps need to be taken in your app to handle local player changes.

> **TIP:** Do not forget to test user switching before shipping your app, as Apple will test it in the review stage.

Working with GKLocalPlayer

The GKLocalPlayer will always exist and be non-nil when authenticated with Game Center; this object is a representation of the user. You will never create an instance of GKLocalPlayer; this is handled through the class method localPlayer. The localPlayer singleton will be the only way that you will interact with the localPlayer.

The GKLocalPlayer has three properties associated with it: authenticated, friends, and underage. We will be dealing with the friends property in the following section. We have already worked with the authenticated Boolean in our authentication code in the previous sections.

The underage property is useful for restricting content in a Game Center–enabled app to users over the age of 17. The following code performs an underage check.

```
if ([GKLocalPlayer localPlayer].underage)
{
        NSLog(@"User is underage");
}
```

The friends property will return nil until we complete the steps required to retrieve the user's friends list. Once this has been done, the friends property will return an array of the local user's friends. This procedure is detailed in the following section.

Retrieving a Friends List

The friends list is an array of user IDs that you have assigned as friends in Game Center.app. With this data, you can do things such as create a friends list only in game voice channel, or highlight your friends' scores in the global scores list.

We will add a call to retrieve the friends list in our sample project, but won't be doing anything specific with the data in this chapter. For the time being, we will simply print it to the debugger console.

We begin by modifying our Game Center Manager class to add a new method for retrieving the local player's friends list. Add the following method to the implementation.

```
- (void)retrieveFriendsList;
{
        if ([GKLocalPlayer localPlayer].authenticated == YES)
        {
```

```
[[GKLocalPlayer localPlayer] loadFriendsWithCompletionHandler:^(NSArray *friends,↩
NSError *error)
                {
[self callDelegateOnMainThread: @selector(friendsFinishedLoading:error:) withArg:↩
 friends error: error];
                }];
        }
        else
{
            NSLog(@"You must authenicate first");
        }
}
```

This method looks a lot like the previous authenticate method that we added earlier in this chapter. After we determine that the GKLocalPlayer is valid, we can call loadFriendsWithCompletionHandler. This method returns an array of player IDs. We will see how we can use these player IDs to retrieve GKPlayer objects in the next section. We then use our thread-safe callDelegateOnMainThread method to return the data to our delegate.

Before this code will execute, we still need to modify the header file and add a new protocol method to our delegate. We modify the header file to look like the following code snippet.

```
@protocol GameCenterManagerDelegate <NSObject>
@optional
- (void)processGameCenterAuthentication:(NSError*)error;
- (void)friendsFinishedLoading:(NSArray *)friends error:(NSError *)error;
@end

@interface GameCenterManager : NSObject <GameCenterManagerDelegate>
{
        id <GameCenterManagerDelegate, NSObject> delegate;
}

@property(nonatomic, retain) id <GameCenterManagerDelegate, NSObject> delegate;

+ (BOOL)isGameCenterAvailable;
- (void)authenticateLocalUser;
- (void)callDelegateOnMainThread:(SEL)selector withArg:(id) arg error:(NSError*) err;
- (void)callDelegate:(SEL)selector withArg:(id)arg error:(NSError*) err;
- (void)retrieveFriendsList;
@end
```

The change we made in the preceding code snippet adds a new optional protocol, which will be called when the friends block is finished executing. We return an array of friend IDs as well as any errors we encounter. We also add a new method called retrieveFriendsList to the class methods.

The last thing that needs to be done before we can run the app is adding a call to retrieveFriendsList and adding the protocol method to UFOViewController.m. Since we are unable to make the call to retrieve the friends list until after we have successfully authenticated with Game Center, we can add the call to do so in the authentication callback. Modify that method to match the following snippet.

```
- (void)processGameCenterAuthentication:(NSError*)error;
{
        if (error != nil)
        {
NSLog(@"An error occured during authentication: %@", [error localizedDescription]);
}
        else
        {
                [gcManager retrieveFriendsList];
        }
}
```

We will also add the protocol method that will print the friends list to the console. Add the following method to UFOViewController.m.

```
- (void)friendsFinishedLoading:(NSArray *)friends error:(NSError *)error;
{
        if(error != nil)
        {
NSLog(@"An error occured during friends list request: %@", [error↵
 localizedDescription]);
        }
        else
        {
                NSLog(@"Friends: %@", friends);
        }
}
```

If you have any friends in your friends list, you should see output that looks similar to the following.

```
2011-02-01 12:56:32.759 UFOs[3328:207] Friends: (
    "G:1093075676"
)
```

> **NOTE:** If you have not yet added any friends to your Sandbox environment, now is a good time to do so. You can create new accounts in the Game Center.App and add them as friends to your test account. Having a populated friends list will be valuable throughout this book in debugging Game Center code.

The next section deals with working with the player data that was retrieved from your friends list.

Friend List Avatars

iOS 5.0 adds support for friends' avatars. Players are required to set their avatar in the Game Center app. If they have not set an avatar, Game Center will assign them a default avatar. To access avatars in your app, you will need to be running on iOS 5.0 or newer, and you will need to implement one new method. The following method is called on an existing GKPlayer object (see the previous section for more information on GKPlayer). There are two options for avatar image sizes: GKPhotoSizeNormal and

GKPhotoSizeSmall. As of iOS 5.0 beta 4, they are undefined sizes, so you will need to experiment with them to see which offers the image size you need.

```
[player loadPhotoForSize:GKPhotoSizeNormal withCompletionHandler: ^(UIImage *photo,↵
 NSError *error)
    {
        if(error == nil)
        {
            playerAvatarImageView.image = photo;
        }
        else
        {
NSLog(@"An error occurred loading player avatar: %@", [error localizedDescription]);
        }
    }];
```

Working with Players

At the heart of the Game Center it is a social service, and as such, it revolves around players. You need to be aware of three properties associated with a GKPlayer object. The isFriend property is a Boolean that returns whether the player is a friend of the current local player. The other two properties handle the name of the player, playerID, and alias. The playerID is static and will always point to the same player. The playerID string should never be shown to the user in your app. The alias, on the other hand, is dynamic and can be changed by the user at any time. It should never be used to test the identity of a user, but it should be the only string used to identify the player to your app's user.

> **CAUTION:** Do not make assumptions about the structure of the player identifier string. Its format and length are subject to change.

When we retrieved the friends list, we did not get back an array of GKPlayers. Instead, we got back an array of their IDs. This is common behavior in Game Center. To help us work with players, we will add two additional convenience methods to translate player IDs into GKPlayers objects.

We need to create two new methods: one will handle an array of player IDs, and the other will handle a single player ID. This will save us extra work down the road. We add the helper methods to our GameCenterManager class. First, add the new protocol method, and modify the relevant section of the GameCenterManager.h file to match the following code.

```
@protocol GameCenterManagerDelegate <NSObject>
@optional
- (void)processGameCenterAuthentication:(NSError*)error;
- (void)friendsFinishedLoading:(NSArray *)friends error:(NSError *)error;
- (void)playerDataLoaded:(NSArray *)players error:(NSError *)error;
@end
```

We will also add the following two new methods to the implementation file of the GameCenterManager class.

```
- (void)playersForIDs:(NSArray *)playerIDs
{
[GKPlayer loadPlayersForIdentifiers:playerIDs withCompletionHandler:↵
^(NSArray *players, NSError *error)
        {
[self callDelegateOnMainThread: @selector(playerDataLoaded:error:)↵
 withArg: players error: error];
        }];
}

- (void)playerforID:(NSString *)playerID
{
[GKPlayer loadPlayersForIdentifiers:[NSArray arrayWithObject:playerID]↵
 withCompletionHandler:^(NSArray *players, NSError *error)
        {
[self callDelegateOnMainThread: @selector(playerDataLoaded:error:) withArg:↵
 players error: error];
        }];
}
```

Both methods will be using loadPlayersForIdentifiers. The only difference is that one will take a string and convert it to a single-item array, and the other will just take in an array. Again, we will use our thread-safe delegate callback.

The last thing that we need to do is to implement the delegate callback in UFOViewController. We start by modifying the friends loaded method. This will translate our friends list into an array of GKPlayer objects. Modify your friendsFinishedLoading method to match the following.

```
- (void)friendsFinishedLoading:(NSArray *)friends error:(NSError *)error;
{
        if (error != nil)
        {
NSLog(@"An error occured during friends list request: %@",↵
 [error localizedDescription]);
        }
        else
        {
                [gcManager playersForIDs: friends];
        }
}
```

You also need to add the new protocol method that we just defined. Add the following to the UFOViewController.m file.

```
- (void)playerDataLoaded:(NSArray *)players error:(NSError *)error;
{
        if (error != nil)
        {
NSLog(@"An error occured during player lookup: %@", [error localizedDescription]);
        }
        else
        {
                NSLog(@"Players loaded: %@", players);
        }
}
```

Now, when the App is run (assuming you have friends associated with your Game Center account), it will pull down a list of your friends' playerIDs, then perform a lookup and print the GKPlayer description to the console. Your output should look similar to the following.

```
2011-02-01 14:20:23.335 UFOs[4038:207] Authenication Changed: <GKPlayer↵
 0x5f46fb0>(playerID: G:1092793231, alias: the_other_kyle, status: (null), rid:(null))
2011-02-01 14:20:23.471 UFOs[4038:207] Players loaded: (
    "<GKPlayer 0x6a201e0>(playerID: G:1093075676, alias: johncash, status: (null),↵
 rid:(null))"
)
```

Summary

In this chapter, you learned how to test for Game Center compatibility and authenticate the local user. You should now have a strong grasp of how we will be using the Game Center Manager class and the benefits it will have on creating a clean code environment that will be easily reusable across multiple projects.

In addition, you should now be comfortable working with GKLocalPlayer, GKPlayer, and the friends list. In the next chapter, we will take an in-depth look at leaderboards and expand on topics learned in this chapter. If you have any difficulty with anything discussed in this chapter, remember that the included sample code contains working examples of all the topics discussed.

Chapter 3

Leaderboards

Leaderboards are older than video games themselves. The leaderboard, as we know it, goes back to the days of the original pinball games of the 1950s. The makers of these pinball games soon realized that adding a high-score list increased competition, which translates to more time played and more money earned.

During the 1970s, when video games began to emerge, leaderboards were quickly adopted into these new games, making their first appearance in Sea Wolf, released in 1976 (see Figure 3–1). Since then, they have played an integral part of the gaming culture. Leaderboards have become so widespread that, in 2007, *The King of Kong*, a full-length documentary, was released about the heated competition over the high score on Nintendo's Donkey Kong. Leaderboards have become so mainstream that they are now an expected part of any video game.

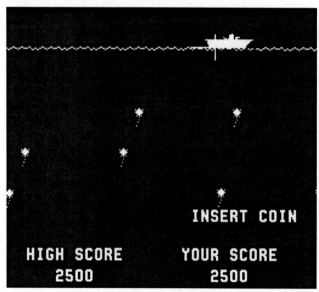

Figure 3–1. *Sea Wolf (1976), the first video game to feature a high score*

Game Center for iOS greatly simplifies adding leaderboards to an app. This is a huge improvement when you consider that, previously, the developer had to write and maintain a server. In this chapter, we examine the steps required to implement multiple leaderboards under Game Center, as well as all the required leaderboard support. You learn how to post scores, retrieve leaderboards, customize the graphical user interface (GUI) of leaderboards, and everything else needed to create leaderboards that are the right fit for your app.

Why a Leaderboard?

Before we get into working with leaderboards themselves, it is important to understand why leaderboards are an integral part of your social app or game.

- Leaderboards create a sense of community in an app or game that, otherwise, might not allow your user to interact directly with other users.

- Leaderboards drive users to return to your app in an effort to beat their own scores or their friend's high scores.

- Leaderboards create a sense of goal and accomplishment in an app.

- Leaderboards make it easier for users to share their app experience and progress with their friends, family, and co-workers.

- Leaderboards in Game Center are easy to implement and can make your app quickly feel more polished and finished.

An Overview of Leaderboards in Game Center

A leaderboard, in the sense of Game Center, is an array of GKScore objects related to a specific leaderboard identifier, of which many can exist per app. Leaderboards can be retrieved and further filtered based on friend status and date submitted.

GKScore objects represent each entry on a specific leaderboard. A GKScore always has a player ID associated with it. When submitting a new GKScore to a leaderboard, the player ID is set automatically by the API and cannot be changed. There are also values for the date and rank that are automatically set and updated. You are required to set only the raw score value and leaderboard category to which the score belongs.

There are two ways to retrieve and display leaderboards. The most common, and easiest, method is by using Apple's leaderboard GUI. This will be the first approach we learn about in the following sections. The second option is to retrieve the raw GKScore values and display them in your own GUI; this method is also discussed later in this chapter.

> **NOTE:** Game Center currently has a limit of 25 leaderboards per bundle ID. There has been a lot of community chatter about it being increased, but as of iOS 5.0, there has not yet been an increase or announced increase to this limit.

Benefits of Using Apple's Leaderboard GUI vs. a Custom GUI

Benefits of using Apple's leaderboard GUI include the following:

- The design was created by some of the best designers in the world.
- It is very simple to implement and present the leaderboard.
- Users will see a familiar interface that they already know how to interact with.

Benefits of using a custom GUI include the following:

- Your leaderboard can match the custom design of your app.
- You have more freedom over the resulting data and can filter using additional criteria.
- You can implement your own custom caching behavior.

As you can see, there are benefits and disadvantages of each system, and there is no right answer in which one you should be using. At the end of this chapter, you will have a strong background in both options and will be able to make the correct decision on which method to implement based on the specific needs of your app.

Configuring a Leaderboard in iTunes Connect

Before working with the code side of leaderboards, you must first set up a new leaderboard in iTunes Connect. Log in to iTunes Connect and select the app that we have already been working with from Chapters 1 and 2. Once you have selected your app from the control panel, go to the Manage Game Center area.

The Game Center portal for your app will have a section labeled "Leaderboards." If this is the first leaderboard that you have set up for this app, you will see a button labeled "Set Up." If you already have leaderboards in place, the steps here will be different and are covered later in this section.

Once you are in the leaderboard section (see Figure 3–2), select the Add Leaderboard button in the upper left-hand corner of the web page. You will be prompted to select either a single leaderboard or a combined leaderboard. A single leaderboard will be one collection of stored score objects that can be queried independently from other leaderboards. A combined leaderboard can also be accessed independently from other leaderboards, but it is a collection of single leaderboards. The combined leaderboard is useful for showing data such as all-time high scores across all levels, or similar combined data.

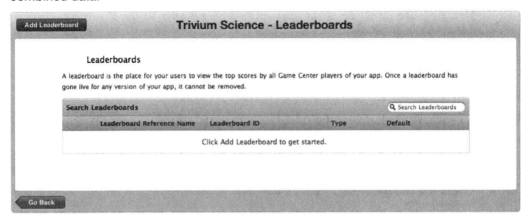

Figure 3–2. *Adding a new leaderboard in iTunes Connect*

We begin by creating a new single leaderboard, as shown in Figure 3–3. The first thing you need to enter is the Leaderboard Reference Name. This value is used solely as a reference within iTunes Connect. The reference name is designed to help you quickly find leaderboards within iTunes Connect; the user never sees it. For this example, you can use the reference name "Leaderboard Foo."

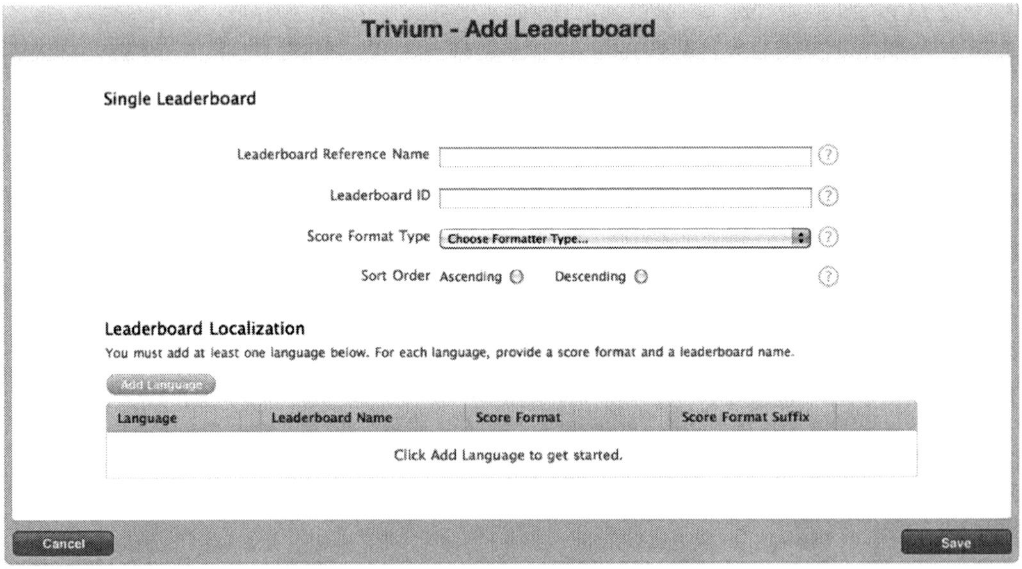

Figure 3–3. *Creating a new single leaderboard in iTunes Connect*

The next field is the Leaderboard ID, the value you will query in your code to retrieve a particular leaderboard. Apple recommends that you use a reverse DNS-type entry for this field, such as com.company.appname.leaderboardname. Fill in the appropriate values for your app here; it is not important what they are, but you will need to remember them throughout the remainder of this chapter.

The Score Format Type is also required when creating a new leaderboard. Select the score format that meets the requirements for your score data. For information on score data formats, see Table 3–1.

Table 3–1. *Score Format Types for Adding a New Leaderboard in iTunes Connect*

Score Format Type	Example Output
Integer	12,345
Fixed Point - To 1 Decimal	12,345.1
Fixed Point - To 2 Decimals	12,345.12
Fixed Point - To 3 Decimals	12,345.123
Elapsed Time - To the Minute	3:45
Elapsed Time - To the Second	3:45:55
Elapsed Time - To the Hundredth of a Second	3:45:55.82
Money - Whole Numbers	$182,121
Money - To 2 Decimals	$182,121.68

> **TIP:** If none of the provided format types match your requirements, select the one that best matches your needs. Later in this chapter, you will see how to customize these values by retrieving the raw score values.

You also need to select whether you want the leaderboard to sort by ascending or descending order. Ascending order will display the lowest score first, as in a golf game or a lap around a track. Descending order will show the highest scores first, as in a game of football or a typical score in a first-person shooter.

The last thing that needs to be done when creating a new single leaderboard is entering the localized score information, as shown in Figure 3–4. iTunes Connect contains built-in localization support for Game Center; you will need to create a new entry for each language you want to support.

The Name field is the display name for your leaderboard in the chosen language. The Score Format field will vary depending on the score format type you selected on the previous screen. (See Figure 3–4 for an example of money formatting.) You also need to provide a Score Format Suffix. This string will be appended to the end of your score value when retrieving the formatted score property.

> **CAUTION:** You will need to add at least one language for every leaderboard you create before it can be considered valid.

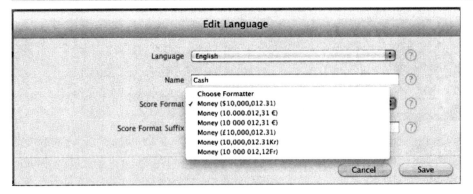

Figure 3–4. *Editing the localization information on a new leaderboard*

> **TIP:** If you want a space to appear between the score and the score format suffix in the formatted score value, don't forget to add a space before the beginning of the score suffix.

You now have a single leaderboard configured for your app. In order to enable the combined leaderboard, we need at least two leaderboards that share the same type of score format. Go ahead and create a second single leaderboard now.

Once you have two leaderboards that share the same score format type, you can create a combined leaderboard. Follow the same procedure for creating a single leaderboard, as described in the previous example. This area is similar to a single leaderboard creation screen. The main difference is that you need to select the leaderboards you want to combine, as shown in Figure 3–5. You will need create a new leaderboard ID, as well as specify the localization data for the new combined leaderboard.

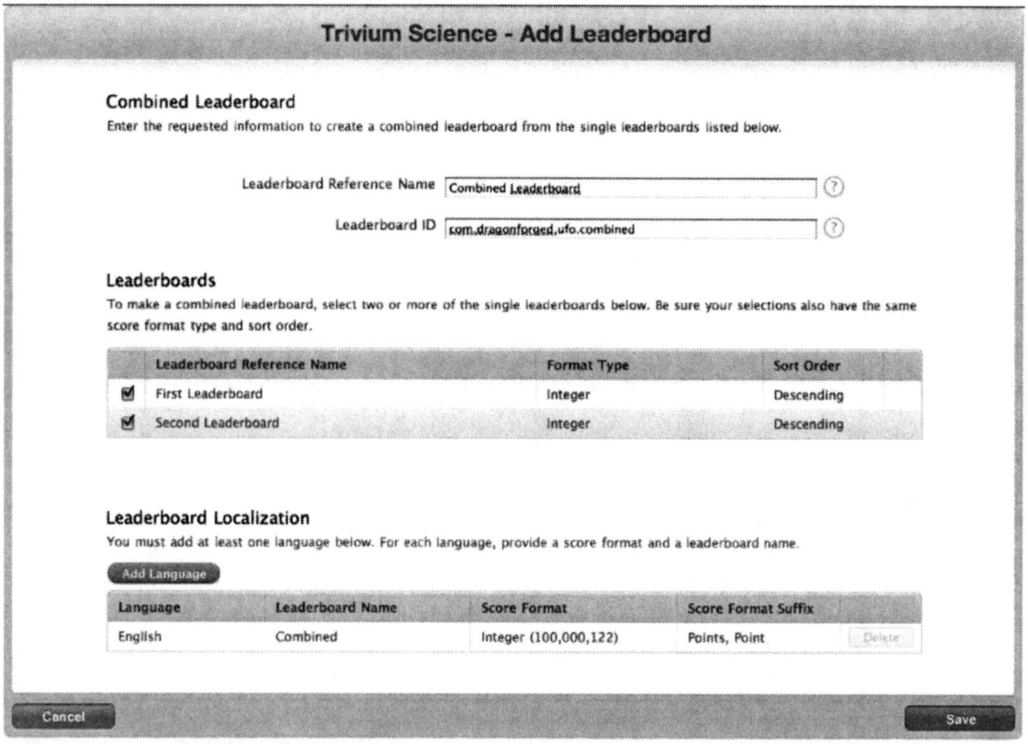

Trivium Science - Add Leaderboard

Combined Leaderboard
Enter the requested information to create a combined leaderboard from the single leaderboards listed below.

Leaderboard Reference Name [Combined Leaderboard] ⑦

Leaderboard ID [com.dragonforged.ufo.combined] ⑦

Leaderboards
To make a combined leaderboard, select two or more of the single leaderboards below. Be sure your selections also have the same score format type and sort order.

	Leaderboard Reference Name	Format Type	Sort Order
☑	First Leaderboard	Integer	Descending
☑	Second Leaderboard	Integer	Descending

Leaderboard Localization
You must add at least one language below. For each language, provide a score format and a leaderboard name.

[Add Language]

Language	Leaderboard Name	Score Format	Score Format Suffix	
English	Combined	Integer (100,000,122)	Points, Point	Delete

[Cancel]   [Save]

Figure 3–5. *Creating a combined leaderboard*

We will also add one last single leaderboard to let us work with a single uncombined leaderboard, as the two previous leaderboards that we had created are now "Attached" type leaderboards. Your leaderboard panel should now have four leaderboards in it: two attached, one combined, and one single leaderboard. Now that we have a handful of valid leaderboards to work with, we can move back to Xcode and begin to work with the leaderboard-specific code.

> **IMPORTANT:** Once a leaderboard has gone live in a shipping app, it can never be removed, so double-check your leaderboard information before shipping an app.

Posting a Score

Before a leaderboard provides any useful functionality, we need to populate it with some score data. We begin this process by modifying our GameCenterManager class once again. Add the following method to the implementation; it should look very familiar as it follows the same pattern that we used when we implemented the authentication methods.

```
- (void) reportScore: (int64_t) score forCategory: (NSString*) category
{
        GKScore *scoreReporter = [[[GKScore alloc] initWithCategory:category]↵
  autorelease];
        scoreReporter.value = score;
        [scoreReporter reportScoreWithCompletionHandler: ^(NSError *error)
        {
                [self callDelegateOnMainThread:@selector(scoreReported:)
                                        withArg:nil
                                        error:error];
        }];
}
```

This new method takes an int64 for the score and an NSString for the category. It then allocates and initializes a new instance of GKScore. The only property that we need to set on the GKScore object is the raw score value. The date and user values are already set for us by the API, and when we initialize the GKScore object, we do so with an argument for the category. We will continue to use the standard callback block to pass the result to our delegate.

We also need to modify the header file to incorporate a new protocol method. Modify the existing protocol declaration area of the GameCenterManager header to include the scoreReported method, as shown in the following code snippet.

```
@protocol GameCenterManagerDelegate <NSObject>
@optional
- (void)processGameCenterAuthentication:(NSError*)error;
- (void)friendsFinishedLoading:(NSArray *)friends error:(NSError *)error;
- (void)playerDataLoaded:(NSArray *)players error:(NSError *)error;
- (void)scoreReported: (NSError*) error;
@end
```

This concludes all of the required modifications to our GameCenterManager class. We can now turn our focus back to the game itself. We will need to first implement some new gameplay dynamics to handle high scores.

Setting a Default Leaderboard

With the release of iOS 5.0 Apple has added just one method to Game Center leaderboards. You now have the ability to set a default leaderboard for the local user. If you set a default leaderboard you can omit setting a category for a leaderboard when submitting and it will default to the correct one. The following method will take an NSString identifier as an argument for the leaderboard that you would like to specify as the default for the local player.

```
[GKLeaderboard setDefaultLeaderboard:@"com.dragonforged.leaderboardToBeDefault"↵
  withCompletionHandler:^(NSError *error)
        {
NSLog(@"An error occurred when setting the default leaderboard: %@",↵
  [error localizedDescription]);

        }];
```

Adding Score Posting to UFOs

There are two obvious ways that we can score in our UFOs game. First, we could implement a system that counted how many cows were abducted and submit that as the score. Although this approach is the easiest to implement for us, it is not a very fun gameplay technique, because there is no logical point at which the game ends. The second, high-score method is harder to implement, but makes more sense. It clocks how long the user took to abduct ten cows; the user with the lowest time is the winner.

These are topics that must be carefully considered for your own app. For the purpose of this book, we will demonstrate the first method in which the number of cows abducted is the user's score. If you were going to implement a timer-based system, the approach is very similar: you would start a timer at the beginning of the round, and when ten cows are abducted, you would submit the time in seconds on the timer.

In order to implement this score-based system, we need to add a way for the player to end a game. In an actual game, this could be handled by something being able to kill your player, or a time limit. However, for the purpose of this example, we will simply add an exit button. This will allow the user to simulate a game-over event, while keeping the code Game Center–focused without adding extra complexity.

We add an exit button in UFOGameViewController.xib, as shown in Figure 3–6. We will need to create a new IBAction for the exit button as well. Add the following code to UFOGameViewController and connect our exit button to it. For the time being, we will just pop the navigation controller back to the root view.

```
-(IBAction)exitAction:(id)sender;
{
        [[self navigationController] popViewControllerAnimated:YES];
}
```

> **NOTE:** You are not required to wait until the end of a game to submit a new score, but it is generally thought of as good practice. You want to avoid submitting a new score multiple times per game if it can be prevented.
>
> A notable exception might be a continuous role-playing game in which the score continually updates and there is no proper ending to submit a score during the game.

Figure 3–6. *Adding the ability to exit the game so a high score can be submitted*

We will also want to add our protocol method from the GameCenterManager class to UFOGameViewController. Add the following code snippet into UFOGameViewController.m.

```
(void)scoreReported: (NSError*) error;
{
        if (error)
        {
                NSLog(@"There was an error in reporting the score: %@",↩
[error localizedDescription]);
        }

else
        {
                NSLog(@"Score submitted");
        }
}
```

The only remaining step is to actually submit the score to Game Center; if you recall, we have already written the method to handle this in our GameCenterManager class. We already have an instance of our GameCenterManager class that we used in UFOViewController to authenticate the user. We will want to keep a pointer to the instance of our object that was already created in the previous class.

Create a new property for UFOGameViewController, make it an instance of GameCenterManager, and name it GCManager as we did in the previous class. Once the property has been synthesized, we can hook into it from our previous class. Modify the playButtonPressed method of UFOViewController to match the following.

```
-(IBAction)playButtonPressed
{
        UFOGameViewController *gameViewController = [[UFOGameViewController alloc]↩
 init];
        gameViewController.gcManager = gcManager; //Changed Code
        [self.navigationController pushViewController: gameViewController animated:YES];
        [gameViewController release];
}
```

Now our game controller class has a reference to the GameCenterManager that we will be using throughout the project. We also have to set a new delegate for gcManager in the viewDidLoad method of UFOGameViewController. We want to make sure that UFOGameViewController will be handling the callbacks for the score submitted. Add the following method to the implementation.

```
- (void)scoreReported: (NSError*) error;
{
        if (error)
        {
                NSLog(@"There was an error in reporting the score: %@",↵
 [error localizedDescription]);
        }

        else
        {
                NSLog(@"Score submitted");
        }

        [[self navigationController] popViewControllerAnimated: YES];
}
```

We will also modify the exitAction method to just submit the score. To do so, replace the old exitAction method with the following. Notice how we are using the leaderboard ID that we set in iTunes Connect; make sure to use the same one that you entered, as it will probably not match this example.

```
-(IBAction)exitAction:(id)sender;
{
        [self.gcManager reportScore:score forCategory:@"com.dragonforged.ufo.single"];
}
```

When you now play and click Exit, you should see a console message that looks similar to the following output.

```
2011-02-10 12:32:47.629 UFOs[15092:207] Score submitted
```

> **TIP:** See the section, "A Better Approach," at the end of this chapter for a more complex, but user-friendly, approach to submitting scores.

Now that we have a score submitted to a leaderboard, in the following sections we will learn how to present this data back to the user. This action has been greatly simplified for the purpose of making this section as easy to learn as possible. This will not be the user experience you want to present to your user; we are simply trapping the user in the game screen while we wait for a network callback. In reality, you will want to handle the delegate callback in the previous view. This ensures the user is not waiting when they do not have to be. For simplicity sake, we will continue to use the easier-to-follow methodology.

> **TIP:** You can only have one score posted per leaderboard category for each player. You might notice that scores that you are submitting never appear on the leaderboard. If you are noticing this behavior, make sure that the score you are submitting is higher than the highest score for that player.

Handling Failures When Submitting a Score

If a score fails to submit, you as the developer are solely responsible for storing the score and resubmitting it when the error has been resolved. Nothing is more frustrating to a user than earning a new high score and losing it due to a network failure. This is also a step that Apple likes to test for during app reviews.

There are many different ways to store the score information for resubmitting it later; however, I feel that the following approach is the easiest for the novice to implement. Feel free to implement your own system if you feel that the provided one does not suit the needs of your app.

We will use NSKeyedArchiver to store our GKScore object for use later. The reason to serialize the object itself is to preserve the data that is created for us once we initialize an instance of GKScore, namely the date. Although you could simply store the raw score data, submitting the raw score with a new GKScore object will use the current timestamp, as opposed to the time when the score was actually earned. The problem with this is that it provides a poor user experience, as the first player to earn a high score might not be recognized as such.

There are three steps that need to be completed to handle and recover from a score submitting failure. The first step is to save the score data. Although we do not inform the user of the failure in this example, it is a good idea to notify the user that their score could not be submitted at this time, and that you will automatically retry later. Modify the following class in GameCenterManager.m to match the following code.

```
- (void) reportScore: (int64_t) score forCategory: (NSString*) category
{
        GKScore *scoreReporter = [[[GKScore alloc] initWithCategory:category]↩
autorelease];

        scoreReporter.value = score;
        [scoreReporter reportScoreWithCompletionHandler: ^(NSError *error)
        {
                if (error != nil)
                {
                        NSData* savedScoreData = [NSKeyedArchiver↩
archivedDataWithRootObject:scoreReporter];

                        [self storeScoreForLater: savedScoreData];
                }

                [self callDelegateOnMainThread: @selector(scoreReported:) withArg:↩
```

```
NULL error:  error];
        }];
}
```

We have added a few additional lines of code that will run if an error is detected. The first line takes the GKScore object and encodes it using NSKeyedArchiver, which will return an NSData object. We will later retrieve the GKScore from this NSData. We also call a new method that we have named storeScoreForLater. Let's take a look at that method now; add the following method to the implementation of the GameCenterManager class.

```
- (void)storeScoreForLater:(NSData *)scoreData;
{
        NSUserDefaults *defaults = [NSUserDefaults standardUserDefaults];

        NSMutableArray *savedScores = [[defaults arrayForKey:@"savedScores"]↵
mutableCopy];

        [savedScoreArray addObject: scoreData];
        [defaults setObject:savedScoreArray forKey:@"savedScores"];

        [savedScoreArray release];
}
```

This snippet of code will save the NSData that represents our score to the user defaults. You could also write this data to a file or even store it in core data. Never assume the user has only one unsubmitted score; they may have racked up a number of scores across many different leaderboards while playing offline.

We caught a posting failure as well as saved the score to disk to be retried later. The last remaining step is to attempt to resubmit the score to Game Center. This step can be very complex, depending on how intelligent you want the system to be. Most failures of score submissions are related to network access issues, but could also be caused by Game Center being down, or even a DNS issue.

There is no correct answer in when to repost a score, but the guideline is that you don't want to hold on to a score that could be submitted. Before we worry about where to tie in the method to resubmit failed scores, let's first implement a method to retry a score posting. Add the following method to your GameCenterManager class.

```
-(void)submitAllSavedScores
{
        NSUserDefaults *defaults = [NSUserDefaults standardUserDefaults];
        NSArray *savedScores = [defaults arrayForKey@"savedScores"];

        [defaults removeObjectForKey: @"savedScores"];

        GKScore *scoreReporter = nil;
        NSData *savedScoreData = nil;

        For (NSData *scoreData in savedScores)
        {
                scoreReporter = [NSKeyedUnarchiver unarchiveObjectWithData: scoreData];

                [scoreReporter reportScoreWithCompletionHandler: ^(NSError *error)
```

```
        {
                if (error != nil)
                {
                        savedScoreData = [NSKeyedArchiver⏎
archivedDataWithRootObject:scoreReporter];

                        [self storeScoreForLater: savedScoreData];
                }
                else
                {
                        NSLog(@"Saved score submitted");
                }
        }];
    }
}
```

The preceding code will loop through all of the saved scores and attempt to resubmit them. Since there is no delegate for this behavior, we do not need to provide a delegate callback. We merely log any successes and failures to add back to our array of non-submitted scores for retrying again later.

As mentioned earlier, there are dozens of ways to tie back in resubmitting failed scores. To keep it simple, we add a call to the submitAllSavedScores after we properly authenticate with Game Center. Modify the authenticateLocalUser method of GameCenterManager.m to match the following.

```
- (void)authenticateLocalUser
{
        if ([GKLocalPlayer localPlayer].authenticated == YES) return;

        [[GKLocalPlayer localPlayer] authenticateWithCompletionHandler:^(NSError *error)
        {
                if (error == nil)
                {
                        [self submitAllSavedScores];
                }

                [self callDelegateOnMainThread: @selector⏎
(processGameCenterAuthentication:)
                                        withArg:nil
                                          error:error];
        }];
}
```

Presenting a Leaderboard

Now that we have a leaderboard in iTunes Connect, and populated a score into that leaderboard, it is time to present the leaderboard to the user. There are two ways of presentation: the first is with Apple's GUI; the second is with a custom GUI. This section will take a look at the implementation using Apple's GUI. In the next section, you will learn how to present a leaderboard with custom graphics.

Before we can begin, we need to create a new button that will trigger the leaderboard. We want to do this outside of the game screen, because you do not want to drag the user away from a game in progress to view a leaderboard. Begin by adding a new button to the UFOViewController view, as shown in Figure 3–7.

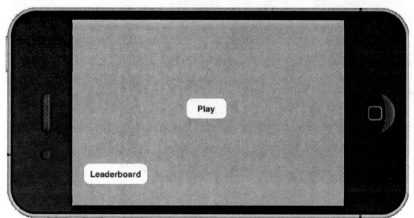

Figure 3–7. *Adding a leaderboard button*

Hook up the button to a new action that matches the one shown next. Do not forget to change the category property to the leaderboard that you set in iTunes Connect.

```
-(IBAction)leaderboardButtonPressed;
{
        GKLeaderboardViewController *leaderboardController = nil;
        leaderboardController = [[GKLeaderboardViewController alloc] init];

        if (leaderboardController == NULL)
                return;

        leaderboardController.category = @"com.dragonforged.ufo.single";
        leaderboardController.timeScope = GKLeaderboardTimeScopeAllTime;
        leaderboardController.leaderboardDelegate = self;
        [self presentModalViewController: leaderboardController animated: YES];
}
```

You also need to add in the delegate call for GKLeaderboardViewController. To do so, add the following required method to your implementation. Don't forget to add GKLeaderboardViewControllerDelegate to your header as well.

```
- (void)leaderboardViewControllerDidFinish:(GKLeaderboardViewController *)viewController
{
        [self dismissModalViewControllerAnimated: YES];
}
```

When you run the program and click on the newly added Leaderboard button, the result should look similar to the image in Figure 3–8. As you can see in the image, the title of our leaderboard (as set in iTunes Connect) is shown in the navigation bar. You can also see the highest submitted score as well as score suffix that was set.

Figure 3–8. *A leaderboard being presented using Apple's GUI*

The GUI provides a back button to take us to a list of all the leaderboards (see initial view in Figure 3–9) that we have configured for the app. If you omit entering a category when you create the GKLeaderboardViewController instance, you will be presented with whatever leaderboard has been selected as the default leaderboard in iTunes Connect.

This is all there is to creating and presenting a leaderboard using Apple's GUI. In the next section, we will look at how to customize a leaderboard to match your own GUI.

> **NOTE:** Remember that you cannot access any Game Center functionality, including leaderboards, before a local user has authenticated. If you try to do so, you will receive a GKErrorNotAuthenticated error.

Figure 3–9. *A collection of leaderboards, shown with Apple's GUI*

> **TIP:** You can change the order that leaderboards appear (see Figure 3–9) by dragging leaderboard entries up and down in iTunes Connect.

Customizing the Leaderboard

As demonstrated in the previous section, presenting a leaderboard to the user is straightforward. However, what if you want to customize the appearance of a leaderboard? In this section, you will be walked through the process of receiving the raw leaderboard information so that you can present it in your app in whatever fashion suits your needs.

We begin the process of adding a custom leaderboard by adding a new button and associated action for it to UFOViewController. Add a new button adjacent to the previous leaderboard button, and create a new action for it.

In the previous example, Apple provides a view controller for us. When we are working with our own custom leaderboards, we need to create a view controller to handle the presentation. Create a new subclass of UIViewController and name it UFOLeaderboardViewController. Modify the action of the new custom leaderboard button to present a new instance of UFOLeaderboardViewController, as seen in the following code snippet.

```
-(IBAction)customLeaderboardButtonPressed;
{
        UFOLeaderboardViewController *leaderboardViewController = nil;
        leaderboardViewController = [[UFOLeaderboardViewController alloc] init];

        [self presentModalViewController:leaderboardViewController animated:YES];
        [leaderboardViewController release];
}
```

The next step is to set up the xib for the new UFOLeaderboardViewController. We will use the setup as shown in Figure 3–10; however, you may provide whatever kind of customization you want here. Create the outlets and objects, as shown in the figure, and hook up connections for all of them, including the delegate and dataSource for the table.

Figure 3–10. *Creating the xib for a custom leaderboard*

The first thing that should be hooked up is the Dismiss button. Add the following code snippet to your action that you connected to the Dismiss button.

```
-(IBAction)dismiss;
{
        [self dismissModalViewControllerAnimated: YES];
}
```

We also want to make sure that the new view controller respects our landscape orientation. Add a shouldAutorotateToInterfaceOrientation call to the implementation of UFOLeaderboardViewController. It should look like the following.

```
- (BOOL)shouldAutorotateToInterfaceOrientation:
(UIInterfaceOrientation)interfaceOrientation
{
        return (UIInterfaceOrientationIsLandscape(interfaceOrientation));
}
```

If you were to run the app at this point and click on the Custom Leaderboard button, it should launch a blank table in the correct orientation and allow you to dismiss it to return to the first view.

Now that we got the view controller overhead out of the way, we can begin to focus on the Game Center–specific features. First, set up the table view delegate and datasource methods that we will be using. We need to create a new class property to hold the score data for display. Create a new NSArray object and name it scoreArray. Also create an associated property for the array and synthesis it. Add the following two methods to your implementation.

```
- (NSInteger)tableView:(UITableView *)tableView numberOfRowsInSection:(NSInteger)section
{
        return [self.scoreArray count];
}

- (UITableViewCell *)tableView:(UITableView *)tableView cellForRowAtIndexPath:
(NSIndexPath *)indexPath
{
        static NSString *CellIdentifier = @"Cell";

        UITableViewCell *cell = [tableView dequeueReusableCellWithIdentifier:
CellIdentifier];

        if (cell == nil)
        {
                cell = [[[UITableViewCell alloc] initWithStyle:
UITableViewCellStyleSubtitle
                                                        reuseIdentifier:
CellIdentifier] autorelease];

                cell.selectionStyle = UITableViewCellSelectionStyleNone;
        }

        GKScore *score = [self.scoreArray objectAtIndex: indexPath.row];

        cell.textLabel.text = score.playerID;
        cell.detailTextLabel.text = score.formattedValue;
```

```
        return cell;
}
```

The first method returns the number of items in our table view. We deal with only one
section in this example, so the number of rows will always equal the number of scores
that are in our array. The next method displays the score into the cell. We use
UITableViewCellStyleSubtitle in this example, but in most cases, you will want to create
a more customized cell. The main label is set to the player ID and the secondary label is
set to the formatted score value. In the previous chapter, it was noted that you should
never show a player ID to the user. We will add a method to convert a player ID to a
player alias in the following section; until then, we will use the player ID for debugging
purposes.

Modifying GameCenterManager

Let's take a moment to switch over to our GameCenterManager class. In the header file,
create a new optional protocol as shown in the following.

```
(void)leaderboardUpdated: (NSArray *)scores error:(NSError *)error;
```

Next, we create a new method to retrieve scores from the Game Center servers. Add the
following method to the implementation of the GameCenterManager class.

```
- (void)retrieveScoresForCategory:(NSString *)category
                    withPlayerScope:(GKLeaderboardPlayerScope)playerScope
                          timeScope:(GKLeaderboardTimeScope)timeScope
                          withRange:(NSRange)range;
{
        GKLeaderboard *leaderboardRequest = [[GKLeaderboard alloc] init];
        leaderboardRequest.playerScope = playerScope;
        leaderboardRequest.timeScope = timeScope;
        leaderboardRequest.range = range;
        leaderboardRequest.category = category;

        [leaderboardRequest loadScoresWithCompletionHandler: ^(NSArray *scores,NSError↩
  *error)
        {
                [self callDelegateOnMainThread:@selector(leaderboardUpdated:error:)
                                        withArg:scores
                                          error: error];
        }];
}
```

We want to keep this call as generic as possible because the ultimate goal of the
GameCenterManager class is to be a reusable class that can easily be dropped into any
of your future projects.

The preceding method takes all the arguments that are required to create a new
GKLeaderboard object. Once we have created the object and set the properties that are
required, we can call the method loadScoresWithCompletionHandler on the
GKLeaderboard object. We will continue to use our standard thread-safe delegate

callback. These are all the modifications that are needed in the GameCenterManager class for this section.

Filtering Results on a Custom Leaderboard

Let's shift our focus back to the UFOLeaderboardCiewController class again. We will next add an action for our segmented controller. This will allow the user to switch between global scores and friends-only scores. Connect the following method to the valueChanged action of the segmented controller.

```
-(IBAction)segementedControllerDidChange:(id)sender;
{
        GKLeaderboardPlayerScope playerScope;

        if ([scopeSegementedController selectedSegmentIndex] == 0)
        {
                playerScope = GKLeaderboardPlayerScopeFriendsOnly;
        }
        else
        {
                playerScope = GKLeaderboardPlayerScopeGlobal;
        }

        self.scoreArray = nil;

        [self.gcManager retrieveScoresForCategory:@"com.dragonforged.ufo.single"
                                                withPlayerScope:playerScope
                                                        timeScope: ↵
GKLeaderboardTimeScopeAllTime
                                                        withRange: ↵
NSMakeRange(1,50)];

        [leaderboardTableView reloadData];
}
```

This method calls the GameCenterManager method to retrieve our score list. The segmented control has two values: one for friends, and one for everyone. You could easily modify the preceding code to retrieve different time scopes as well, but in this example we request only the all-time scope. An important step here that can be easy to overlook is setting the array to nil and reloading the table. Doing so will remove the scores that are in the table when the segmented controller value is changed.

The retrieve scores call is fairly straightforward. We use the category we set in iTunes Connect for the leaderboard we wish to retrieve, and set our time and player scope. The last argument on the method is a range. In the previous example, we return scores from 1st place to 50th place.

You also need to create a new property for the UFOLeaderboardViewController class; this will be a pointer to our GameCenterManager class. This is done exactly the same as when we did it for the UFOGameViewController class.

NOTE: Score ranges always start at an index of 1. You could modify the above example with a new range of NSMakeRange(50,50); this will retrieve scores from 50th place to 100th place. Make sure you don't request too many scores at a time, as the time it takes to retrieve the score data is related to how many scores you are attempting to retrieve.

Displaying the Custom Leaderboard

If you were to run this project now, you would notice the table is always blank. This is caused by two different omissions. The first is that we never set a value for our gcManager, and the second is that we never called the retrieveScore method. To rectify this, modify the viewDidLoad method of the UFOLeaderboardViewController implementation to match the following.

```
-(void)viewDidLoad
{
        [super viewDidLoad];

        self.gcManager.delegate = self;
        [self segementedControllerDidChange:nil];
}
```

The last step is to pass a reference to the gcManager to our leaderboard class. We do this in the UFOViewController class. Modify the existing IBAction method to set the property for gcManager to the instance that exists in the UFOViewController. Your code should look like the following example.

```
-(IBAction)customLeaderboardButtonPressed;
{
        UFOLeaderboardViewController *leaderboardViewController = nil;
        leaderboardViewController = [[UFOLeaderboardViewController alloc] init];
        leaderboardViewController.gcManager = gcManager;
        [self presentModalViewController:leaderboardViewController animated:YES];
        [leaderboardViewController release];
}
```

If you were to now run the app again, you would see output similar to that shown in Figure 3–11. The number of scores, the score values, and the player IDs will be different, but you should be able to see at least one score listed.

Figure 3–11. *An initial view of our custom leaderboard*

> **IMPORTANT:** It cannot be guaranteed that you will not be returned cached data for a
> leaderboard request. You should assume that the data you are retrieving is cached and might not
> be the most up to date.

Mapping a Player ID

In the previous section, we learned how to pull down the raw score values of a
leaderboard. However, we ended up with a leaderboard that contained only player IDs
rather than the aliases (which the user expects to be shown). In this section, we will
create a new method that will translate player IDs into player aliases. We will begin this
process by adding some new methods to our GameCenterManager class. These will
enable searching for a single name and an array of names. Add the following two
methods to the GameCenterManager class.

```
- (void)mapPlayerIDtoPlayer:(NSString*)playerID
{
        [GKPlayer loadPlayersForIdentifiers: [NSArray arrayWithObject: playerID]
                        withCompletionHandler:^(NSArray *playerArray, NSError↩
    *error)
            {
                GKPlayer* player = nil;
                for (GKPlayer* tempPlayer in playerArray)
                {
                        if ([tempPlayer.playerID isEqualToString: playerID] == nil)
    continue;

                        player = tempPlayer;
                        break;
                }
```

```
[self callDelegateOnMainThread:@selector(mappedPlayerIDToPlayer:error:)
                                                withArg:player
                                                  error:error];
        }];
}

- (void)mapPlayerIDstoPlayers:(NSArray*)playerIDs
{
[GKPlayer loadPlayersForIdentifiers: playerIDs withCompletionHandler:^(NSArray↵
 *playerArray, NSError *error)
        {
[self callDelegateOnMainThread: @selector(mappedPlayerIDs:error:) withArg: playerArray↵
 error: error];
        }];
}
```

The first method will return a single GKPlayer object, while the second method will return an array of GKPlayer objects. We also need to add two new protocol methods to handle the delegate callbacks.

Though we could use the same callback and return a single-item array for the first call, we will want to keep both methods around. Nothing prevents you from passing a single player ID into the second method; however, the first method will serve useful purposes from time to time as well. Do not forget we are building a reusable library of Game Center calls.

Your protocols for GameCenterManagerDelegate should now look like the following code, assuming you have been following along since the beginning of this book.

```
@protocol GameCenterManagerDelegate <NSObject>
@optional
- (void)processGameCenterAuthentication:(NSError*)error;
- (void)friendsFinishedLoading:(NSArray *)friends error:(NSError *)error;
- (void)playerDataLoaded:(NSArray *)players error:(NSError *)error;
- (void)scoreReported: (NSError*) error;
- (void)leaderboardUpdated: (NSArray *)scores error:(NSError *)error;
- (void)mappedPlayerIDToPlayer:(GKPlayer *)player error:(NSError *)error;
- (void)mappedPlayerIDsToPlayers:(NSArray *)players error:(NSError *)error;
@end
```

Once you have a GKPlayer object for a given playerID, there are many ways to look up one based on the other. For simplicity's sake, we will store all fetched players into an array and use a simple lookup.

The first thing we need to do is add a new NSMutableArray to our UFOLeaderboardViewController class. Let's name this new object playerArray. Don't forget to allocate and initialize it in the viewDidLoad method. Add a method for the new protocol that we just set up, initialize shown in the following.

```
- (void)mappedPlayerIDToPlayer:(GKPlayer *)player error:(NSError *)error
{
        if (error != nil)
        {
                NSLog(@"Error during player mapping: %@", [error localizedDescription]);
        }
        else
```

```
          {
                    [playerArray addObject: player];
          }

          [leaderboardTableView reloadData];
}
```

This method merely stores the retrieved GKPlayers into an array for future reference. If you were using the method that returns an array of players, your delegate callback would look like the following instead.

```
- (void)mappedPlayerIDsToPlayers:(NSArray *)players error:(NSError *)error
{
          if (error != nil)
          {
                    NSLog(@"Error during player mapping: %@", [error localizedDescription]);
          }
          else
          {
                    [playerArray addObjectsFromArray:players];
          }

          [leaderboardTableView reloadData];
}
```

We also need to add a new method that will handle iterating through our array and looking for a player match.

```
-(NSString *)playerNameforID:(NSString *)playerID;
{
          for (GKPlayer *player in playerArray)
          {
                    if ([player.playerID isEqualToString: playerID])
                              continue;

                    return player.alias;
          }

          return nil;
}
```

The preceding method searches through the player array for a match on the playerID and returns the alias for that player. You could just as easy return the entire GKPlayer object if you wanted more information in your table cell, such as whether they are underage or are one of your friends.

The final step is to modify our cellForRow method to handle the new name lookup code. The following method will replace our old cellForRow method in UFOLeaderboardViewController.

```
- (UITableViewCell *)tableView:(UITableView *)tableView
          cellForRowAtIndexPath:(NSIndexPath *)indexPath
{

                    static NSString *CellIdentifier = @"Cell";

                    UITableViewCell *cell = [tableView dequeueReusableCellWithIdentifier:↵
```

```
CellIdentifier];
  if (cell == nil)
      {
                        cell = [[[UITableViewCell alloc] initWithStyle: ↵
          UITableViewCellStyleSubtitle reuseIdentifier:CellIdentifier]
autorelease];

                        cell.selectionStyle = UITableViewCellSelectionStyleNone;
      }

  GKScore *score = [self.scoreArray objectAtIndex: indexPath.row];

      NSString *playerName = [self playerNameforID: score.playerID];

  if (playerName == nil)
      {
                        [self.gcManager mapPlayerIDtoPlayer: score.playerID];
                        cell.textLabel.text = @"Loading Name...";
      }
      else
{
              cell.textLabel.text = playerName;
      }

  cell.detailTextLabel.text = score.formattedValue;

  return cell;
}
```

> **TIP:** You can access the raw score data with the value property on GKScore. This will allow you to perform even more customization than is available in the score format type in iTunes Connect.

As you can see in the preceding method, we get a GKScore as we did in the previous example. We created a new string called playerName and use our new method to populate it. The first time this method is called, playerNameforID will return nil. During that event, we call our mapPlayerIDtoPlayer method and set the text in the cell to "Loading Name...". This serves as a placeholder until we can load in the full username. When we get a callback from the GameCenterManager, we reload the table. At this point, playerNameforID should return the alias for the player.

If the app is run again, you will see that we are now displaying proper player aliases as opposed to the player IDs (see Figure 3–12).

> **NOTE:** Remember that the user can change their alias at any time, and you should always display the most up-to-date alias. With this in mind, you should always attempt to update the alias whenever displaying it. Do not cache once and never request an update.

Figure 3–12. *A custom leaderboard that properly maps player aliases*

Local Player Score

There are often times that you will want to know the local players score on a given leaderboard. Maybe you want to display their score at the top of your leaderboard, or perhaps you want to fetch a leaderboard that shows other player scores that are close to your local player's score.

Apple has provided an easy technique for determining the local players score. During any GKLeaderboard request, it contains a property for localPlayerScore. We create a new method in our GameCenterManager to handle retrieving the local player score for us. Add the following method to your GameCenterManager class.

```
-(void)retrieveLocalScoreForCategory:(NSString *)category
{
        GKLeaderboard *leaderboardRequest = [[GKLeaderboard alloc] init];
        leaderboardRequest.category = category;

        [leaderboardRequest loadScoresWithCompletionHandler: ^(NSArray *scores,NSError↵
  *error)
        {
                [self callDelegateOnMainThread:@selector(localPlayerScore:error:)
                                                 withArg:↵
leaderboardRequest.localPlayerScore
                                                          error:error];
        }];
}
```

This method functions almost the same as our previous score function. However, we care about only the local player score for the category we are requesting. We also need to add a new protocol method to pass this data back to our delegate. Go ahead and set it, as shown in the following code snippet.

```
(void)localPlayerScore:(GKScore *)score error:(NSError *)error;
```

We now need to add our protocol implementation to UFOLeaderboardViewController. That method is presented next. We will not be directly using the local player's score in this demo, so we just print the value to the console.

```
- (void)localPlayerScore:(GKScore *)score error:(NSError *)error;
{
        if (error != nil)
        {
                NSLog(@"Error getting local score: %@", [error localizedDescription]);
        }
        else
        {
                NSLog(@"Local User Score: %@", score);
        }
}
```

Next, we call the GameCenterManager method for retrieving our local user score. Let's add that code to the viewDidLoad method of UFOLeaderboardviewController. Don't forget to change the category to match the one for the leaderboard you want to request.

```
[self.gcManager retrieveLocalScoreForCategory: @"com.dragonforged.ufo.single"];
```

If you run the app again, now you should see console output that looks similar to the one here.

```
2011-02-14 14:38:41.940 UFOs[22485:207] Local User Score: GKScore player=G:200192907
rank=2 date=2011-02-14 04:08:04 +0000 value=3 formattedValue=3 Points
```

A Better Approach

In the section, "Posting a Score," earlier in this chapter, we discovered how to post new scores to Game Center. Our methodology, while simple, was not the best approach from a user-interaction standpoint. It is now time to refactor the posting new score code to improve usability. This approach is more complex, but delivers better performance and has less of an impact on the user.

The first thing we need to do is move our scoreReported method from UFOGameViewController to UFOViewController. We also want to modify the exit action in the UFOViewController. Modify that method to match the following.

```
-(IBAction)exitAction:(id)sender;
{
        [[self navigationController] popViewControllerAnimated: YES];
        [self.gcManager reportScore:score forCategory:@"com.dragonforged.ufo.single"];
}
```

We also need to add a single line of code the UFOViewController viewWillAppear method, as follows.

```
gcManager.delegate = self;
```

This resets the delegate for our Game Center calls back to the UFOViewController. This allows us to exit the game without waiting for a network callback from the Game Center delegate. This method is more user friendly, but involves some delegate switching.

Summary

This chapter introduced leaderboards in Game Center. We covered the benefits of using a leaderboard, as well as the two available types. We learned how to post a score and recover for any errors that occurred during posting. We also looked at the requirements of getting leaderboards up and running in your app, using either Apple's provided GUI or a custom one.

Throughout the chapter, we continued to build our GameCenterManager class, adding the required methods to post scores, retrieve scores both local and global, map playerIDs to GKPlayer objects, and display custom and built-in leaderboards.

You should now feel confident in adding a leaderboard to any existing or new iOS app. In the next chapter, we will explore all that Game Center achievements offer.

Chapter 4

Achievements

The relatively new gaming concept, achievements, came along much later than leaderboards and has gained a dramatic rise in popularity with the release of Microsoft's Xbox 360. Achievements offer a level of detail overlooked in leaderboards. Leaderboards show who possesses the leading score; on the other hand, achievements demonstrate a player's skills and strengths by rewarding the player for completing tasks or levels. When the achievements start to serve in-game purposes, they become more of a power-up over other players. The ability to view the achievements by others gives players a type of "bragging rights."

As social network–enabled gaming spreads and becomes prevalent, the achievement system feature has skyrocketed into even more popularity.

Foursquare was one of the first to bring achievements out of the gaming world and into the social app universe. Foursquare calls its achievements "badges," (see Figure 4–1) but the basic concept is the same. Players receive a reward for completing a task, but the number of badges does not affect gameplay, or in this case, the ability for the user to use the app in any direct manner.

Figure 4–1. *Foursquare for iPhone showing badges or achievements*

Game Center has made adding an achievement system to your iOS app simple. In this chapter, we will learn how to add achievements to our demo game, UFOs. You will learn everything needed to fully integrate an achievement system into your app quickly and easily. Notably, you will learn how to:

- Create new achievements
- Display achievement progress
- Add achievement hooks into your app
- Progress and reset achievements
- Customize the appearance of achievements

Why Achievements?

If it is not already apparent what achievements can add to your social app or game, let's take a moment to review some of the many benefits.

- Achievements give your users an extra sense of accomplishment.

- Achievements bring users back into your app more often. Users are more apt to return to your app to complete more achievements, making completing the game a more rewarding and fun process.

- Achievements add an easy way for users to share experiences with other users.

- Achievements in Game Center provide a polished look and feel to the shipping product.

- Achievements give users a greater sense of progression as they make their way through your app or game.

- Achievements provide an alternative way to play the game. If users do not enjoy the campaign, they can enjoy a sense of accomplishment through your achievement system.

- Achievements attribute game brand awareness. As users share their accomplishments on Twitter and Facebook, name recognition increases, and with it sales.

An Overview of Achievements in Game Center

Achievements, also known as badges in certain circles, function slightly differently in Game Center than on other platforms. As with leaderboards, achievements first need to be configured in iTunes Connect on a per-app basis. You will be creating new instances of a GKAchievement object to report progress (more on this object later). Unlike leaderboard entries, which are created when a score is reached and submitted, achievements can report incremental progress.

Another notable change from working with leaderboards (see Chapter 3 for more on leaderboards) is that you will use two different types of objects to submit and retrieve achievements. GKAchievement is used to submit new achievements or update progress on achievements, and GKAchievementDescription is used to display achievement data to the user. This is contrary to what we saw when working with leaderboards, in which GKScore objects were used to submit data as well as retrieve it.

As with leaderboards, achievement progress can be shown using either Apple's included graphical user interface (GUI) or a customized one that better matches the look and feel of your app. The benefits and disadvantages of each system are the same as with leaderboards. Those benefits and disadvantages follow for your convenience, with minor achievement-specific information added where appropriate.

Benefits of Using Apple's Achievement GUI vs. a Custom GUI

The following are some of the benefits that you will gain by using Apple's included GUI for working with achievements.

- The look and feel of your achievements is created by some of the best designers in the world.

- The GUI is very simple to implement, making it easy to present the achievement progress to your users.

- Users appreciate a familiar interface with which they already know how to interact.

- Your app is more future-proof than it otherwise would be if you implemented your own system.

The following are a few of the benefits of using your own GUI when working with achievements on iOS devices.

- Your achievement progress can match the custom design of your app.

- You have more freedom over the returned data and can filter using additional criteria.

- You can implement your own custom caching behavior.

- You can use custom images for incomplete or in-progress achievements.

As you can see, there are advantages and disadvantages of each system, and there is no right answer in which one you should be using. By the end of this chapter you will have a better understanding of the options and be better equipped to decide which approach is the best fit for your app.

As mentioned in the beginning of this section, you will need to begin with achievements in the same manner as we did for leaderboards, in iTunes Connect.

Configuring Achievements in iTunes Connect

As we saw with leaderboards, you cannot begin working with achievements without first setting up at least one new achievement in iTunes Connect. Log in to iTunes Connect (itunesconnect.apple.com) using your Apple connect username and password, and select the app that we have already been working with from the previous chapters (see Chapter 2 for more information). Once you have selected your app from the control panel, return to the Manage Game Center area that was introduced earlier in this book.

The Game Center portal for your app will have a section labeled "Achievements." If this is the first time working with achievements in this app, a button labeled "Set Up" will appear. If you already have achievements in place, the steps are different and will be covered later in this section.

Clicking the Set Up button will bring up the Achievements Configuration Screen. Select the Add New Achievement button in the upper left-hand corner of the page, as shown in Figure 4–2. This will bring you to the view shown in Figure 4–3.

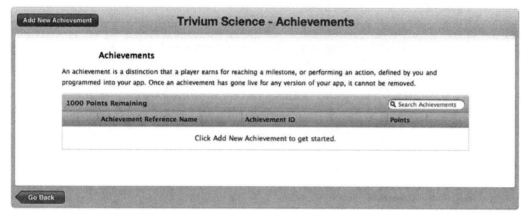

Figure 4–2. *Adding a new achievement through the iTunes Connect Portal*

You might notice that there are a lot of similarities between this portal page and the leaderboard portal page. I break down the attributes in Table 4–1.

Table 4–1. *Achievement Attributes in iTunes Connect.*

Attribute	Description
Achievement Reference Name	A string that is not used outside of iTunes Connect, this string is used to easily locate and reference this achievement within iTunes Connect.
Achievement ID	This is the identifier that you will refer to in your code. As with leaderboard categories, Apple recommends that you use a reverse DNS system such as com.company.appname.achievementname.
Hidden	If an achievement is hidden, the user will not see it in the achievement list until they have either completed it or increased the progress.
Points	Achievements can be assigned points. Your app is allocated 1,000 points. Each completed achievement progresses the user toward that total. Once the user has reached 1,000 points, he or she has unlocked all achievements.
	You should assign more points to achievements that are more difficult to complete. This provides the user with a better sense of how valuable the achievement is.
	Point values are optional and can be ignored if you do not want to use them within your app.

TIP: You aren't required to have your achievements add up to 1,000 total points, but you cannot exceed 1,000 points.

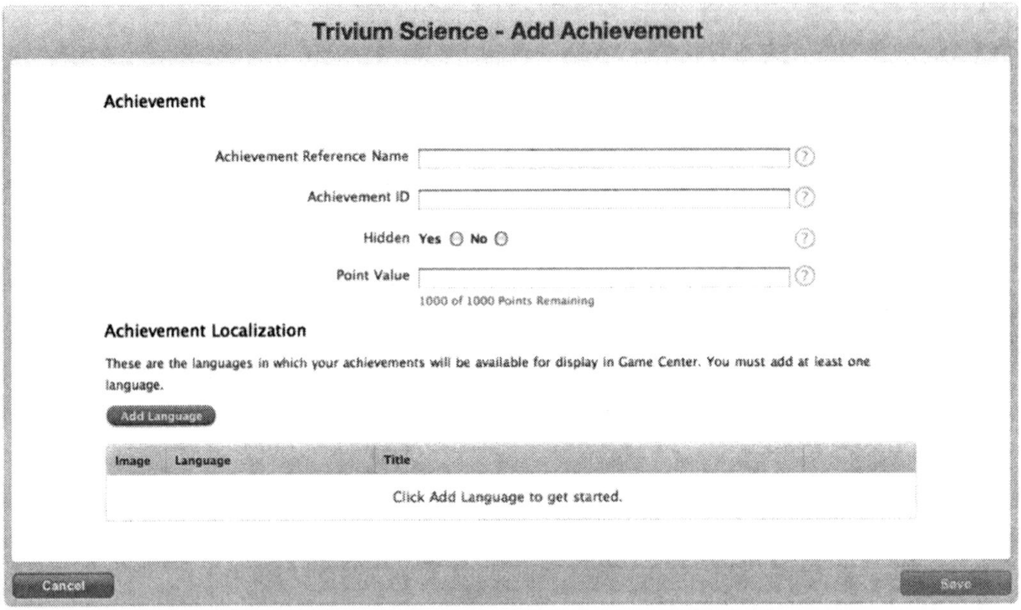

Figure 4–3. *The configuration view for new achievements in iTunes Connect*

It is now time to make a new achievement. We will create an achievement that will be reached when the user abducts 25 cows. We will use "Abduct 25" for the achievement name so it will be easy to find when we have dozens of achievements. For our achievement ID, we will use "com.dragonforged.ufo.abduct25." Feel free to use whatever ID you want here, but make sure to substitute it for com.dragonforged.ufo.abduct25 in the upcoming examples. We will make this an unhidden achievement, and assign it a point value of 10.

IMPORTANT: No achievement can have more than 100 points awarded for completing it.

For an achievement to be valid, you must configure at least one language. As you can see in Figure 4–4, the localization area of achievements is much different than that encountered when creating leaderboards in the previous chapter. Refer to Table 4–2 for information on each attribute.

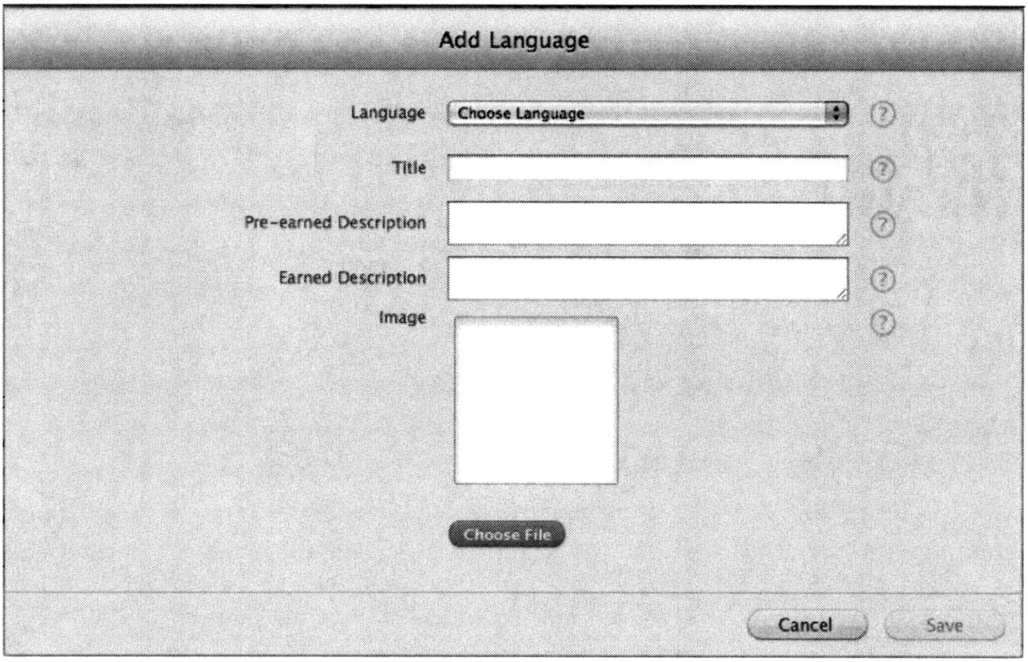

Figure 4–4. *Localizing an achievement in iTunes Connect*

> **NOTE:** Each game owns its achievement descriptions; you may not share achievement descriptions between multiple games.

Table 4–2. *Localized Achievement Attributes in iTunes Connect*

Attribute	Description
Language	Select the language in which this achievement will appear. You must set up a language for each localization that you will support in your shipping product.
Title	This is the title that will appear within the app to describe this achievement.
Pre-earned Description	This is the description that appears when the achievement is unhidden and is unearned or only partially completed.
Earned Description	This is the description that is shown when the achievement has been fully unlocked and completed.
Image	This is the image that will be displayed to the user when the achievement is earned. Apple will supply the unearned image, or you can specify your own when working with a custom achievement GUI. This image must be 512 × 512 and 72 DPI.

For our purposes, we will configure this achievement for English. I will use "Abduct 25 Cows" as the title, but you may use any title that you prefer. For the pre-earned description, I chose "Abduct 25 cows with your UFO." For the earned description, I used "You have mastered the art of cow abduction." I will also use a cow crossing road sign as the image. When you are done, you should have a fully set up achievement, which should look similar to the view shown in Figure 4–5.

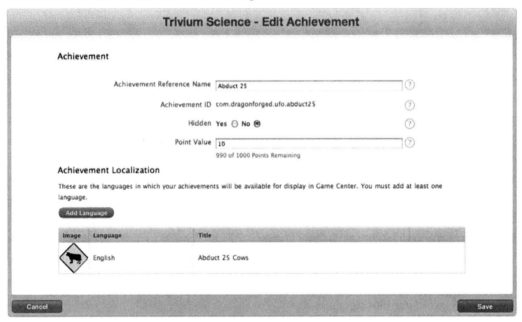

Figure 4–5. *A new achievement, as shown in iTunes Connect*

We will want to work with a couple of different achievements setups for our game. Go ahead and create another new achievement for abducting a single cow; this will be our non-progressive achievement. Then, make a third achievement for five-minute play time and set it to hidden. This last achievement will let us work with timers, progressive achievements, and hidden achievements. You may select any point values, descriptions, titles, and images you want for these achievements, but make sure you remember the achievement IDs.

You should now have three achievements configured in iTunes Connect for our game. We can now get back into Xcode and begin working with these achievements.

Presenting Achievements

Unlike leaderboards, there will be plenty to preview GUI-wise before we populate user data into our achievement system. It is helpful to see the effects that modifying achievements have on how they are displayed through the default GUI. In this chapter, we will begin by presenting Apple's achievement GUI, then move on to submitting user data. We will also cover custom GUI achievements later in this chapter.

Before we can begin, we need to create a new UIbutton that will trigger the achievement view. We most likely want to do this outside of the game screen, as we did with our two leaderboard buttons. We begin by adding a new button to the UFOViewController view, as shown in Figure 4–6.

You also need to create and hook up an IBAction to our new achievement button. Insert the following code into the action that you hooked up to the achievement button.

```
-(IBAction)achievementButtonPressed;
{
  GKAchievementViewController *controller = nil;
  controller = [[GKAchievementViewController alloc] init];
  [achievementViewController setAchievementDelegate:self];
  [self presentModalViewController:controller animated:YES];
  [controller release];
}
```

Figure 4–6. *Adding a new button to trigger our achievement view*

In addition, we need to hook up a delegate callback used with the GKAchievementViewController. Add the following method to your implementation file.

```
- (void)achievementViewControllerDidFinish:(GKAchievementViewController *)viewController
{
  [self dismissModalViewControllerAnimated:YES];
}
```

If you were to run the App and tap on the achievement button, you would now see a view similar to the one shown in Figure 4–7. The achievements shown are using Apple's unearned image. Apple recommends that you always use its unearned image, but when working with a custom achievement GUI, you can override this image and return your own.

Next, recall that we set up three achievements, one of them hidden. As you can see in Figure 4–7, the provided view shows us only two achievements. Because we have not submitted any kind of progress to the third achievement, its details are hidden from the user. However, you can see that the top information line reflects that there is a hidden achievement (0 of 3 Achievements). Also notice that the achievements are using the localized unearned description that was set in iTunes Connect.

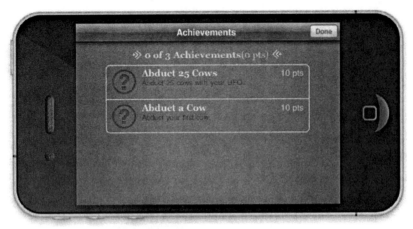

Figure 4–7. *Our achievements, as shown with Apple's default GUI*

These are the only necessary steps to show the user his or her achievement progress through Apple's built-in GUI. In the next section, we will look at how to update and progress these achievements. Later in this chapter, you will learn how to present achievement using a custom GUI.

> **NOTE:** A user can always see his or her achievement progress in Game Center.app, but it is recommended allowing your user a way to view their progress from within your app as well.

Modifying Achievement Progress

Unlike a leaderboard entry, achievements can be constantly modified and progressed through user interaction. As with the other Game Center functionality we have been working with, we will create a new method in our GameCenterManager class to handle interacting with achievements. Once the following method has been added, we will review the method to understand exactly how it functions.

> **TIP:** Remember that all this source code is made available to you online. When dealing with large methods, it might be easier to copy it from the source code downloaded from apress.com.

```
- (void)submitAchievement:(NSString*)identifier percentComplete:(double)percentComplete
{
  if ([self earnedAchievementCache] == NULL) {
    [GKAchievement loadAchievementsWithCompletionHandler:^(NSArray *achievements,↵
NSError *error) {
      if (error == NULL) {
        NSMutableDictionary *tempCache = [NSMutableDictionary dictionaryWithCapacity:↵
```

```
[achievements count]];

        for (GKAchievement* achievement in achievements) {
          [tempCache setObject: achievement forKey: [achievement identifier]];
        }

        [self setEarnedAchievementCache:tempCache];
        [self submitAchievement:identifier percentComplete:percentComplete];
      } else {
        [self callDelegateOnMainThread:@selector(achievementSubmitted:error:)↩
withArg:NULL error:error];
      }
    }];
  } else {
    GKAchievement *achievement = [[self earnedAchievementCache]↩
objectForKey:identifier];

    if (achievement != NULL) {
      if (((([achievement percentComplete] >= 100.0) ||↩
([achievement percentComplete] >= percentComplete)) {
        achievement = NULL;
      }
      [achievement setPercentComplete:percentComplete];
    } else {
      achievement = [[[GKAchievement alloc] initWithIdentifier:identifier] autorelease];
      [achievement setPercentComplete:percentComplete];
      [[self earnedAchievementCache] setObject:achievement forKey:[achievement↩
identifier]];
    }

    if (achievement != NULL) {
      [achievement reportAchievementWithCompletionHandler:^(NSError *error) {
        [self callDelegateOnMainThread: @selector(achievementSubmitted:error:)↩
withArg: achievement error:error];
      }];
    }
  }
}
```

Before this code can be executed, you need to add a new class property. Create a new mutable dictionary (and don't forget to synthesize it). The relevant section of the header of GameCenterManager should now look like the following.

```
@interface GameCenterManager : NSObject <GameCenterManagerDelegate>
{
  id <GameCenterManagerDelegate, NSObject> delegate;
  NSMutableDictionary* earnedAchievementCache;
}

@property(nonatomic, retain) id <GameCenterManagerDelegate, NSObject> delegate;
@property(nonatomic, retain) NSMutableDictionary* earnedAchievementCache;
```

Now look at the submitAchievement:percentComplete: method we added. There are two primary if/else blocks. The first one is executed if [self earnedAchievemenetCache] is NULL, which it will always be the first time this code is executed. Let's take a look at that block of code now.

```
[GKAchievement loadAchievementsWithCompletionHandler:^(NSArray *achievements, NSError↵
 *error) {
  if (error == NULL) {
    NSMutableDictionary *tempCache = [NSMutableDictionary dictionaryWithCapacity:↵
[achievements count]];

    for (GKAchievement *achievement in achievements) {
      [tempCache setObject:achievement forKey:[achievement identifier]];
    }

    [self setEarnedAchievementCache:tempCache];
    [self submitAchievement:identifier percentComplete:percentComplete];
  } else {
    [self callDelegateOnMainThread:@selector(achievementSubmitted:error:) withArg:NULL↵
error:error];
  }
}];
```

> **IMPORTANT:** The array that is returned by loadAchievementsWithCompletionHandler will not
> show any achievements that you have not yet submitted a percentageCompleted for.

The primary function of this code snippet is to load a list of achievements into the
earnedAchievementCache. We call loadAchievementsWithCompletionHandler on
GKAchievement. This call returns an array of all the achievements that were set up in
iTunes Connect. We then store the GKAchievement object into the dictionary with the
identifier as the key. At this point, the code calls submitAchievement:percentComplete
again. This time, earnedAchievementCache is not NULL and the second set of code is
executed. If we encounter an error during this process, we use our standard delegate
callback to send the error back to our delegate.

You will need to add a new protocol method to GameCenterManager to handle this
delegate callback; this is a good time to do that. Add the following optional protocol to
the header file.

```
- (void)achievementSubmitted:(GKAchievement*)achievement error:(NSError*)error;
```

Now let's take a look at the second section of code. The following code, when
successfully executed, submits the achievement to the Game Center servers.

```
GKAchievement *achievement = [[self earnedAchievementCache] objectForKey:identifier];
if (achievement != NULL) {
  if ((achievement.percentComplete >= 100.0) || (achievement.percentComplete >=↵
percentComplete)) {
        achievement = NULL;
  }

  [achievement setPercentComplete:percentComplete];
} else {
  achievement = [[[GKAchievement alloc] initWithIdentifier: identifier] autorelease];
  [achievement setPercentComplete:percentComplete];

  [[self earnedAchievementCache] setObject:achievement forKey:[achievement identifier]];
}
```

```
if (achievement != NULL) {
  [achievement reportAchievementWithCompletionHandler: ^(NSError *error) {
    [self callDelegateOnMainThread:@selector(achievementSubmitted:error:)↵
 withArg:achievement error:error];
        }];
}
```

The first line of code retrieves a GKAchievement object from our earnedAchievementCache, based on the identifier string that is passed into this method. If the achievement is completed or the reported progress is equal to what we have on the Game Center server, we set the achievement to NULL. This prevents us from tying up networking time by submitting progress on something that will be ignored. We also set the property for percentComplete on the GKAchievement object to the double that was passed into this method.

In the event that the achievement doesn't exist in the cache, we allocate and initialize a new instance of it. In this event, we also want to add it to our local achievement cache.

The final step, after doing a NULL check, is to submit the achievement. We call reportAchievementWithCompletionHandler on the achievement object. We then pass the results back to our delegate using our existing protocol.

> **NOTE:** All achievements have a percentageComplete regardless of whether they allow a percentage to be completed at a time. If your achievement can only be completely earned or unearned, then you will want to pass 100 for earned.

The last thing that we need to do in this section is implement our protocol method in UFOGameViewController. Add the following method to the implementation of that file; all we will worry about right now is printing the error and success information to the console.

```
- (void)achievementSubmitted:(GKAchievement *)achievement error:(NSError *)error;
{
  if (error) {
    NSLog(@"There was an error in reporting the achievement: %@", [error↵
 localizedDescription]);
  } else {
    NSLog(@"achievement submitted");
  }
}
```

Resetting Achievements

There are circumstances when you might want to reset user achievements. Besides being extremely helpful in debugging, you might find it useful to provide users with an option to reset. You might want to add a prestige mode or give the users a chance to start your game over from the beginning. The following code snippet will completely reset all achievements in your app for the local user.

```
- (void)resetAchievements
{
  [self setEarnedAchievementCache:NULL];

  [GKAchievement resetAchievementsWithCompletionHandler:^(NSError *error) {
     if (error == NULL) {
       NSLog(@"Achievements have been reset");
     } else {
       NSLog(@"There was an error in resetting the achievements: %@", [error↵
localizedDescription]);
     }
  }];
}
```

> **IMPORTANT:** Don't forget to remove the cached information you have stored on the achievements,
> or you will not be able to progress the reset achievements until the app is restarted.

Adding Achievement Hooks

The biggest challenge in implementing achievements into your app is adding the hooks
to activate and progress those achievements into your normal routines. In my personal
experience, I have found that adding these hooks when the program is almost finished is
easier than trying to add them in as you go. In this section, I will provide a number of
examples of how to tie in achievements; your own app may differ significantly, but you
should be able to easily adapt the examples to suit your needs.

To make achievements easier to retrieve progress details, we first add a few
convenience methods to our GameCenterManager class. This is the first method we will
use to populate the local achievement cache.

```
-(void)populateAchievementCache
{
  if ([self earnedAchievementCache] == NULL) {
    [GKAchievement loadAchievementsWithCompletionHandler:^(NSArray *achievements,↵
NSError *error) {
      if (error == NULL) {
        NSMutableDictionary* tempCache= [NSMutableDictionary dictionaryWithCapacity:↵
[achievements count]];

        for (GKAchievement *achievement in achievements) {
          [tempCache setObject:achievement forKey:[achievement identifier]];
        }

        [self setEarnedAchievementCache:tempCache];
      } else {
        NSLog(@"An error occurred while loading achievements: %@", [error↵
localizedDescription]);
      }
    }];
  }
}
```

The preceding method functions very similarly to the cache population code in the submit achievement progress method previewed in the previous section. We will need to populate the local cache in order to work with the other two convenience methods. We will want to call the populateAchievementCache as soon as we can after authenticating; in our demo app, I have added a call to it from the local player did authenticate method in GameCenterManager. Add the following method as well.

```
- (double)percentageCompleteOfAchievementWithIdentifier: (NSString*)identifier
{
  if ([self earnedAchievementCache] == NULL) {
    NSLog(@"Unable to determine achievement progress, local cache is empty");
  } else {
    GKAchievement *achievement= [[self earnedAchievementCache] objectForKey:identifier];

    if (achievement != NULL) {
      return [achievement percentComplete];
    } else {
      return 0;
    }
  }
  return -1;
}
```

The preceding method returns a double for the percent complete for the achievement with the identifier passed to it. If it cannot find a copy of the achievement in the local cache, we can assume the percent complete is 0. The next method uses the preceding method to return either YES or NO on whether an achievement has been completed.

```
- (BOOL)achievementWithIdentifierIsComplete: (NSString*)identifier
{
  if ([self percentageCompleteOfAchievementWithIdentifier:identifier] >= 100) {
    return YES;
  } else  {
    return NO;
  }
}
```

> **NOTE:** Do not forget to call populateAchievementCache as soon as possible after authentication. Otherwise, these convenience methods will not return correct information.

Now that we have some helper methods in place, we can begin to hook up the achievement hooks for UFOs. We have three different achievements we need to tie in. The first two both have to do with the number of cows that we have abducted, so let's start there. Modify the finishAbducting method of UFOGameViewController to match the following.

```
- (void)finishAbducting
{
  if (!currentAbductee || !tractorBeamOn) return;

  [cowArray removeObjectIdenticalTo:currentAbductee];

  [tractorBeamImageView removeFromSuperview];
```

```
    tractorBeamOn = NO;

    score++;
    [scoreLabel setText:[NSString stringWithFormat:@"SCORE %05.0f", score]];

    [[currentAbductee layer] removeAllAnimations];
    [currentAbductee removeFromSuperview];

    currentAbductee = nil;

    [self spawnCow];

    if (![[self gcManager] achievementWithIdentifierIsComplete:↩
@"com.dragonforged.ufo.aduct1"]) {
        [[self gcManager] submitAchievement:@"com.dragonforged.ufo.aduct1"↩
    percentComplete:100];
    }
}
```

We are concerned with only the last few lines of this method at this time. First, we call
our convenience method achievementWithIdentifierIsComplete on our identifier string for
a single abduction. Because this is an earned or unearned achievement, we don't need
to worry about current percentage complete. To mark the achievement as complete, we
set its percent complete to 100.

> **NOTE:** Don't forget to change the identifier string from the example to the one that you used in
> iTunes Connect for a single abduction.

The next achievement is hooked up in a similar fashion; the only difference is that we
use incremental progress. Add the following code snippet onto the end of the
finishAbducting method.

```
if (![[self gcManager] achievementWithIdentifierIsComplete:↩
 @"com.dragonforged.ufo.abduct25"]) {
   double percentComplete = [[self gcManager]↩
 percentageCompleteOfAchievementWithIdentifier: @"com.dragonforged.ufo.abduct25"];

   percentComplete += 4;
   [[self gcManager] submitAchievement:@"com.dragonforged.ufo.abduct25"↩
 percentComplete:percentComplete];
}
```

In the preceding code snippet, we use the same methodology that we did for submitting
a complete achievement, but with one main difference. We first need to determine the
current progress on the achievement. We then add 4 to it, since 4 percent of 25 is 1. To
increment by 1 abduction out of 25, we need to add 4.

> **TIP:** Do not forget about the resetAchievement method that we added to GameCenterManager. It is very useful in debugging the submit code. I find it is helpful to keep a call to this in the didAuthenticate section to always put the app back to a clean state during debugging.

Go ahead and run the game and abduct a few cows. When you are done, you will notice that the achievement screen now shows progress similar to that shown in Figure 4–8. If you abducted at least one cow, you should have a complete achievement. If you abducted less than 25 cows, you should have one progressed achievement. Notice that the user is not informed when he or she completes an achievement; we will discuss a method of notification in the later section, "Achievement Completion Feedback."

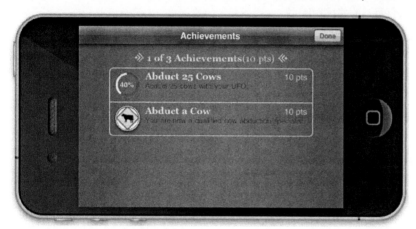

Figure 4–8. *Progressing achievements*

The last hook we add for this project handles the player for the five-minutes achievement. Your first instinct is probably to keep track of time played, and submit it as progress when your user exits the game. This might not be the best approach. We want to inform the user when he or she completes an achievement. You don't want them to have to wait until they finish a game to see which achievements they have earned. There are many approaches to this problem. For this example, we will fire an NSTimer every three seconds (which is one percent of five minutes) and update the achievements progress. Add the following to UFOGameViewController.

```
- (void)tickThreeSeconds
{
  if ([[self gcManager]↵
achievementWithIdentifierIsComplete:@"com.dragonforged.ufo.play5"]) return;

  double percentComplete = [[self gcManager]↵
percentageCompleteOfAchievementWithIdentifier:@"com.dragonforged.ufo.play5"];
  percentComplete++;
  [[self gcManager] submitAchievement:@"com.dragonforged.ufo.play5"↵
percentComplete:percentComplete];
}
```

As well as modifying the viewDidAppear and ViewWillDisappear methods to match the following, we will start a three-second timer. Every time the timer fires, we call tickThreeSeconds. This gives us our current progress of the achievement, to which we add one percent, then submit it back to the server. In the event that the achievement is already complete, we simply return.

```
-(void)viewDidAppear:(BOOL)animated
{
  [super viewDidAppear: animated];

  timer = [NSTimer scheduledTimerWithTimeInterval:3.0 target:self↩
 selector:@selector(tickThreeSeconds) userInfo:nil repeats:YES];
}

- (void)viewWillDisappear:(BOOL)animated
{
  [super viewWillDisappear: animated];
  [timer invalidate];
  timer = nil;
}
```

Another Convenience Method

There might be occasions where you would like to get GKAchievement when all you have available is an achievement identifier. The following method will return a GKAchievement when passed an achievement identifier.

```
- (GKAchievement*)achievementForIdentifier:(NSString*)identifier
{
  GKAchievement *achievement = [[self earnedAchievementCache] objectForKey:identifier];

  if (achievement == nil) {
    achievement = [[[GKAchievement alloc] initWithIdentifier:identifier] autorelease];
    [[self earnedAchievementCache] setObject:achievement forKey:[achievement↩
 identifier]];
  }

  return achievement;
}
```

Achievement Completion Feedback

It is important to let users know when they have completed an achievement. However, you don't want to just present a UIAlertView, as that would be very distracting, considering most achievements are going to be completed in the middle of an action, such as completing 20 laps in a racing game. You wouldn't want to take the user away from any interaction, so we need a better system. I have always been a fan of the small view that slides in from the bottom or top to inform the user of the accomplishment— very similar to the fashion in which you get feedback from logging in to Game Center.

The first thing we need to do in order to implement a feedback system is add a new protocol method to GameCenterManager. We will use this to inform the delegate that an achievement has been completed for the first time. Add the following method to the header file, as an optional protocol.

```
-(void)achievementEarned:(GKAchievementDescription*)achievement;
```

In addition, we need to modify our existing submitAchievement:percentComplete: method. Take a look at the last if statement block of that method. We want to modify it as follows, but add an if statement to determine whether we have a percentageComplete over 100, which will call our new protocol. Also notice that we are using GKAchievementDescription instead of GKAchievement. We will discuss this further in the next section, "Custom Achievement GUI.".

```
if (achievement != NULL) {
  [achievement reportAchievementWithCompletionHandler:^(NSError *error) {
    if (percentComplete < 100) {
      [self callDelegateOnMainThread: @selector(achievementSubmitted:error:)↵
withArg:achievement error:error];
      return;
    }

    [GKAchievementDescription loadAchievementDescriptionsWithCompletionHandler:↵
^(NSArray *descriptions, NSError *error) {
      for (GKAchievementDescription *achievementDescription in descriptions) {
        if (![[achievement identifier] isEqualToString:[achievementDescription↵
identifier]]) continue;

        [self callDelegateOnMainThread:@selector(achievementEarned:)↵
withArg:achievementDescription error:nil];
      }
    }];

    [self callDelegateOnMainThread: @selector(achievementSubmitted:error:)↵
withArg:achievement error:error];
  }];
}
```

This completes the modifications that we need to make to the GameCenterManager class. Now we need to hook up the visual feedback for the user. Move back into UFOGameViewController.m and add our new protocol method achievementEarned:. You could add any type of feedback here including a standard UIAlertView, but we will be exploring something a little more user friendly in this section.

We need to create some new IBOutlets as part of our UFOGameViewController. Make a new view and set its dimensions to 480 × 25. Then, set the background of the view to black with 70% opacity. We also create a new label, place it in the center of this view, and set the text alignment to center. Your view should look similar to that shown in Figure 4–9.

Figure 4–9. *Achievement earned view and label*

Hook up both the view and the label to IBOutlets. I have named mine achievementCompletionView and achievementCompletionLabel, respectively. We then modify our achievementEarned: method, as well as add an additional method to handle the animations.

```
- (void)achievementEarned:(GKAchievementDescription *)achievement;
{
    [achievementCompletionView setFrame:CGRectMake(0, 320, 480, 25)];
    [[self view] addSubview:achievementCompletionView];
    [achievementcompletionLabel setText:[achievement achievedDescription]];

    [UIView beginAnimations:@"SlideInAchievement" context:nil];
    [UIView setAnimationDuration:0.5];
    [UIView setAnimationDelegate:self];
    [UIView setAnimationDidStopSelector:@selector(achievementEarnedAnimationDone)];
    [achievementCompletionView setFrame:CGRectMake(0, 295, 480, 25)];
    [UIView commitAnimations];
}

-(void)achievementEarnedAnimationDone
{
    [UIView beginAnimations:@"SlideInAchievement" context:nil];
    [UIView setAnimationDelay:5.0];
    [UIView setAnimationDuration:1.0];
    [achievementCompletionView setFrame:CGRectMake(0, 320, 480, 25)];
    [UIView commitAnimations];
}
```

Both of these methods are fairly straightforward. When we get a delegate callback from completing the achievement, we add our achievementCompletionView to our game view. Then, we animate it onto the bottom of the view. After a five-second delay, we animate it back off the view. You also have access to the images used in GKAchievementDescription. We will look more into these properties in the next section.

> **TIP:** You might need to reset your achievements to see any completion progress. I find it is helpful to create a new button that resets achievements for use during testing.

If you run the app now and abduct a single cow (assuming you haven't yet accomplished that achievement), you should see output very similar to that shown in Figure 4–10.

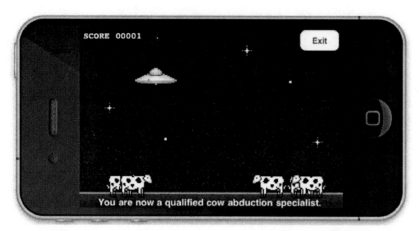

Figure 4–10.

iOS 5 Completion Banners

In iOS 4 you were responsible for creating and displaying achievement feedback for your users. Apple has added a very easy-to-use property onto the GKAchievement class to allow you to quickly implement this step: setting the showsCompletionBanner property as seen in the following code snippet with display a message to the user when an achievement has been completed. The default property of showsCompletionBanner is NO.

```
myAchievement.showsCompletionBanner = YES;
```

Custom Achievement GUI

There might be times when you will want to customize the appearance of your achievement system to match the custom GUI in your app. As we saw with leaderboards in the previous chapter, we have the ability to work with the raw data and present it in whatever fashion we choose. This section focuses on adding achievements to your app using your own GUI. As with the leaderboard section, the first thing that we need to do is to add a new button to get to our custom achievement progress view. Add a new button and associated action, as shown in Figure 4–11.

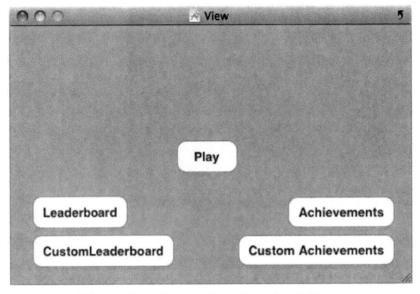

Figure 4–11. *Adding a custom achievement button in Interface Builder*

We will need to create a new class to handle processing and displaying the achievement progress information. Create a new class named UFOAchievementViewController and make it a subclass of UIViewController. Set up actions and outlets in the XIB for a table view, a navigation bar, and a dismiss button. Don't forget to set the datasource and delegate for the table view as well. Your XIB should look like the one shown in Figure 4–12.

Figure 4–12. *Custom achievement progress view, as shown for interface builder*

We also want to create an array that will be used to hold onto the achievement data. Create a new NSArray object and name it achievementArray. We also want to import the GameCenterManager header and conform to its protocol. The header file for UFOAchievementViewController should now look similar to the following one.

```
#import <UIKit/UIKit.h>
#import "GameCenterManager.h"

@interface UFOAchievementViewController : UIViewController <UITableViewDelegate,↵
 UITableViewDataSource, GameCenterManagerDelegate>
{
  GameCenterManager *gcManager;

  UITableView *achievementTableView;

  NSArray *achievementArray;
}

@property (nonatomic, retain) GameCenterManager *gcManager;
@property (nonatomic, retain) NSArray *achievementArray;
@property (nonatomic, retain) IBOutlet UITableView *achievementTableView;

- (IBAction)dismissAction;

@end
```

Next, hook up the action to present our new UFOAchievementViewController class. Edit
the action that was created in UFOViewController to reflect the following changes.

```
- (IBAction)customAchievementButtonPressed;
{
  UFOAchievementViewController *achievementViewController =↵
 [[UFOAchievementViewController alloc] init];

  [achievementViewController setGcManager:gcManager];

  [self presentModalViewController:achievementViewController animated:YES];

  [achievementViewController release];
}
```

Let's take a minute to switch over to the implementation file for
UFOAchievementViewController. First, add a method to ensure the view is properly set
for landscape orientation. Add the following method.

```
-(BOOL) shouldAutorotateToInterfaceOrientation:↵
 (UIInterfaceOrientation)interfaceOrientation
{
  if (UIInterfaceOrientationIsLandscape(interfaceOrientation)) return YES;

  return NO;
}
```

we also need a dismiss action, add that method as well.

```
- (IBAction)dismissAction
{
  [self dismissModalViewControllerAnimated:YES];
}
```

If you were to run the app now, you should see a plain and boring table view, similar to
the one shown in Figure 4–13. In addition, the dismiss button should now be working.

Figure 4–13. *The blank custom table that we will be using for our custom achievements*

Before we can go on with our UFOAchievementViewController, we need to move back into our GameCenterManager class. Add the following method as an optional protocol to the GameCenterManagerDelegate.

```
- (void)achievementDescriptionsLoaded:(NSArray *)descriptions error:(NSError *)error;
```

Then add the following new method to the implementation of GameCenterManager.

```
- (void)retrieveAchievementMetadata
{
  [GKAchievementDescription loadAchievementDescriptionsWithCompletionHandler:↵
^(NSArray *descriptions, NSError *error) {
    [self callDelegateOnMainThread:@selector(achievementDescriptionsLoaded:error:)↵
 withArg:descriptions error:error];
  }];
}
```

This method will return all the GKAchievementDescriptions that are found on the Game Center server. We can now move back to our UFOAchievementViewController class and finish implementing the custom achievement table.

> **IMPORTANT:** The retrieveAchievementMetadata method will return hidden achievements as well. If you want to hide these from the user, you will have to filter them out of the results.

Modify the viewWillAppear: method of UFOAchievementViewController to match the following.

```
- (void)viewWillAppear:(BOOL)animated
{
  [[self gcManager] setDelegate:self];

  [super viewWillAppear: YES];

  [[self gcManager] retrieveAchievementMetadata];
}
```

In addition, add the new protocol method that we created earlier. If we do not encounter any errors, we simply set the returned descriptions to our local array. When we get the new data, we will also want to refresh the table to show the data to the user.

```objc
- (void)achievementDescriptionsLoaded:(NSArray *)descriptions error:(NSError *)error;
{
  if (error == nil) {
    [self setAchievementArray:descriptions];
  } else {
    NSLog(@"An error occurred when retrieving the achievement descriptions: %@",↵
[error localizedDescription]);
  }

  [achievementTableView reloadData];
}
```

For our numberOfRowsInSection method, we simply return the count on the achievementArray, as follows.

```objc
- (NSInteger)tableView:(UITableView *)tableView numberOfRowsInSection:(NSInteger)section
{
  return [[self achievementArray] count];
}
```

We also need to implement a cellForRowAtIndexPath method. Add the following method to the implementation as well. After it is added, we will look at it in more detail.

```objc
- (UITableViewCell *)tableView:(UITableView *)tableView↵
 cellForRowAtIndexPath:(NSIndexPath *)indexPath
{
  static NSString *CellIdentifier = @"Cell";
  UITableViewCell *cell = [tableView dequeueReusableCellWithIdentifier:CellIdentifier];

  if (cell == nil) {
    cell = [[[UITableViewCell alloc] initWithStyle:UITableViewCellStyleDefault↵
reuseIdentifier:CellIdentifier] autorelease];
    [cell setSelectionStyle:UITableViewCellSelectionStyleNone];
  }

  GKAchievementDescription *achievementDescription = [[self achievementArray]↵
objectAtIndex:[indexPath row]];
  [[cell textLabel] setText:[achievementDescription title]];

  if ([achievementDescription image] == nil) {
    [[cell imageView] setImage:[GKAchievementDescription↵
placeholderCompletedAchievementImage]];
    [achievementDescription loadImageWithCompletionHandler:^(UIImage *image, NSError↵
*error) {
      if (error == nil) {
        [[cell imageView] setImage:image];
      }
    }];
  } else {
    [[cell imageView] setImage:[achievementDescription image]];
  }

  return cell;
}
```

The first half of this method is rather standard; we create a new table cell or we use one from our reusable collection. We are using the default built-in table cell to save some time as well. We create a new GKAchievementDescription and populate it based on the row number from our achievementArray.

The first property we work with is the title, which we use to set the textLabel of the cell. In most circumstances, you will want to use the achievedDescription or unachievedDescription as well as the title. For the sake of simplicity, we use only the title here. Next, we need to set the image for the achievement. This is slightly more complex.

GKAchievementDescription has an image property associated with it, which is nil until you populate it. First, check to see whether the property is populated; we can accomplish this with a simple nil check. If it is populated, we set the cell image to the one that we have cached. If not, we need to load an image from the Game Center servers. To populate it, we call loadImageWithCompletionHandler on the GKAchievementDescription object. This returns the earned image. Notice that we used the default placeholder image, which we can access through a class method on GKAchievementDescription.

> **TIP:** When setting an image in the UITableViewCellSytleDefault cell, do not set the image to nil. This will cause the cell to left align the text and remove the image view. If we then use our block to load the image, it wouldn't appear until the cell or table has been reloaded. This is the reason we set the placeholder image first.

If we were to run the app and visit our custom achievement view, it should look similar to the one shown in Figure 4–14.

Figure 4–14. *Achievement data, as displayed in a custom GUI*

We are able to view only a list of achievements and associated images, but not how far the user has progressed toward unlocking the achievements. If you recall, earlier in this chapter we wrote a few convenience methods, which can be useful here. We have two methods that will return just the progress for the achievement, percentageCompleteOfAchievementWithIdentifier: and achievementWithIdentifierIsComplete. In addition, if we want access to the entire GKAchievement object, we can use achievementForIdentifier. Let's use the percentageCompleteOfAchievementWithIdentifier: to display the percentage complete here. Modify the section of code in the cellForRowAtIndexPath: that sets the text label of the cell. The new code snippet should look like the following.

```
NSString *percentageCompleteString = [NSString stringWithFormat: @" %.0f%% Complete",↵
 [[self gcManager] percentageCompleteOfAchievementWithIdentifier:↵
[achievementDescription identifier]]];

[[cell textLabel] setText:[[achievementDescription title]↵
 stringByAppendingString:percentageCompleteString]];
```

If you run the game again, you will notice a more helpful output, as shown in Figure 4–15.

Figure 4–15. *Achievements with custom GUI and completion percentage*

Recovering from a Submit Failure

You as the developer are solely responsible for handling achievement-submitting failures. You do not want your users to lose any achievement progress. Losing an achievement is very frustrating to your users and should be avoided at all cost. To prevent this, take the same approach that we used when working with score failures. The primary difference is that there is no need to store the GKAchievement object because it does not contain any date information or time-sensitive information. We just need to store the percentageComplete. We will create a new method to handle this behavior for us. Add the following method to the GameCenterManager class.

```
-(void)storeAchievementToSubmitLater:(GKAchievement *)achievement
{
  NSMutableDictionary *achievementDictionary = [[NSMutableDictionary alloc]↵
 initWithArray:[[NSUserDefaults standardUserDefaults]↵
 objectForKey:@"savedAchievements"]];
```

```
    if ([achievementDictionary objectForKey:[achievement identifier]] == nil) {
        [achievementDictionary setObject:[NSNumber numberWithDouble:[achievement↵
percentComplete]] forKey:[achievement identifier]];
    } else {
        double storedProgress = [[achievementDictionary objectForKey:↵
achievement.identifier] doubleValue];
        if ([achievement percentComplete] > storedProgress) {
            [achievementDictionary setObject:[NSNumber numberWithDouble:[achievement↵
percentComplete]] forKey:[achievement identifier]];
        }
    }

    [[NSUserDefaults standardUserDefaults] setObject:achievementDictionary↵
forKey:@"savedAchievements"];

    [achievementDictionary release];
}
```

This method will treat an achievement as an argument, and verify whether it is not already stored as a reference in our achievements that have failed to properly be submitted. If it has, then we need to see which one is progressed further so we do not have any instances in which we delete a user's progress. Once that is done, we store it into userDefaults as a dictionary, using the identifier as the key and the percentage completed as the value. We add a call to this method from an error in the submitAchievement:PercentComplete: method. You can find the relevant snippet of code, as follows.

```
if (achievement!= NULL) {
    [achievement reportAchievementWithCompletionHandler: ^(NSError *error) {
        if (error != nil) {
            [self storeAchievementToSubmitLater: achievement];
        }

        if (percentComplete >= 100) {
            [GKAchievementDescription loadAchievementDescriptionsWithCompletionHandler:↵
^(NSArray *descriptions, NSError *error) {
                for (GKAchievementDescription *achievementDescription in descriptions) {
                    if (![[achievement identifier] isEqualToString:[achievementDescription↵
identifier]]) continue;
                    [self callDelegateOnMainThread:@selector(achievementEarned:)↵
withArg:achievementDescription error:nil];
                }
            }];
        }

        [self callDelegateOnMainThread: @selector(achievementSubmitted:error:)↵
withArg: achievement error: error];
    }];
}
```

> **TIP:** I recommend informing your users their achievement could not be submitted at this time, but it has been saved and will be submitted later. This lets the user know that any progress has not been lost.

We also need a new method that will check to see whether we have uncommitted achievement progress. There is no right answer for when it is a good time to call this method. You can typically get away with calling it after a user authenticates with Game Center, but you may want to add additional methods that it is called from, such as whenever the reachability status is updated. Add the following method to your GameCenterManager class.

```
- (void)submitAllSavedAchievements
{
  NSMutableDictionary *achievementDictionary = [[NSMutableDictionary alloc]↵
 initWithArray:[[NSUserDefaults standardUserDefaults]↵
 objectForKey:@"savedAchievements"]];
  NSArray *keys = [achievementDictionary allKeys];

  for (int x = 0; x < [keys count]; x++) {
    [self submitAchievement:[keys objectAtIndex:x] percentComplete:↵
[[achievementDictionary objectForKey:[keys objectAtIndex:x]] doubleValue]];

    [[NSUserDefaults standardUserDefaults] removeObjectForKey:[keys objectAtIndex:x]];
  }

  [achievementDictionary release];
}
```

This method loads a copy of our unsubmitted progress and loops through each item, attempting to resubmit them as they go. In the event that they fail to be submitted again, they will be added back to our saved data.

Summary

You now have all the tools you need to add rich and complex achievements into your Game Center–enabled app. You now know the value of adding achievements, as well as how to set up and configure them in the iTunes Connect Portal. We have discussed the pros and cons of using both Apple's default GUI and a custom GUI that you have designed. You now know how to expand our GameCenterManager class to include posting achievement progress, getting achievement feedback, and resetting achievement progress all together.

The most important step completed in this chapter is expanding the reusable GameCenterManager class, which will allow you to easily add achievements in future projects. In the next chapter, we will explore Game Center's matchmaking and invitation systems so you can add multiplayer capabilities and other networking features.

Chapter 5

Matchmaking and Invitations

Beginning with this chapter, and through the next few chapters, we will discuss how to add networking with Game Center, and later Game Kit, into your app or game. Adding networking capability to your app is almost considered essential technology in the modern era. Virtually all modern software has some sort of networking component associated with it today, whether it is talking to an online service to retrieve or post information, or talking directly to a peer device to exchange data.

In the following chapters we will discuss communicating with other peer devices, although not all of our networking configurations will be peer to peer (see Chapter 7 for details on network design).

This chapter, in particular, explores how to use Game Center to find and invite peers into your app using Game Center's invitation system.

Game Center provides an amazingly undervalued selling and distribution tool to you for very little overhead, in regards to handling invitations. When inviting non-local users to begin a multiplayer experience in your game or app, you have the option to invite any of your Game Center friends. If the friends that you invite do not currently have the app installed, they will be prompted to purchase the app instantly and begin playing. There are no other methods on the iPhone to send a "buy now" link to another user in this manner. This functionality provides a great way to grow your user base—just let your users do the selling for you.

Why Add Matchmaking and Invitations to Your App?

When looking at the list of the top-ten selling PC or console games for any recent year, you will find it heavily dominated by games that demonstrate a strong focus on multiplayer interaction. Let's take a quick look at the number one selling PC game for 2010, *Call of Duty: Black Ops*. While this game does feature a single-player mode, this is considered more of an add-on to the game as opposed to the primary selling point. The focus was obviously the multiplayer gaming, even at the sacrifice of the single-player campaign. In recent years, the industry's focus has shifted from creating rich and in-depth single-player campaigns to putting more effort into the multiplayer. There is a perfectly reasonable answer for this new phenomenon: you get more bang for the buck with multiplayer.

Humans are, by nature, social creatures. We crave social interaction for healthy mental development. Video games and other social software are increasingly becoming an outlet for that interaction. Whether you agree with the politics of that statement is not what is important here, but the fact remains that multiplayer games are becoming more and more popular. Software users have grown increasingly fond of multiplayer interaction, be it a massive multiplayer online role-playing game, or your garden-variety first-person shooter.

Adding a multiplayer element to your game can increase user playtime by a hundredfold. If you need proof, look at *Quake 3* or *Unreal Tournament,* both of which were released in 1999 and both of which still had users logging in for many years after. If these games had focused solely on single-player, they most likely wouldn't have had such a devoted fan base. Listed here are some additional reasons why adding matchmaking and invitations through Game Center should be a simple business decision for your products.

- Adding a multiplayer component to a game is a great way to add additional polish. Depending on the type of game you are working with, it might be very minor additional work to add a multiplayer element.

- Users have come to expect multiplayer from top-notch games on the App Store.

- You can justify a higher selling point if you have a well done multiplayer component.

- There is no better way to have users download your app on the fly than the auto-buy invitation system. If you can set up perspective users for a situation in which they are invited to play and can purchase immediately, you will have a much better chance of closing the sale.

- You can increase playtime or use-time in your app or game, if you are using an ad-supported system. This will result in more income. If you are selling a paid app, users will feel like they have gotten more for their money.

- Humans like to compete, so encourage your users to do what they enjoy. Multiplayer might not be for everyone, but for many, it is all they are interested in when shopping for a new game.

> **TIP:** Whenever possible, also provide your users with a single-player option for your game, as there is still a noticeable user base that prefer single-player campaigns.

Common Matchmaking Scenarios

Before we begin working with matches and invitations themselves, it is important to understand some of the scenarios that you might encounter in your quest to implement multiplayer networking into your iOS app or game.

- The first, and probably most common, scenario that you could encounter would be players who are already in your app and want to create an auto-matched game. Both players will already have the app installed and loaded, as well as be in a place where it is expected that they will want to begin a networked session with each other. The invitee player will receive a notification asking whether he or she wants to join a game with the inviter. When both agree, the matchmaking GUI is dismissed and a new match is created.

- Another common scenario that you could encounter would be if the user creates a new matchmaking event and invites other players from their Game Center friends list. The invited friends will receive a push notification informing them that they have been invited to a game; if they already have the game installed and accept the invitation, the game will be launched. Once all invited players have entered the match, the game will begin. If they do not yet have the game installed, they will be prompted to install it and it will automatically be launched after it has been successfully installed.

- A slightly different event path would occur if a friend is invited, and they do not yet have the app installed, and have decided to install the app. After the install process, the app will automatically launch and you can continue with the normal flow of the matchmaking event.

- A player can also create a new matchmaking event from within the Game Center.app itself. In this scenario, All players are launched into the app and receive an invitation to join the match. The best part about this scenario is that if your app already supports invitations, you don't need to write any additional code to support this scenario.

- A player can also invite a friend or multiple friends and fill any remaining slots with the auto-matcher. This is a mix and match of the first two scenarios and, if support for both of them is added, you shouldn't have any additional programming to do for this scenario.

- The last scenario you could encounter (optionally) is to programmatically auto-match players. In this case, a request would be sent to the Game Center servers and matches would be returned for you. The player would not see any standard GUI and you have the option to implement your own interface.

> **NOTE:** Matchmaking can only be done between two of the same apps. If the bundle identifier doesn't match, the apps will not be able to communicate over the matchmaking system.

Creating a New Match Request

To create a new match, you first have to create a new GKMatchRequest object. This object represents the desired parameters for the new match that you will be creating. A GKMatchRequest is used both when presenting a GUI as well as when creating matches programmatically. When working with the GUI, you will pass the GKMatchRequest object to a new instance of GKMatchmakerViewController; on the other hand, if you are handling the matchmaking programmatically, you will pass the object to an instance of GKMatchmaker. See the following sections for more details on programmatic match interaction. For the time being, let's focus on how to create a new match request in your code. Take a look at the following code snippet.

```
GKMatchRequest *request = [[GKMatchRequest alloc] init];
request.minPlayers = 2;
request.maxPlayers = 2;
```

This example is the simplest demonstration of how to create a new match. You must specify the maximum number of players as well as the minimum. In this example, we are creating a new request that will require exactly two players.

A GKMatchRequest also has a property titled playersToInvite, in which you can use an array of GKPlayer identifiers to automatically populate into a new match. This can be very helpful when playing multiple games that are chained back to back and you want to keep the same groups of players together. This property is also prepopulated when your app is launched from the Game Center.app with the players that invited you into the app.

> **NOTE:** When accepting an invite to a match with a friend, the event is handled from the Game Center.app and the playersToInvite property will be populated.

GKMatchRequest also has an additional two properties that you will be working with in later sections of this chapter. These are playerAttributes and playerGroup. These two properties are discussed in length in the sections that share their names.

> **NOTE:** If you are using Game Center as your server for hosting games, you are limited to a maximum of four players. However, if you implement your own server as discussed in the "Using Your Own Server" section of this chapter, you can include up to 16 players.

Presenting Match GUI

We begin by first working with the standard matchmaking GUI provided to us by Apple. Start by first adding a new button to handle presenting the view on the main screen of our test game. I have also gone ahead and renamed the old Play button to Single Player, and created a new button called Multiplayer (see Figure 5–1). We will use the UFOViewController to act as the delegate for our matchmaking behavior, so set the view controller to conform to GKMatchmakerViewControllerDelegate. Additionally, modify the action method of the multiplayer button we just added to match the following code.

```
- (IBAction)multiplayerButtonPressed;
{
    GKMatchRequest *request = [[GKMatchRequest alloc] init];
    request.minPlayers = 2;
    request.maxPlayers = 2;

    GKMatchmakerViewController *mmvc = [[GKMatchmakerViewController alloc]
initWithMatchRequest:request];
    mmvc.matchmakerDelegate = self;
    [request release];

    [self presentModalViewController:mmvc animated:YES];
    [mmvc release];
}
```

We create a new instance of GKMatchRequest, as we did in the previous section. Our demo game will consist of exactly two players, so we set the max and the min both to two.

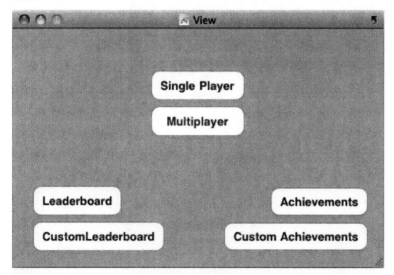

Figure 5–1. *Adding a new button for multiplayer in the UFOViewController.xib*

In the next part of the code snippet, we create a new instance of GKMatchViewController and alloc and init it with the GKMatchRequest we just created.

We also set the delegate to our UFOViewController class. When that is done, we present it as we present any other modal view. You should have output that looks similar to that pictured in Figure 5–2.

If you haven't already done so, now would be a good time to populate your friends list on your sandboxed Game Center account. It is helpful to have several unused email addresses available for this process, as you don't want to use any email addresses that have previously been used with iTunes Connect or with Game Center. Once you have populated a friend or two, you can go ahead and tap on the Invite Friend button pictured in Figure 5–2. You should now see a list of your friends and have the ability to invite them into your app, as shown in Figure 5–3.

> **REMINDER:** Do not use any email addresses you have previously used in iTunes Connect or Game Center when creating sandboxed accounts, as it can cause strange and unexpected behavior.

Figure 5–2. *MatchmakerViewController creating a new match GUI with two players*

Figure 5–3. *Inviting a friend from your Game Center friends list*

Before we can continue, we need to implement the required delegate methods for the GKMatchmakerViewController. We need to implement the following three methods before we can continue working with matchmaking.

```
- (void)matchmakerViewControllerWasCancelled:(GKMatchmakerViewController↵
 *)viewController
{
        [self dismissModalViewControllerAnimated:YES];
}

- (void)matchmakerViewController:(GKMatchmakerViewController *)viewController↵
 didFailWithError:(NSError *)error
{
        [self dismissModalViewControllerAnimated:YES];

        if (error != nil)
        {
                NSString *message = [NSString stringWithFormat:@"An error occurred:↵
%@", [error localizedDescription]];

                UIAlertView *alert = [[UIAlertView alloc] initWithTitle:@""
                                               message:message
                                               delegate:nil
                                               cancelButtonTitle:@"Dismiss"
                                               otherButtonTitles:nil];

                        [alert show];
                        [alert release];
        }
}

- (void)matchmakerViewController:(GKMatchmakerViewController *)viewController↵
 didFindMatch:(GKMatch *)match
{
        [self dismissModalViewControllerAnimated:YES];
}
```

The first two methods handle user cancellations and failures, while the third method handles the successes. The last method will return a GKMatch object upon success; we will use this object in the following chapters to begin a new match.

When working with a variable number of players allowed per match, the user will have the option of adding and removing player slots from the matchmaker view controller as seen in Figure 5–4. When inviting friends into a Game Center match, you will have the option of supplying a short message to be displayed with the invitation, as seen in Figure 5–5.

Figure 5–4. *A matchmaker screen with a variable number of players. Notice the Remove Player and Add Player buttons, and the modified navigation bar.*

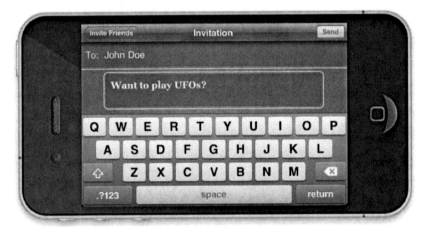

Figure 5–5. *Sending an invitation method to a friend asking them to begin a match with you. This message will be sent as a push notification and displayed in the fashion of an incoming text message on the invitee's device, as shown later in Figure 5–6.*

Handling Incoming Invitations

When implementing matchmaking into your app, you also have to implement a system to handle invitations from friends. The invitee's device will receive a push notification informing them that one of their friends has invited them to play a game. Assuming they have the game installed and accept the invitation, you will be required to handle connecting the two players together via a new match. If the invitee does not have the game or app installed, they will be instructed to download it. After the download is finished, the normal invitation process is followed.

> **NOTE:** You will also need to process invitations from new matches created within Game Center.app. You most likely won't need to write any additional code; however, you do want to thoroughly test this interaction path.

We will process invitations using an invitation handler (special thanks to Apple for the naming). The invitation handler accepts two parameters; only one of these parameters will be non-nil, depending on the type of invitation you are handling.

- The acceptInvite parameter is non-nil when the app receives an invitation from a Game Center friend. The match request has already been created by the player who invited you, so your app will not need to create its own when accepting the invitation.

- The playersToInvite parameter, which we discussed earlier in this chapter, is non-nil when Game Center.app launches your app. The property contains an array of player identifiers for the player to invite with a new GKMatchRequest. When playersToInvite property is non-nil, you will be required to create a new GKMatchRequest and populate it with the players that you received here.

> **IMPORTANT:** When working with the sandboxed mode and invitations, there can be some quirkiness. If you find yourself never getting the invited push notification, open up the app on both devices and invite the other player on both devices. After this has been done once, it normally restores the ability to test invitations from the Springboard.

Now that we know what kind of parameters that we will be working with, as well as the scenarios that we will encounter, we can begin to write a new invitation handler. GKMatchmaker has a singleton method called sharedMatchmaker, which accepts a property for inviteHandler. We use a block here to set up and handle the invitations as they are received. To keep things clean and simple, we wrap our invitation handler in its own method in our GameCenterManager class. Add the following new method to GameCenterManager.

```
- (void)setupInvitationHandler:(id)inivationHandler;
{
    [GKMatchmaker sharedMatchmaker].inviteHandler = ^(GKInvite *acceptedInvite,↵
NSArray *playersToInvite)
    {
        GKMatchmakerViewController *mmvc = nil;
        if (acceptedInvite)
        {
            mmvc = [[GKMatchmakerViewController alloc] initWithInvite:acceptedInvite];
        }
        else if (playersToInvite)
        {
            GKMatchRequest *request = [[GKMatchRequest alloc] init];
            request.minPlayers = 2;
            request.maxPlayers = 2;
            request.playersToInvite = playersToInvite;
            mmvc = [[GKMatchmakerViewController alloc] initWithMatchRequest:request];
            [request release];
        }
        mmvc.matchmakerDelegate = inivationHandler;
        [inivationHandler presentModalViewController:mmvc animated:YES];
        [mmvc release];
    };
}
```

Let's break down this method to see exactly what is happening at each step of the process. The first thing we do is set a block to the inviteHandler property on the shareMatchmaker singleton. When this block is executed, which will happen when a user accepts an invite, we have two possible outcomes.

The first is acceptedInvite is not nil. In this scenario, we create a new instance of GKMatchmakerViewController and init it with the invite that was accepted. We then present the view controller to the user.

In the second scenario, playersToInvite is non-nil, in which case we then need to create a new instance of GKMatchRequest. In our example game, we only ever allow two players, but you will set this to the total maximum players that can be played against here. We set the playersToInvite property of the request to the array of player IDs that was passed in from the block. After we have created the new request object, we can create a GKMatchmakerViewController to present the information to our user. They will see the standard matchmaker view with the players prepopulated for them.

> **IMPORTANT:** You cannot accept or otherwise process an invitation formally until you have authenticated a local user with Game Center. It is, therefore, important to register an invitation handler as soon after a successful authentication as possible.

Because we want this to be called as soon as possible after authenticating with Game Center, we add a call to our new method after we have successfully authenticated. Modify the processGameCenterAuthenication method of UFOViewController to match the following one.

```
- (void)processGameCenterAuthentication:(NSError*)error;
{
        if (error != nil)
        {
                NSLog(@"An error occured during authentication: %@",↩
 [error localizedDescription]);
        }
        else
        {
                [gcManager setupInvitationHandler:self];
        }
}
```

> **TIP:** If you don't have two devices to test invitations on, you can use the simulator as one of the
> devices. Don't forget to sign in to the simulator and your device from two different Game Center
> accounts, or you won't be able to invite each other.

We will use self (UFOViewController) as the delegate for our invitation handler. If you
completed the required delegate calls in the last section, "Presenting Match GUI," you
will not need to make any additional changes to this class.

Congratulations! You can now handle incoming invitations to your app (see Figure 5–6).
In the next section, we will explore how to configure auto-matching to populate invitees
for you.

> **NOTE:** The buy now feature of invitations cannot be tested in the sandboxed environment; this
> can be used only in live apps. The app must be installed on every device being used in order to
> test invitations while in sandbox.

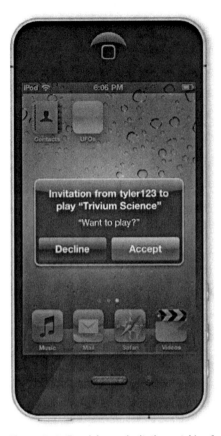

Figure 5–6. *Receiving an invitation outside of your App. The name of your app is automatically populated into the alert view. While inviting, you have the option of specifying a message, as shown previously in Figure 5–5.*

Auto-Matching

Auto-matching is a great feature provided to you for no extra work when working with Game Center. Game Center keeps an online queue of people who are waiting to join a multiplayer game in your app. If you do not fill up a new match request with all invited friends, the auto-matching feature will automatically populate the remaining spots with other unmatched players online.

You can filter down the auto-matched results using player groups and player attributes, which will be discussed later in this chapter. In addition, you can query the activity of any live player group to see what the average wait time is to be paired up with a new match; this is also discussed more in a later section.

Matching Programmatically

It is also possible for your app to find matches programmatically, without using the matchmaker interface. You could use this methodology to implement your own custom GUI for matchmaking or create an "instant match" type action, in which users are automatically paired and a game begins with no additional user interaction. We will not be using this style of matchmaking in our demo app, but the following method will allow you to implement a match programmatically.

```
- (void)findProgrammaticMatch
{
        GKMatchRequest *request = [[GKMatchRequest alloc] init];
        request.minPlayers = 2;
        request.maxPlayers = 4;

        [[GKMatchmaker sharedMatchmaker] findMatchForRequest:request⏎
 withCompletionHandler:^(GKMatch *match, NSError *error)
        {

                if (error)
                {
                        NSLog(@"An error occurrred during finding a match: %@",⏎
 [error localizedDescription]);
                }

                else if (match != nil)
                {
                        NSLog(@"A match has been found: %@", match);
                }
        }];
        [request release];
}
```

The preceding is fairly straightforward. We create a new GKMatchRequest and set the minimum players to two, as well as set the maximum players to four. We then call a new method, findMatchesForRequest. This will call our block when a match is found, so it might be a good idea to provide an activity indicator if a match isn't returned quickly. After you have a GKMatch, you can begin a new multiplayer game, as discussed in the following chapters.

When working with programmatically added matches, it is important to allow users a way to cancel the match request if it is taking too long or if they have changed their minds. That action can be accomplished with the following line of code.

```
[[GKMatchmaker sharedMatchmaker] cancel];
```

Adding a Player to a Match

There might be occasions in which you will want to add a new player to a match after it has already been created. For example, maybe you have a player drop from a game and want to replace him without starting the game over, or a player fails to connect after a game starts and you want to substitute in a replacement. The following method will automatically add a new player to the match using the auto-matching behavior.

```
- (void)addPlayerToMatch:(GKMatch *)match withRequest:(GKMatchRequest *)request
{
        [[GKMatchmaker sharedMatchmaker] addPlayersToMatch:match matchRequest:request⏎
completionHandler:^(NSError *error)
        {
                if (error)
                {
                        NSLog(@"An error occurred during adding a player to match:⏎
%@", [error localizedDescription]);
                }

                else if (match != nil)
                {
                        NSLog(@"A player has been added to the match");
                }
        }];
}
```

After a player has been added to a match, you will need to sync that player up with the current match. Adding a player will now allow the player to receive and send data, but they will not have any access to data that has already been sent through the match.

iOS 5 Reinvites

With the release of iOS 5.0, Apple added the ability to automatically try to reinivite a disconnected player. This method is only supported in two-person Game Center matches. The following method is called when a player is disconnected; Game Center will automatically try to reconnect to that player. If successful, you will receive an additional call to match:player:didChangeState:. This functionality is only available in iOS 5 or greater.

```
-(BOOL)match:(GKMatch *)match shouldReinvitePlayer:(NSString *)playerID
{
        return YES;
}
```

Player Groups

Player groups allow you to specify different classifications for each player. Game Center, by default, auto-matches everyone into the same group. With player groups, you can specify that certain players are looking for groups that contain only other players of that group.

For example, players who want to play a certain level of a dungeon or a specific racetrack will be grouped together so they are paired up with other people who want to play that same level. Player groups can be used to segregate players into many different types of groupings, such as:

- Players who wish to play the same level of a map (such as a racecourse), area in an RPG, map in a first-person shooter, or level in an action game.

- Separate players based on skill level. Either have players choose the skill level that they wish to play at, or automatically determine their skill level based on past performance.

- Type of game that is being played. For example, players can be broken down into who wants to play Capture the Flag, Team Deathmatch, Domination, or Last Man Standing.

- Players of the same Clan, Guild, Team, or Network who want to play together.

- Players who have purchased additional in-app content and can no longer be paired up with those who have not.

A player group isn't restricted to these items, and can be used to group players together in whatever fashion meets the needs of your app. A player group is represented by the playerGroup property on a GKMatchRequest. The only restriction placed on this property is that it must be represented by an NSUInteger. Specifying a playerGroup is rather straightforward, as seen in the following code snippet.

```
#define kMyForestMap 123456789
GKMatchRequest *request = [[GKMatchRequest alloc] init];
request.minPlayers = 2;
request.maxPlayers = 4;
request.playerGroup = kMyForestMap;
```

Under most circumstances, you will want to let your users select the playerGroup that they belong to; however, there might be instances in which this is not true, such as automatically determining a player's skill level.

> **CAUTION:** After you set playerGroup to any non-zero value, players will only be matched with other players of that group.

Player Attributes

Like player groups, player attributes are used during matchmaking to narrow down the possible available games to the user. Player attributes, which generally function the same as player groups, do handle some things in a different manner. Some of the many uses for player attributes include the following.

- Often, in role-playing games, characters pick a class. It is common to require a group of multiple classes—such as a healer, a fighter, and a mage—in order to complete a quest.

- Sports games often have various positions on a team, such as goalkeeper, fullback, midfielder, and forward. A team will require a mix of all of these to be able to play.

- In a submarine simulator game, you could also have various players, such as a captain, sonar operator, pilot, and weapons systems.

- In a first-person shooter game, you could need players in roles such as close-quarter combat specialist, sniper, medic, and platoon leader.

Understanding Player Attribute Limitations

Player attributes can be used to assign these values to each player so that you can balance a team that contains the required players. However, as of iOS 4.3, there are a number of limitations when using player attributes; it is important that you familiarize yourself with them before you begin working with player attributes.

- Only a single player may fill a role. For example, you cannot require three midfielders in a soccer game.

- All roles must be filled before the game is considered ready to start. For example, you can't have a first-person shooter without a sniper (based on the preceding example).

- Each player can fill only one role at a time; players cannot offer to join a game in a position that would fill more than one role. For example, you couldn't have a player in a first-person shooter willing to play either a sniper or a medic; they will need to pick one before the match request is finalized.

- Player attributes are used during auto-matching. If you invite a friend into a game, they are not tested to see whether they match the role that needs to be filled. Instead, they will automatically be assigned a random, unassigned role. In short, friends do not get to pick their player attributes.

- Roles are not displayed anywhere in the standard matchmaking graphical user interface. You will need to implement your own system prior to entering this view to allow users to select their roles.

- The GKMatch object does not contain information about which players have been assigned which roles. You will need to implement your own system after the match is connected to determine who is playing which role.

- There is no system in place to determine which roles are overfilled or which are harder to find matches for. For example, everyone might want to play a mage in a role-playing game and no one might want to be a healer; therefore, it would be much harder for a mage to find an open game, while a healer can easily find one.

Working with Player Attributes

Don't let the long list of limitations scare you off from player attributes. Even with the listed limitations, they can be extremely valuable in creating a better multiplayer experience. Let's look at an example of how to build a match using player attributes.

```
#define class_SquadLeader       0xFF000000
#define class_Breacher          0x00FF0000
#define class_Grenadier         0x0000FF00
#define class_LightMachineGun   0x000000FF
```

We begin by defining a mask for each of our player attributes, which we will refer to as "classes" for the rest of this section. This example represents a standard squad in a modern military-style game. Each class is assigned a different value of a mask. Game Center uses an algorithm to match these players together, using the following rules.

- A match's mask will always begin with the mask of the inviting player.

- Game Center will ignore all players who have not set a player attribute mask if the inviting player has set a player attribute mask.

- A player will be added to a match only if their player attribute mask doesn't overlap any section of a mask from any players already invited into the match.

- After adding a player to the match, the value of that player's attributes value is logically ORed into the match's mask.

- If a match's mask value is equal to FFFFFFFFh, then the match is considered complete and can begin; if the mask does not equal FFFFFFFFh, then Game Center will continue searching for a player who can fill the match.

- There is no way to query Game Center to see which player is still currently being waited on.

The following is based on the classes we just defined.

A blank match will have the player attribute mask shown in Figure 5–7.

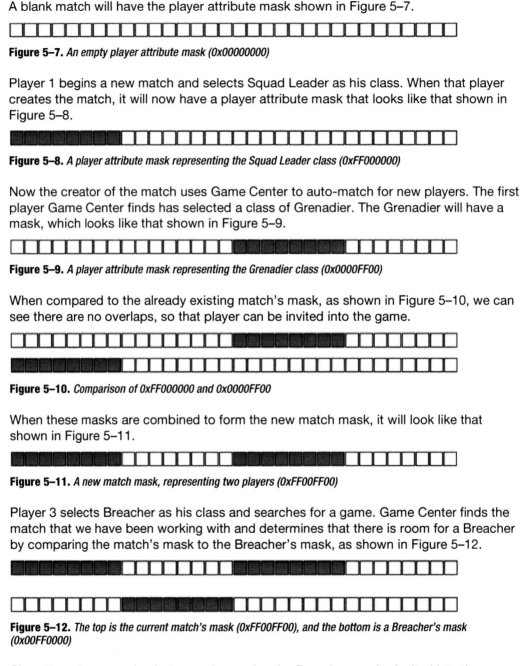

Figure 5–7. *An empty player attribute mask (0x00000000)*

Player 1 begins a new match and selects Squad Leader as his class. When that player creates the match, it will now have a player attribute mask that looks like that shown in Figure 5–8.

Figure 5–8. *A player attribute mask representing the Squad Leader class (0xFF000000)*

Now the creator of the match uses Game Center to auto-match for new players. The first player Game Center finds has selected a class of Grenadier. The Grenadier will have a mask, which looks like that shown in Figure 5–9.

Figure 5–9. *A player attribute mask representing the Grenadier class (0x0000FF00)*

When compared to the already existing match's mask, as shown in Figure 5–10, we can see there are no overlaps, so that player can be invited into the game.

Figure 5–10. *Comparison of 0xFF000000 and 0x0000FF00*

When these masks are combined to form the new match mask, it will look like that shown in Figure 5–11.

Figure 5–11. *A new match mask, representing two players (0xFF00FF00)*

Player 3 selects Breacher as his class and searches for a game. Game Center finds the match that we have been working with and determines that there is room for a Breacher by comparing the match's mask to the Breacher's mask, as shown in Figure 5–12.

Figure 5–12. *The top is the current match's mask (0xFF00FF00), and the bottom is a Breacher's mask (0x00FF0000)*

Since there is no overlap between the masks, the Breacher can be invited into the game. Player 4 selects the class of Grenadier and has Game Center look for a match. Game Center again will find our match in progress and attempt to add the new player to it.

Since the mask supplied by Player 4 overlaps a part of the match's mask (see Figure 5–13), that player is not allowed to join. If Game Center cannot find an open match for that player, then it will begin looking for new players to fill in the holes on that player's match.

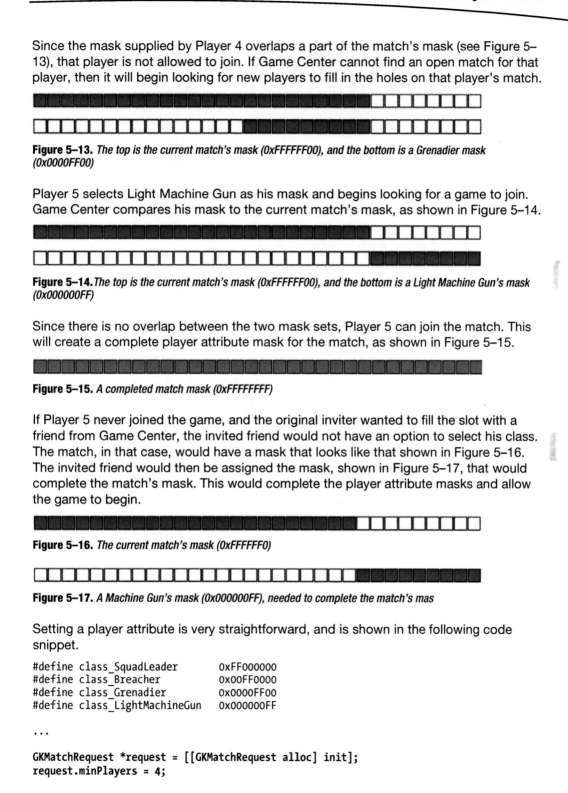

Figure 5–13. *The top is the current match's mask (0xFFFFFF00), and the bottom is a Grenadier mask (0x0000FF00)*

Player 5 selects Light Machine Gun as his mask and begins looking for a game to join. Game Center compares his mask to the current match's mask, as shown in Figure 5–14.

Figure 5–14. *The top is the current match's mask (0xFFFFFF00), and the bottom is a Light Machine Gun's mask (0x000000FF)*

Since there is no overlap between the two mask sets, Player 5 can join the match. This will create a complete player attribute mask for the match, as shown in Figure 5–15.

Figure 5–15. *A completed match mask (0xFFFFFFFF)*

If Player 5 never joined the game, and the original inviter wanted to fill the slot with a friend from Game Center, the invited friend would not have an option to select his class. The match, in that case, would have a mask that looks like that shown in Figure 5–16. The invited friend would then be assigned the mask, shown in Figure 5–17, that would complete the match's mask. This would complete the player attribute masks and allow the game to begin.

Figure 5–16. *The current match's mask (0xFFFFFFF0)*

Figure 5–17. *A Machine Gun's mask (0x000000FF), needed to complete the match's mas*

Setting a player attribute is very straightforward, and is shown in the following code snippet.

```
#define class_SquadLeader        0xFF000000
#define class_Breacher          0x00FF0000
#define class_Grenadier         0x0000FF00
#define class_LightMachineGun   0x000000FF

...

GKMatchRequest *request = [[GKMatchRequest alloc] init];
request.minPlayers = 4;
```

```
request.maxPlayers = 4;
request.playerAttributes = class_SquadLeader;
```

Player Activity

Game Center provides a method to query for recent player activity. Your users will often want as much information as possible about how long of a wait they could experience while looking for a multiplayer match. It is important to establish that player activity is recent activity and not current activity. There is no Apple-provided method for determining exactly how many players are waiting for a match, but Apple does provide a way to determine how many users have recently looked for a match. Let's take a look at the required source code to get player activity. Add the following two new methods to your GameCenterManager class's implementation file.

```
- (void)findAllActivity
{
        [[GKMatchmaker sharedMatchmaker] queryActivityWithCompletionHandler:↵
^(NSInteger activity, NSError *error) {
                [self callDelegateOnMainThread:@selector(playerActivity:error:)↵
 withArg:[NSNumber numberWithInt: activity] error:error];
        }];
}

- (void)findActivityForPlayerGroup:(NSUInteger)playerGroup
{
        [[GKMatchmaker sharedMatchmaker] queryPlayerGroupActivity:playerGroup↵
withCompletionHandler:^(NSInteger activity, NSError *error) {

                NSDictionary *activityDictionary = [[NSDictionary alloc]↵
 initWithObjects:                        [NSArray arrayWithObjects:↵
 [NSNumber numberWithInt: activity],
                                [NSNumber numberWithInt: playerGroup], nil]
                                forKeys:[NSArray arrayWithObjects:@"activity", @"group", nil]];


                [self callDelegateOnMainThread: @selector(playerActivityForGroup:↵
 error:) withArg: activityDictionary error:error];

                [activityDictionary release];
        }];
}
```

We also need to add two new protocol methods in GameCenterManager's header file. Add the following two optional protocols.

```
- (void)playerActivity:(NSNumber *)activity error:(NSError *)error;
- (void)playerActivityForGroup:(NSDictionary *)activityDict error:(NSError *)error;
```

When you implement these new protocol methods in your UFOViewController as follows:

```
- (void)playerActivity:(NSNumber *)activity error:(NSError *)error
{
        if (error != nil)
```

```
        {
                NSLog(@"An error occurred while querying player activity: %@",↵
[error localizedDescription]);
        }

        else
        {
                NSLog(@"All recent player activity: %@", activity);
        }


}

- (void)playerActivityForGroup:(NSDictionary *)activityDict error:(NSError *)error
{
        if (error != nil)
        {
                NSLog(@"An error occurred while querying player activity: %@",↵
[error localizedDescription]);
        }

        else
        {
                NSLog(@"All recent player activity: %@ For Group: %@", [activityDict↵
objectForKey:@"activity"], [activityDict objectForKey:@"group"]);
        }
}
```

You should get output similar to the following.

```
2011-03-08 11:11:04.007 UFOs[3000:207] All recent player activity: 3 For Group: 12345
2011-03-08 11:11:04.008 UFOs[3000:207] All recent player activity: 3
```

So now that we have player activity for a specified player group, what do these numbers mean? Apple has never specified the exact meaning of these numbers, but through careful research, it appears that they represent the number of users who attempted to connect to a game using the auto-matching feature in the last one to three minutes. The numbers seem to reset at an undeterminable interval somewhere within that time frame. In addition, there appears to be a 15–30 second delay until new numbers are reflected from users attempting to join a match.

Even with the limitations imposed by player activity, it can still be a very valuable tool in determining possible wait times for your users to find a match. However, you want to make sure these numbers are used for informational purposes only, as they tend to be just unreliable enough to depend upon.

> **NOTE:** You can implement your own server system to keep track of exactly how many players are waiting for a match if the Apple system does not provide specific enough information on player activity for the needs of your app.

Using Your Own Server (Hosted Matches)

Under normal circumstances, Game Center will host your match for you; however, Apple has provided a technique for implementing your own server to host a match. This approach is called a "hosted match," and can be implemented in any app to add increased flexibility to Game Center–based multiplayer networking.

When using Game Center to host a match, every device that is connecting to that match creates an instance of GKMatch. The GKMatch class does all the legwork of connecting, handshaking, sending and receiving data, and handling errors. However, there are times when you will need to implement your own server, most notably if you want to allow more than four people to connect to a single match at a time. In this scenario, you can use Game Center to find peers for your match and use your own server to connect those peers.

> **TIP:** Using a hosted match allows you to connect up to 16 users, as opposed the limit of four while using Game Center hosting.

There are several downsides to using your own server, however, most notably that you are now responsible for all the legwork that was previously given to you for free by Game Center. Specifically the following:

- You must design and implement all of your own networking code to connect the peers together. Game Center will find the matches for you, but its involvement stops there.

- If your app is using the standard matchmaking interface, your server must inform the app when a new peer successfully connects, so that is can update the GUI.

- Voice chat is no longer provided for you for free. You can still, however, use the GKVoiceChatService class to send voice data over your own networking system. See Chapter 9 for more information.

We will need to make a handful of minor changes to our code base in order to support hosted matches on the device side. We begin by modifying our multiplayer button action method that we set up earlier in this chapter.

```
- (IBAction)multiplayerButtonPressed
{
        GKMatchRequest *request = [[GKMatchRequest alloc] init];
        request.minPlayers = 2;
        request.maxPlayers = 4;

        GKMatchmakerViewController *mmvc = [[GKMatchmakerViewController alloc]↵
initWithMatchRequest:request];
        [request release];

        mmvc.matchmakerDelegate = self;
```

```
        mmvc.hosted = YES;

        [self presentModalViewController:mmvc animated:YES];
        [mmvc release];
}
```

As you can see, we added a new line—matchmakerViewController.hosted = YES—
which tells the matchmaker GUI that this match will be hosted on our own servers. In
addition to setting the matchMakerViewController to hosted, you will need to have each
device connect to your server. This section does not deal with how to code the server
itself, as there are dozens of languages and approaches that can be taken here.
However, after a device has connected to your server, it needs to call the following with
the playerID of the player who is joining.

```
[matchmakerViewController setHostedPlayerReady: playerID];
```

This will update the GUI on all the connected players' screens, informing them that a
new player is ready to begin a match. After all the players are connected to your server,
and have confirmed that they are ready, your delegate is called to begin the game.
When working with Game Center matches, we used the delegate callback
matchmakerViewController:didFindMatch: to begin a match. However, for a hosted
game we use the following.

```
- (void)matchmakerViewController:(GKMatchmakerViewController *)viewController↩
 didFindPlayers:(NSArray *)playerIDs
{
        [self dismissModalViewControllerAnimated:YES];

        NSLog(@"Players: %@", playerIDs);

        //Begin Hosted Game
}
```

At this point, you can begin the game with your server handling the communication
between the connected players. In addition, you can begin a hosted match
programmatically, as we saw with a Game Center–hosted match earlier in this chapter.

```
- (void)findProgrammaticHostedMatch
{
        GKMatchRequest *request = [[GKMatchRequest alloc] init];
        request.minPlayers = 2;
        request.maxPlayers = 16;

        [[GKMatchmaker sharedMatchmaker] findPlayersForHostedMatchRequest:request↩
withCompletionHandler:^(NSArray *playerIDs, NSError *error)
        {
                if (error)
                {
                        NSLog(@"An error occurrred during finding a match: %@",↩
[error localizedDescription]);
                }

                else if (playerIDs != nil)
                {
                        NSLog(@"Players have been found for match: %@", playerIDs);
                }
```

```
    }];
    [request release];
}
```

As you can see, it is very similar to our previous method; however, instead of getting back a GKMatch object, we are returned an array of playerIDs. You will also note that we can also increase the maximum players to 16.

Summary

In this chapter you were introduced to the concepts of matchmaking and invitations. We discussed the overwhelming benefits of adding multiplayer to your iOS app or game, as well as some of the hurdles you might need to jump along the way. We explored the matchmaking process from presenting the standard Apple GUI to highly customized matches using player groups and player attributes. We reviewed how to process invitations in every possible scenario, as well as how to query for player activity. Finally, we discovered how it is possible to implement your own server to remove some of the limitations placed on Game Center. We expanded our reusable Game Center Manager to handle matchmaking, invitations, and the required overhead, so that you can quickly add multiplayer ability to your apps.

In this chapter, we deeply explored how to create matches and populate them with peers. In the upcoming chapters, we will not only learn how to communicate between the peers, but also explore new methods for locating peers with whom to communicate. The next chapter covers information on how to use Game Kit to find peers using the Peer Picker.

Chapter 6

The Peer Picker

In the last chapter, we explored how to find matches using Game Center. In this chapter, we will look at the other provided system for finding peers to connect to. This system is called the Peer Picker and can be used to create a connection between two iOS devices using either Bluetooth or a local Wi-Fi network.

Before we begin working with the actual code, we let's take a quick look at the history surrounding Game Kit and Game Center. When Apple released iOS 3.0, at the time called iPhone OS 3.0, it implemented a new set of API calls, collectively referred to as Game Kit. Game Kit, in the 3.0 days, handled Bluetooth, LAN networking, and voice chat services. When Game Center was added in iOS 4.0/4.1, it brought with it significant improvements to Game Kit. Game Center can really be thought of as an extension to Game Kit, as opposed to a completely new API.

In this chapter, we will look at how to establish new connections using Bluetooth and a LAN. In Chapter 8, "Exchanging Data," we will learn how to use shared methods to send data, regardless of whether the peer was found via Game Center or Game Kit.

Benefits of the Peer Picker

With the introduction of iOS 4.0, Game Kit networking has become generally neglected by the developer community. This is a great injustice, as Game Kit remains an extraordinarily helpful tool for iOS developers. Game Kit remains the easiest way to add peer-to-peer networking to an iOS app.

In most of the multiplayer type apps that I have developed, I have implemented both systems of iOS networking. Game Center networking and Game Kit networking both have different strengths and weaknesses, and it is normally easier to provide both to your users than to be forced into a corner by the limitations of one. The following offer some reasons for including both.

- Your users might not have access to an outside network connection, but still want to engage in multiplayer activity. Such a scenario might occur with passengers in a car or in a plane that allows Bluetooth devices to be turned on during the flight.

- You might want to allow users to easily connect to other nearby (location based) users. Although this can be done through player groups with Game Center, it is much easier to do with Game Kit.

- You are looking for a lower latency connection between two devices.

- You want to target users who have iPod touches or Wi-Fi iPads who might not have consistent access to Wi-Fi or no access to a cellular network.

- Implementing Game Kit networking is quicker and easier than a full multiplayer system done with Game Center.

As you can see, the Peer Picker approach to finding peers has some important differences from the Game Center matchmaker system. There is nothing in place from stopping you from implementing both and is highly encouraged by at least me, if not by Apple as well.

In the upcoming chapters, you will learn some methods for making it easy to have both systems side by side. However, if you choose to implement only one or the other, carefully consider your options for which one will better suit the needs of your users.

Real-World Examples

Since the release of iOS 3.0, we have seen Game Kit networking used in very unexpected ways. Here, we discuss some of the notable examples of apps that use Game Kit networking to enhance user experience. Both of the apps that we show you in this section are better suited for Game Kit networking than Game Center networking.

First, let's take a look at Bristomath (see Figure 6–1) from Black Pixel. The central purpose of this app is to split up a bill among multiple diners at a restaurant. This idea has been done to death on the iPhone and there are literally dozens of apps on the App Store that provide this service. Bristomath remains hugely popular, even at a higher price point than most of the competition. Why is this?

Bristomath sets itself apart. Not only is it well designed and visually appealing, but it offers something that no other check splitter does: Game Kit networking. Bristomath uses Game Kit to establish a Wi-Fi or Bluetooth connection between multiple devices, allowing a user to log in to the "host" app and enter their meal items.

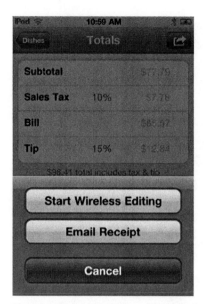

Figure 6–1. *Bristomath from Black Pixel, which uses Game Kit networking to split checks*

This simple feature has put Bristomath ahead of the curve in this niche. Adding in Game Kit networking removed the need for a user to pass an iPhone around the table and have everyone enter what they ordered. Small additions such as this to your app can make a major difference in the perceived value of your app.

Handshake (see Figure 6–2) was an app that was developed by Skorpiostech in the early days of the App Store. It was the first app that allowed a user to send his or her business cards to another user. More than six months of work was put into the server that powered Handshake's network connections. The server needed to support a large number of clients logging in and provide matches to other clients who were physically located within a certain distance of each other.

Figure 6–2. *Handshake from Skorpiostech, which uses its own server system to share data between two local devices*

Each device would determine its location and inform the server where it was and that it was looking for peers. The server would then return nearby peers and allow the app to establish a connection between them. This process could have been accomplished in days rather than months if Game Kit networking had been available at the time Handshake was being written. Handshake was never rewritten to support Game Kit; however, it was considered end-of-life when Apple introduced contact sharing alongside Game Kit in iOS 3.0.

> **REMINDER:** Game Kit and Game Center are not restricted to just games, while Apple has recently cracked down on using Leaderboards and Achievements in non-games, the argument can always be made that they add gaming functionality to your app. Game Kit networking remains unrestricted in any app.

Working with Sessions

When working with Game Kit networking, you will be using a GKSession object (see Figure 6–3) to tie everything together. This object is used to create and manage an ad-hoc Bluetooth or local wireless network connection between devices. Copies of your app, running on multiple devices, can use these services to discover each other, connect, handshake, exchange data, and gracefully disconnect.

IMPORTANT: Bluetooth networking is not supported on the original iPhone or the original iPod touch.

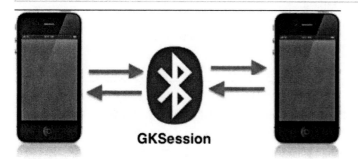

Figure 6–3. *Peer-to-peer networking over Bluetooth using GKSession*

A GKSession object primarily works with peers. A peer, in this context, is any iOS device made visible by creating and configuring a GKSession object of its own. Peers can only see other peers on apps that have the same bundle identifier as each other.

Each peer is represented by a peerID string, which will always be unique. Your app can use a peer's peerID to obtain a user-readable handle or name for that peer. Similarly, when your app begins a GKSession, it creates a peer to represent the local user, and this peer becomes visible to all nearby devices. Nearby devices, in this sense, would be any devices on the same local Wi-Fi network or within the range of Bluetooth, as detailed in Tables 6–1 and 6–2.

NOTE: As of iOS 5, the only Apple-approved way of using Bluetooth is via Game Kit. Apple does not support custom implementations of Bluetooth in App Store apps.

Table 6–1. *Range of Standard Bluetooth Devices*

Bluetooth Class	Milliwatts (mW)	dBm (dBmW)	Approximate Range
Class 1	100	20	~100 Meters, or ~320 Feet
Class 2 (iPhone)	2.5	4	~10 Meters, or ~32 Feet
Class 3	1	0	~1 Meter, or ~3 Feet

Table 6–2. *Data Rates for Standard Bluetooth Versions*

Version	Data Rate	Maximum Application Throughput
Version 1.2	1 Mbit/s	0.7 Mbit/s
Version 2.0 + EDR (iPhone)	3 Mbit/s	1.4 Mbit/s
Version 3.0 +HS	24 Mbit/s	N/A

> **NOTE:** Apple has recently enabled support for Bluetooth connections between a device and the iOS Simulator. However, it does have some limitations: most notably, a device cannot find the Simulator through Bluetooth, so the Simulator will have to initiate the connection.

Additionally, the iOS Simulator doesn't detect whether the Mac has Bluetooth enabled. Finally, when the device receives a connection, it appears to come from the bundle ID string and not the device name, as shown in Figure 6–10 later in this chapter. Peers are discovered by other peers by using a unique string to identify the service that they are implementing. This unique string is the sessionID property. Sessions can be configured in one of three ways. A session can be configured to broadcast its sessionID, making it a server; or to search for other peers advertising with a sessionID, making it a client; or, finally, as both a server and a client simultaneously, referred to as a peer. In the next chapter we will explore network design on iOS in more depth.

GKSession has an associated GKSessionDelegate protocol. The delegate is called whenever a new remote peer is discovered, attempts to connect, or when the connection state of a peer has changed. In addition, you will have to set a data-received handler to specify a delegate callback when new data is received. This can be different than the main GKSessionDelegate. We will explore exchanging data in complete detail in Chapter 8.

> **NOTE:** GKSession and its associated methods are thread-safe; however, the session will always call its delegate methods on the main thread.

Presenting a Peer Picker

We will begin, as we have in the past, by adding a new button for our Peer Picker in our UFOViewController.xib, as shown in Figure 6–4. Create a new action for the button and name it localMultiplayerGameButtonPressed. In addition, you need to create two new class variables, one instance of GKPeerPickerController and another for a GKSession. Name these peerPickerController and currentSession, respectively. You also need to conform the UFOViewController to the delegate GKPeerPickerControllerDelegate.

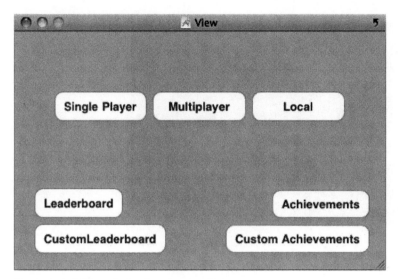

Figure 6–4. *Adding a button for a local multiplayer game*

Add the following code to the action that you created for the new local button.

```
- (IBAction)localMultiplayerGameButtonPressed
{
  peerPickerController = [[GKPeerPickerController alloc] init];
  [peerPickerController setDelegate:self];

[peerPickerController setConnectionTypesMask:GKPeerPickerConnectionTypeNearby];

  [peerPickerController show];
}
```

This code is fairly self-explanatory: we alloc and init a new instance of GKPeerPickerController, and set its delegate to self.

We do need to specify a connection type mask. There are two options available to us, GKPeerPickerConnectionTypeNearby and GKPeerPickerConnectionTypeOnline. In this example, we are using GKPeerPickerConnectionTypeNearby, which will allow Bluetooth connections. The GKPeerPickerConnectionTypeOnline constant will allow online connections through the local wireless network.

You can also supply both and allow the user to select. After the user selects an option, you can continue as if you had provided only one choice to the user. If you were to run the app now and select Local, you should see a new UIAlert that looks like that shown in Figure 6–5.

Figure 6–5. *The alert shown while searching for Bluetooth peers. Notice how the alert is gray instead of the typical blue usually seen with UIAlerts.*

Go ahead and install the app on a second device, or the Simulator if you don't have a second device. When the app is ready on both devices, launch it and select the Local game option. You will, at first, see an image similar to that shown in Figure 6–5. After several seconds, the devices should find each other, and you should see an alert similar to that shown in Figure 6–6.

NOTE: It can take up to 30 seconds for two Bluetooth devices to find each other. The farther away the devices are, the longer it can take to establish a connection.

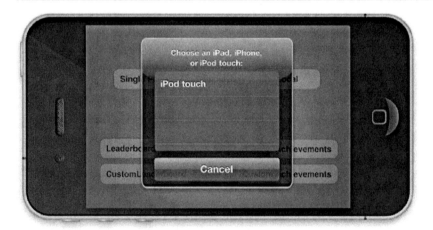

Figure 6–6. *Finding a peer with the Peer Picker*

TIP: If Bluetooth is turned off on the user's device and you begin a GKSession, the user will be prompted to enable Bluetooth, as shown in Figure 6–7.

Figure 6–7. *Prompting the user to enable Bluetooth on a device. You cannot enable Bluetooth through any other manner from inside of your apps.*

If you select one of the peers from the list of available peers, you will get a waiting message, as shown in Figure 6–8. The device that was invited will see a message, as shown in Figure 6–9; or, if invited by the Simulator, the device will show a message such as that shown in Figure 6–10.

With the relatively small amount of code we have written, all the functionality is provided to us via the API. If you happen to tap on the Accept button, you will notice that nothing happens. In the section "The Peer Picker Delegate," we will implement the delegate calls required to complete the functionality of the Peer Picker.

Figure 6–8. *Bluetooth waiting on a connect to be established*

Figure 6–9. *Incoming invitation to a device from a peer device*

Figure 6–10. *Incoming invitation to a device from the Simulator. Notice the bundle ID as the device name.*

Advanced GKSession Interaction

There might be times when you want to get your hands dirty and dig into your GKSession object a little deeper than we saw with the initial configuration. Table 6–3 lists the available properties for customization of the GKSession object.

Table 6–3. *Properties Available on a GKSession Object*

Property Name	Description
available	The available property is used to determine whether your peer is visible to other peers looking for a connection. This property is typically set for you through the Peer Picker, but you can set it yourself.
	After the Boolean is set to YES, you will remain connected to any peer that you have already connected to, but you will not receive new connection requests.
delegate	The GKSession delegate property is discussed at length in the following section.
disconnectTimeout	The disconnectTimeout property is the time amount that your session will wait before it disconnects a non-responsive peer. Apple provides a default number for this value, which through testing, appears to be between 20 and 30 seconds. The exact number is not disclosed in the documentation.
displayName	The displayName property is a read-only NSString that represents the peer's human-readable name; this is the property that should be displayed to other users through your GUI.
peerID	The peerID property is a read-only string that identifies your session peer to other devices. This value is unique.
sessionID	The sessionID property is used by sessions configured as servers to advertise themselves to other peers, and by sessions configured as clients to search for compatible servers. The sessionID should be the short name of an approved Bonjour service type.
sessionMode	The sessionMode property is the session used to find other peers. This value is read-only and is configured when you first initialize a new session. It has three possible values: GKSessionModeServer, GKSessionModeClient, and GKSessonModePeer.

The Peer Picker Delegate

In the previous sections, we saw that we get a lot for free when using a GKPeerPickerController. However, after we accepted a connection from another user, our app didn't yet know how to proceed.

In this section we, discuss the GKPeerPickerControllerDelegate. The GKPeerPickerControllerDelegate is called by the Peer Picker to create a new session object and used to handle state changes that occur thoughout the course of normal networking.

The GKPeerPickerControllerDelegate has three main responsibilities that you need to implement and respond to. It needs to create the session, respond to new connection messages, and handle the user cancelling out of the Peer Picker.

First, let's look at peerPickerController:didSelectConnectionType:. This delegate method informs us what connection type the user has selected. If you recall from the earlier sections, we worked with connectionTypeMask. If you provide the user with an option for selecting whether they want to connect using the LAN or Bluetooth, this delegate method will return the selection. If the user selects an online connection, you should dismiss the peerPicker controller and display your own LAN connection view; see the following code snippet for an example of this behavior.

```
- (void)peerPickerController:(GKPeerPickerController*)picker
     didSelectConnectionType:(GKPeerPickerConnectionType)type
{
  if (type == GKPeerPickerConnectionTypeOnline)
  {
    [picker dismiss];
    [picker release];

    // Display your own user interface here.
  }
}
```

The GKPeerPickerControllerDelegate is also responsible for returning a GKSession. When your Peer Picker needs a session object, it will call peerPickerController:session ForConnectionType:. If you are implementing this method, you must either create or return an existing GKSession.

> **IMPORTANT:** If you are creating a new GKSession as part of peerPickerController:sessionForConnectionType:, the session that you create must advertise itself as GKSessionModePeer.
>
> If you do not need to implement peerPickerController:sessionForConnectionType:, and the session is using the Bluetooth protocol, the peer controller allocates a new session with the default sessionID and displayName parameters. If you are creating a new LAN connection, you will need to implement peerPickerController:sessionForConnectionType: and return the required GKSession.

You also need to implement peerPickerControllerDidCancel:. Even though this method is optional, Game Kit expects it to be implemented. After this method is returned, the Peer Picker will automatically be dismissed, so you will not need to add code to handle this event.

The last delegate method we need to implement when working with the GKPeerPickerControllerDelegate is peerPickerController:didConnectPeer:toSession:. This method is called whenever a new peer is connected to the session.

```
- (void)peerPickerController:(GKPeerPickerController*)picker
            didConnectPeer:(NSString*)peerID
                 toSession:(GKSession*)session
{
  currentSession = session;

  //hold onto session and peerID
  [self dismissModalViewControllerAnimated:YES];
}
```

When this method is called, we will want to keep a reference to the session and peerID. We will use these in the upcoming chapters when we begin to work with sending data back and forth. Once a peer has successfully connected, your app should take ownership of the session and dismiss the Peer Picker.

Figure 6–11 represents an iPhone that has entered the connected state and set its availability flag to NO.

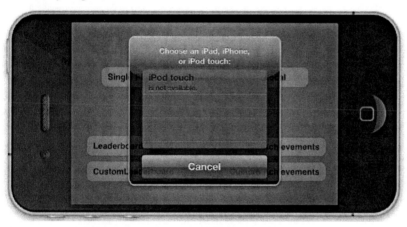

Figure 6–11. *The iPod touch has set its availability status to false*

> **IMPORTANT:** Although peerPickerController:didConnectPeer:toSession: is optional, you will be required to implement it before you can fully enable Game Kit networking.

Summary

In this chapter we learned about using Game Kit networking to connect two devices together using either the local area network or Bluetooth. In the previous chapter, we worked with matchmaking and invitations. Between these two technologies we have completely covered all the available methods to find and connect to peers using Game Center and Game Kit technology on the iOS platform.

We also looked at some real-world examples of iOS apps that have benefited from Game Kit networking integration, and you saw how easy it was to move your app up to the next tier of quality with only a small amount of invested time.

In addition, we explored the workings of the Peer Picker, including how to request a new session using either Bluetooth or the LAN, and how to connect peers together. We also covered all the required delegate and controller overhead to get these systems up and running quickly in your own apps.

In the next chapter, we will discuss how to design a network for mobile devices, the dos and don'ts of network design, and overview. In Chapter 8, we will learn how to tie together all the peers that we have been establishing connections with and have them begin to talk to each other.

Chapter 7

Network Design Overview

In previous chapters, we learned how to find and establish connections to peers through a variety of methods using both Game Center and Game Kit. In this chapter, we will look at how to design a networking experience for not just an iOS game but also a game on any platform. This chapter is designed slightly different than the previous chapters you have encountered in this book. Primarily, there will be no associated source code with this chapter and we will only briefly touch on Game Kit networking topics themselves. This chapter will focus on the concepts of network design, as opposed to actually implementing the network itself. In the next chapter, you will discover how to tie everything together and have your peers begin to communicate with each other.

While it is entirely possible (and often done) to go ahead and just start writing your network logic, it is probably not a great idea. After all, you wouldn't begin writing a new app or game without first planning out how it will function. Networking is a complex topic and you should approach it with a plan; otherwise, you could find yourself rewriting the entire system after you put a lot of work and effort into it. You don't want to find yourself up against a wall because the approach you took limited your options for future expandability. Just like with software, you shouldn't jump right into writing code on the first day. You should whiteboard things out a little and get a feel for the requirements of the project.

Take, for example, a desktop role-playing game called Clan Lord that was written in the late 1990s for the Mac. Clan Lord has maintained a very dedicated fan base that has kept the game active and continual to the present day. However, when the game was originally written, many network-related issues were not properly thought through.

Clan Lord uses frame-by-frame syncing for all of its network calls. This means that every frame, every element visible on the player's screen, has to be transmitted. This approach works, and works well while you have a small game, a small user base, and limited functionality. However, when you are designing software, you cannot have a limited vision for the future. Always plan for the best, or depending on your perspective, the worst case. When designing a network, you must take into account what you will want to do six months, a year, or even ten years from now with your game or app.

Clan Lord now suffers from long-ingrained problems, such as an eight frames per second rendering engine, due to the fact that you cannot sync more than eight full frames of data per second on the average home network. This could have been prevented by implementing some logic into the client when the project was first started; for example, it would have been much more efficient to inform the client where objects are and when they move, as opposed to fully syncing everything each frame. In addition, player movement is limited to eight frames per second because actions have to be synced back to the server, making it hard to react to events. This also could have been prevented by using prediction algorithms, discussed later in this chapter, to determine where a player will end up during movement.

Clan Lord is one example of a game that was much more popular than planned, and lived a lot longer than anyone expected. Sadly, when this happens, you are limited to the vision and design that you had when the project was first started. It is much harder to undo something later than to do it initially. When designing your network, take time to do it carefully and intentionally, as it can follow you around for a very long time.

Three Types of Networks

Although there are many different types of network designs available, there are three primary kinds of networks that you can implement when designing your network. Picking a primary type of network is a good place to start, as it will guide you toward the next step in the design process.

We will be focusing on just three of the primary types of network designs, but keep in mind that there are dozens of other well known network configurations, some of which we will briefly touch on in this section. The three types of networks we will be discussing in length throughout this chapter are peer-to-peer, client-to-host, and ring networking.

Peer-to-Peer Network

A peer-to-peer network (see Figure 7–1) is the most common network that you will see on the iOS platform. No device is treated any differently than any other device, and each device is in charge of sending and receiving data to all the other peers it wishes to communicate with.

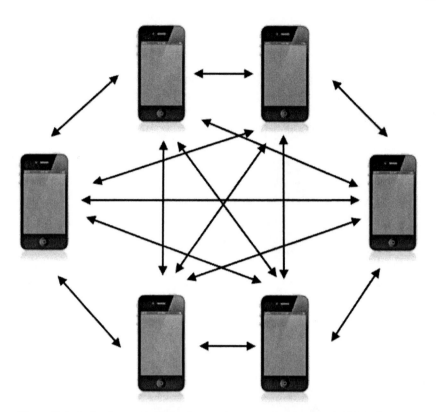

Figure 7–1. *A visual representation of a peer-to-peer network using six iOS devices*

A peer-to-peer network is commonly used when dealing with Game Center networking because it is the easiest to implement on the iOS platform. While this approach has the benefit of being extremely easy to set up, it has an equal amount of weaknesses. Primarily, it can cause a lot of redundant overhead. Each peer needs to inform every other peer about its actions. In a six-way network like the one shown in Figure 7–1, this means that each device needs to send out five messages every time it wants to update the game state. In addition, if you are implementing a system in which each peer confirms a successful message, you will also need to receive five messages.

Another disadvantage of a peer-to-peer network is that it can become very confusing to work with a large number of peers. As you can see from Figure 7–1, things can get messy pretty quickly. Unlike the other primary types of networks that we will discuss in this section, the peer-to-peer approach is the only one without a clear flow. Each peer can message any other peer, by definition. This also means that you have to keep track of what every peer needs to know. Under most circumstances, this is a perfectly acceptable approach. However, when you begin to deal with more complex types of networks, this configuration might no longer be ideal.

In addition, no one device is in control of the state of the game. If there are artificial intelligence components, then you will need to figure out a system that will allow them to stay in sync between all the devices.

Client-to-Host Network

A client-to-host network designates one device to be the host. This device is responsible for sending information to all the connected clients. The clients never speak to each other; they speak only to the host who then relays the required information back to the other clients. An example of what a client-to-host setup looks like is shown in Figure 7–2.

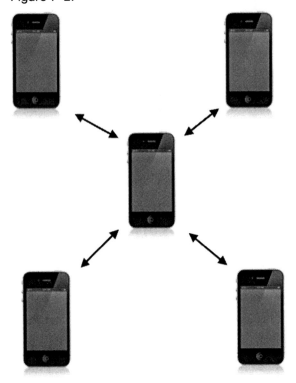

Figure 7–2. *A visual representation of a client-to-host network using five iOS devices*

A client-server network simplifies the flow of data. Each peer or client only needs to worry about itself and the host; they do not need to be aware of the other devices that might exist on the network. The benefit of this type of network is that one device keeps everything in sync and handles the flow of information; this makes it a very secure network (in the sense of anti-cheating). Cheating, however, is not a large concern on the iOS platform because it's a sandboxed system to begin with.

There are other benefits to this system as well, such as the fact that only one device needs to worry about the state of the network, and that sole device is in charge of the behavior of the network. This type of network simplifies events such as connections, disconnections, transmission errors, and other state changes such as computer-controlled objects like artificial intelligence. However, this same setup could be troublesome on the iOS platform; if the host device has too much information to process, that device could run slower or use more battery.

Ring Network

A ring network (see Figure 7–3) has no host and no clients. It works similarly to a peer-to-peer network, but a peer is in charge of communicating with only one designated peer and will receive information from only another separately defined peer. The information flows through a group of devices in the shape of a ring, hence the name.

This type of network isn't very common on the iOS platform, as there is not a lot of argument for the redundancy that it typically provides for disconnected peers. Apple has done a lot of the groundwork to ensure that networks remain active and stable, without the need for the developer to spend additional design hours ensuring that there won't be instances where peers lose contact with other peers that are currently joined together. There are times, however, were you might find this type of configuration useful when designing your network on the iOS platform.

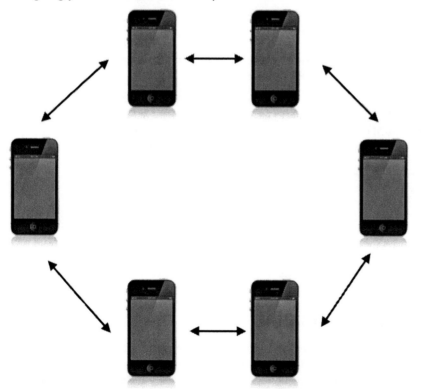

Figure 7–3. *A visual representation of a ring network using six iOS devices. Notice how much simpler this diagram appears than the peer-to-peer network shown in Figure 7–1.*

Less Common Networks

There are many additional types of network designs available in computer science. Some are more practical than others and some are mostly theoretical. In this section, we cover some of the better known "uncommon" networks. Although some of these can be implemented on iOS devices, most will likely not have any real benefit for the average project.

- Headless Client—The client has no data whatsoever, and is controlled by a host device. You can think of this type of setup as a computer terminal that is booted from a server disk.

- Dedicated Server—The host in this example does not participate in the game or activity and is dedicated to sending the information out from the peers and collecting new input. This is typically seen deployed by large companies creating a gaming community.

- Mesh/Partial Mesh Network—This is a peer-to-peer network in which each peer may not be aware of the other peers that exist on the network. The packets are tagged with a destination and every hop attempts to get the packet closer to the destination. A full-mesh network means that every peer is interconnected, which is more or less the same as a peer-to-peer network.

- Tree Network—This type of network consist of a tree of peers interconnected to each other and each controlled by a centralized point. The central point passes messages to other central points and each tree branch passes messages back and forth along that branch.

- Hybrid Network—This type of network combines two or more technologies, such as two groups of peers who are linked together through a centralized server.

This covers most of the networks you will encounter during a career of software engineering. There is really no limit to the type of network that you can design, and every year better designs and flows become available. In the next section, we will look at the actual packets that will be sent and received on your network.

Reliable Data vs. Unreliable Data

When dealing with network design, packet reliability is an important topic. When discussing packet reliability outside of the iOS platform, we are specifically referring to the priority of the data, the ordering of the packets, and the retry determination factor. Let's look at all these attributes separately and how they relate to network design (see Table 7–1) before we dig into the specifics we need for our implementation when dealing specifically with iOS.

Table 7–1. *Common Packet Attributes and How They Affect Network Behavior*

Attribute	Relationship to Network Design
Priority	When you are working with low-level networking, you are dealing with packets. Each packet is a predetermined sized and contains information about the event that you want to send to another peer. Packets are typically sent to a queue and then sent out to the peer they are addressed for, but because networking isn't precise (especially if you are trying to get the lowest latency), packets might not always be received in the order that they are generated.
	For example, in a standard online game, you might be passing two types of information, game state changes and chat information. Obviously, your character requesting an action, such as attacking an enemy or dodging an attack, is more important to have in a timely manner than a chat message.
	The solution to this type of problem is to set priority for packets. The peer will send cycle through all its pending messages and send the highest priority ones first. This allows the vital messages to be retried in the event of failure first, as well as bump the important packets to the top of the queue.
Ordering	The order in which packets are received can be crucial. For example, if you are sending 10 packets, which together make up a very long chat message, then the order in which those packets are received is important to the receiving peer.
	If the packets aren't received and processed in order, your message could appear scrambled. When this happens with a state engine, very unpredictable behavior may follow. There is a certain cost overhead involved when ensuring packets are ordered, however. If you are waiting for packet 1 of 10, then you can't do anything with the packets you might have already received. This creates a situation in which your network is only as fast as your slowest packet. If ordering isn't critical to your network functioning correctly, then you should not worry about the order.
Retry	Networks are, by nature, unreliable. Even a desktop machine hooked up to a dedicated connection will have lost packets and experienced other failures. When you are dealing with network reliability on a mobile device, the only thing you can count on is failure. When you send a packet to another peer, you can handle it two ways: the first is a send-and-forget system; the second is a send-and-verify system.
	In the first approach, you send a packet and you don't really care if it gets there. Let me clarify: you do care, but if it fails, there is nothing you can do about it. A good example of this type of acceptable failure is a voice chat packet. If it fails to reach the end of the line successfully, resending it will merely bring things out of sync; it is better to just continue on streaming the data.
	In the second approach, the packet is considered vital, such as player opening a chest, searching a slain foe for treasure, or updating their direction of movement. The peer needs this data to be sent to continue smoothly executing the commands. If you skip this packet, it will be frustrating to the user, as they will have to retry the action themselves instead of having the network retry it for them.

Now that we have covered the issues that are important when dealing with sending the actual data packets from one device to another, we can look at how these principles apply to the iOS platform itself.

There are two types of modes that data can be sent in with Game Kit: the first is GKSendDataReliable; the second is, naturally, GKSendDataUnreliable. Let's take a look at what each one of these modes do for us and how they fit in with the topics we just discussed. See Table 7–2.

Table 7–2. *Packet Attributes and How They Apply to Game Center*

Attribute	GKSendDataReliable	GKSendDataUnreliable
Priority	Game Kit networking doesn't factor in any type of priority when dealing with packets. Packets are sent in the order that they are fed into the system.	Game Kit networking doesn't factor in any type of priority when dealing with packets. Packets are sent in the order that they are fed into the system.
Ordering	Packets will be received in the order that they are sent.	Packets using this method are not guaranteed to be received in the same order that they were sent.
Retry	A packet will be continuously retried until it is successfully received. The next packet will not be sent until the first one has been confirmed received.	A packet is sent and then removed from the queue. The API does not wait to receive a received notification before it sends the next packet. This is naturally faster than waiting for a response between each packet.

Sending Only What Is Needed

One of the vital mistakes that first-timers make when designing a network is sending too much data. It is easy to just send everything. In the beginning of this chapter, we talked about a game that exhibited this very problem.

> *"If I had more time I would write a shorter letter."*

> — Blaise Pascal

Pascal could have very well been talking about network packets, in this often-misattributed quote. The size of the packet can be directly related to the speed, stability, and scalability of your network. It is important to spend the time to figure out what the absolute bare minimum is that can be sent.

Take a look at a hypothetical example that some of you might encounter while designing a game. For this example, let's say you are working on a role-playing game. You control your hero and guide him or her through a series of dungeons. In these dungeons, you can interact with items and encounter various enemies, which you will fight in real time.

Well, we know we will have some static data; for example, the layout of the dungeon probably will not be changing while you are inside it, so instead of sending the map tiles to the client every frame or even periodically, we should send that data when the player first enters the zone. There might be elements that will be moving, but we can predict their behavior infinitely, such as a river flowing or a torch flickering. These items can also be loaded once with the information they need to stay in sync.

There are, of course, items that will need to be updated throughout the player's adventures in the dungeon. The player himself will need to be updated every time the user creates a new action. For example, if you are running east, you could send a packet every frame to tell the server that you are running east. However, a much more efficient way to handle this interaction is to tell the server to begin moving east at full speed. When you are done moving east, you should inform the server that you want to stop. This type of interaction drastically reduces the number of messages that need to be sent to the server to accomplish the same task. Optimizations such as these is why, when playing modern games, you sometimes see disconnected players running into walls—the server never received a stop-running command before the client disconnected.

Take the time to carefully design how you will structure your network data. You can always add more information, but it becomes very difficult to remove data as you dig deeper into your network design. Always look for a way to reduce packet size, as there is no downside to packets being too small, but a packet that is too large will cause you a lot of suffering down the road.

Prediction and Extrapolation

Let's take another example into consideration: this time, a racing game. Each player controls a car that is guided around a track. We know where each car is at the start of the race. We also know that any messages we send to the server will have an inherited latency due to the round-trip network time. Should we not update the car positions until the server tells us to? That would result in a very choppy racing game. To account for this very common issue, we use predictive technology.

We know that racecars will, more than likely, continue on a current course for the next handful of frames. We will assume things will continue doing what they are doing until the server tells us otherwise; if the user steers slightly to the left or right, that is a minor correction we will need to make when the server informs us of the update. The fact that an object in motion will stay in motion until acted on by an outside force is not just a law of physics; it is also the first rule of designing a predictive network.

The chances of an object completely reversing its current course are much less likely than slightly modifying its current course. This makes it easier to account for minor changes if the server informs you that things are out of sync. In the event that a player does completely change direction or otherwise break your prediction about what actions were going to continue, you are only off the mark by as much as your current latency, which is typically only a small fraction of a second. If you have an object that is likely to continue doing what it is doing—such as a player moving, objects in a falling state, bullet trajectory, or any type of physics simulation—the best bet is to continue assuming that those actions will continue until the server informs you that they have changed.

Formatting Messages

Whenever you are dealing with designing a network for a game or game-like application, you are guaranteed to be dealing with at least two types of messages. These are often referred to as state messages and server messages. A state message is a message that will directly affect your game engine, such as a player moving or opening a chest. Server messages deal with the glue that holds everything together, such as connections, disconnections, pings, and errors.

It becomes important to quickly sort these messages to different handlers. It is a good design pattern to keep the parsing of these messages in different places. After all, you don't want to be scanning all your chat messages in a first-person shooter for client timeout messages. There are many different methods to handle this segregation, but I have found a simple prefix is suitable for most cases. If you prefix all of your state messages with a character that you will not see in server messages, you can quickly check the first character in incoming messages to make sure they are delivered to the correct parser. If you are designing a more complex network, you can use a large number of possible prefixes to make sure things get to the correct place. In Chapter 8, we will look at practical examples of message formatting when we begin to send and receive data.

Preventing Cheating and Preventing Timeout-Related Disconnections

One thing that has not become a big concern on the iOS platform, as of yet, is cheating through network exploits. If you are an online gamer, you are probably all too familiar with this behavior. A clever user will determine how the network behaves, and then send commands that the client itself would never send, such as increase hit points to max float or decrease respawn time to zero. Although you might need to have your server respond to things such as increase or decrease hit points, you want to make sure the server is in control. For example, instead of letting the client say "increase moment speed to fifty," you should set up the message to something like "request increase moment speed" and then have the server return the new speed. If you put clients in charge of variables, at some point someone will take advantage of this and exploit your system.

If your client doesn't have any updates to send out to the server or its peers, it is good practice to send a message that simply states, "I'm still here don't disconnect me," which is known as a "keep alive" message. Although you don't have to worry about timeout disconnection on the iOS platform, it is still a good idea to make sure that you keep your own line of communication open between idle peers.

When you are designing a message architecture, you can really think of it as designing an API; there are a lot of similarities and you have to follow the same guidelines. If you ship version one of your app with a command that lets users query for their movement speed, you can't easily pull out that command in version two, because previous clients might still be depending on it. Follow the same guidelines that API developers do: test everything thoroughly, because after it is out in the wild, it is very hard to get it back.

What to Do When All Else Fails

An issue that is bound to come up when you have been working with networks long enough is that of what to do when the system you have designed no longer meets your needs. Let's discuss something that might be familiar to those of you who have taken some logic or business courses. There is a syndrome known as the "Sunk Cost Fallacy," where when dealing with non-refundable resources, such as time, those cost are weighed as equally as refundable costs.

Take a look at the following equation.

Payoff = project revenue – open cost

Now let's look at the same example using some real-world data. In 1968, Knox and Inkster approached 141 horse bettors: 72 of the people had just finished placing a $2.00 bet within the past 30 seconds, and 69 people were about to place a $2.00 bet within the next 30 seconds. The hypothesis was that people who had just committed themselves to a course of action would reduce post-decision dissonance by believing more strongly than ever that they had picked a winner. Knox and Inkster asked the bettors to rate their horse's chances of winning on a seven-point scale. What they found was that people who were about to place a bet rated the chance that their horse would win at an average of 3.48, which corresponded to a "fair chance of winning," whereas people who had just finished betting gave an average rating of 4.81, which corresponded to a "good chance of winning." This hypothesis was confirmed: after making a $2.00 commitment, people became more confident that their bet would pay off. Knox and Inkster performed an ancillary test on the patrons of the horses themselves and managed to repeat their finding almost identically.[1]

What we are talking about is accepting when it is time to give up and start over. Giving up is never a popular solution; our brains are wired against it. We look at the non-refundable cost and calculate that into our favor. Once you have already made an investment, it is easier to justify that investment and try to defend it. No one wants to be the person to call it quits and throw away all the time and money already invested into a project; however, when you spend time and resources on a development project, they are spent and they cannot be recouped. You cannot justify more time simply based on time spent.

---

[1] Knox, R. E., & Inkster, J. A. (1968). "Postdecision dissonance at post time". *Journal of Personality and Social Psychology, 8,* 319–323.

There is no right answer on when to give up and start over, and there is no wrong answer. The only thing you can do is look at the problem objectively. If you hadn't already invested into this problem, what solution would you pick?

Summary

In this chapter, we looked at the design of the actual network, as opposed to the iOS-specific information that we have dealt with in the rest of this book so far. You could easily design a working network without the information in this chapter, through common sense and gut instinct, but keep in mind the lesson learned throughout this chapter: just because it works, doesn't mean it works well. Designing a network is easy; designing a network correctly is very difficult.

There is significantly more information on network design than can easily fit into a single chapter, or even a single book. If I can leave you with a final piece of advice: when you begin to look at how to structure your network, think through everything as you go, and never feel the need to be satisfied with your first solution.

In the next chapter, we will finally get to work with sending our messages from one device to another. Chapter 9 will also be an extension of that technology where we look into how to add voice chat services to your iOS app.

Chapter 8

Exchanging Data

In the past few chapters, we explored how to connect to peers through a variety of methods. So far, we have not been able to do much with that connection. In this chapter, we will learn all that there is to know about exchanging data between sets of peers using Game Kit and Game Center networking. We have already added the ability to find peers using both Game Center and the Peer Picker (Game Kit) to our UFO game. We will now add the ability to actually play a multiplayer match.

Because all the groundwork has already been laid out in previous chapters, there are only two items that we need to worry about in regards to exchanging data. First, we need to send the actual data; second, we need to receive and process that data on the other side. Everything else that you need to do is already done, except some logic for disconnecting. Let's jump right into it by modifying our source code from Chapter 6.

Modifying a Single-Player Game

There are a few modifications that we need to make to our single-player game in order to transform it into a multiplayer game.

- Once we connect to a new peer, we need to begin the game. We also need a way to inform our existing engine that the new game is multiplayer.

- One device needs to be designated the host device. We will have this one device control the movements of the cows, since both devices can't control cow movement themselves. This is an important step if we want both devices to appear in sync.

- Each peer needs to inform the other peer(s) about its actions, such as movement and tractor beam usage.

- Each peer needs to parse the other peer's device and update its own game state to keep both devices in sync with each other.

These steps are a representation of the bare minimum that is typically required to turn a single-player game into a multiplayer game. Your particular game or app might be much more complex. For example, your multiplayer experience might be so different from your single-player gameplay that you cannot reuse the same class for both modes. On the other hand, your game might be even simpler. For example, a multiplayer game of battleship wouldn't require either device to be the host because there are no computer-controlled elements that you need to worry about keeping track of.

Setting Up Our Engine for Multiplayer

The very first thing that we need to do is let our game engine know whether the state should be set to multiplayer or single player. There are complex ways and simple ways of doing this. Depending on your needs, you will most likely be able to get away with a simple state variable.

A state variable is the approach that we will use for our example, since our game is extremely straightforward. In UFOGameViewController.h, we create a new ivar to represent a BOOL, which will be set to inform the class whether we are in single-player or multiplayer mode. Add the following two bold lines into our already existing header file, and don't forget to synthesize gameIsMultiplayer in the implementation.

```
@interface UFOGameViewController : UIViewController <UIAccelerometerDelegate,↵
 GameCenterManagerDelegate>
{
  BOOL gameIsMultiplayer;
}

@property(nonatomic, assign) BOOL gameIsMultiplayer;
```

We will use this property throughout our code base to determine whether the game is running in multiplayer mode.

We have two existing methods that will be called when our game begins a new multiplayer match. The first method is called when Game Center finds a match, and the second will be used when we find a peer through our Peer Picker. We will deal with two different identifiers for our peers: Game Center returns a GKMatch object, and the Peer Picker returns an NSString to represent the peer. We will also add some new methods in our GameCenterManager class to handle using the same code to communicate to both of these systems at once. For now, we will simply focus on getting the game up and running in a new state.

```
- (void)matchmakerViewController:(GKMatchmakerViewController *)viewController↵
 didFindMatch:(GKMatch *)match
{
        [self dismissModalViewControllerAnimated:YES];
}

- (void)peerPickerController:(GKPeerPickerController *)picker didConnectPeer:(NSString↵
 *)peerID toSession:(GKSession *)session
{
        currentSession = session;
        [self dismissModalViewControllerAnimated: YES];
}
```

Next, we add a section of code to the end of each one of these methods to begin a new multiplayer game after we find a peer that we want to play against. Go ahead and add the following snippet of code into each method.

```
UFOGameViewController *gameVC = [[UFOGameViewController alloc] init];
gameVC.gcManager = gcManager;
gameVC.gameIsMultiplayer = YES;
[self.navigationController pushViewController:gameVC animated:YES];
[gameVC release];
```

We also need to hold onto either the GKMatch or the NSString that represents a peer. Create two new properties in the UFOGameViewController, named peerIDString and peerMatch. Set these up in the same fashion that you did for the gameIsMultiplayer ivar. The new section of your header should look like the following abstracted snippet.

```
@interface UFOGameViewController : UIViewController <UIAccelerometerDelegate,↵
 GameCenterManagerDelegate>
{
        //…

        NSString *peerIDString;
        GKMatch *peerMatch;
}

@property(nonatomic, retain) NSString *peerIDString;
@property(nonatomic, retain) GKMatch *peerMatch;
```

Now we need to add logic to set these properties in both of the methods for beginning a new multiplayer game. These methods should now look like the following ones. As you can see, we nil out the unused property; we will always have one of the two properties being set to nil, because you can never have a game that is using both the Peer Picker and Game Center at the same time.

When we load our game view controller, we know whether it is multiplayer or not, as well as having a reference to our peer or peers. Our GameViewController now has all the information it needs to begin a new multiplayer game.

```
- (void)matchmakerViewController:(GKMatchmakerViewController *)viewController↵
 didFindMatch:(GKMatch *)match
{
        [self dismissModalViewControllerAnimated:YES];
         UFOGameViewController *gameVC = [[UFOGameViewController alloc] init];
        gameVC.gcManager = gcManager;
        gameVC.gameIsMultiplayer = YES;
        gameVC.peerIDString = nil;
        gameVC.peerMatch = match;
        [self.navigationController pushViewController:gameVC animated:YES];
        [gameVC release];
}

- (void)peerPickerController:(GKPeerPickerController *)picker didConnectPeer:↵
(NSString *)peerID toSession:(GKSession *)session
{
        currentSession = session;
        [self dismissModalViewControllerAnimated: YES];
        UFOGameViewController *gameVC = [[UFOGameViewController alloc] init];
```

```
        gameVC.gcManager = gcManager;
        gameVC.gameIsMultiplayer = YES;
        gameVC.peerIDString = peerID;
        gameVC.peerMatch = nil;
        [self.navigationController pushViewController:gameVC animated:YES];
        [gameVC release];
}
```

Picking a Host

Picking which device will be the host is harder than it sounds. Both devices, when first connected together, are treated as equals. How do we then determine which device will have more control than the other?

The most straightforward and foolproof system that I have discovered is having each device generate a random number. Whichever device has the largest random number becomes the host. In the very rare event that both devices generate the same random number, we simply try again.

After we have determined the random number a device has picked for its chance at being the host, we need to send that data to the other device. On the other side, we need to process the data and have both devices come to the same conclusion about which one has been selected as the host. This section deals only with generating the host number; the next two sections handle how to send and receive this data. We now add the following method to our UFOGameCenterViewController class.

```
-(void)generateAndSendHostNumber;
{
        double randomHostNumber = arc4random();
        NSString *randomNumberString = [NSString stringWithFormat: @"%d",↩
 randomHostNumber];
        [self.gcManager sendStringToAllPeers:randomNumberString reliable: YES];
}
```

For the purpose of this particular example, we will work with an NSString for sending the data back and forth. You could easily send this as an NSNumber as well, but whatever we send will first need to be converted to NSData, which we will cover in the next section. In addition, we want to make sure this method is called whenever we are dealing with a multiplayer game. To do so, we need to add the following to the end of our viewDidLoad method. We also need to slightly modify our logic to spawn cows. If it is a multiplayer game, only the host is responsible for spawning and updating cow paths.

> **TIP:** When you begin to deal with more complex networking, it is often beneficial to switch to a data type that can easily store more data with less parsing, such as a dictionary or an array.

```
-(void)viewDidLoad
{
        //…
```

```
            [self generateAndSendHostNumber];
            if (self.gameIsMultiplayer == NO)
            {
                    for (int x = 0; x < 5; x++)
                        {
                                    [self spawnCow];
                        }

                    [self updateCowPaths];
            }
}
```

Sending Data

We will work with two primary methods to send data to other connected peers. One will
handle sending data to every peer we are connected to, and the other will send data
only to specified peers, such as teammates or other groups of players. First, add the
following two methods to our GameCenterManager class.

```
-(void)sendStringToAllPeers:(NSString *)dataString reliable:(BOOL)reliable;
-(void)sendString:(NSString *)dataString toPeers:(id)peers reliable:(BOOL)reliable;
```

We will use these methods to send strings back and forth, but you can add additional
methods to accept any type of input you want. Keep in mind that everything will need to
be converted to NSData along the way. You might also notice that the first method is the
same method we called previously from our generateAndSendHostNumber.

> **TIP:** It is a good idea to implement methods to handle arrays and dictionaries. These are both
> very common data types when working with networking messages.

Before we can really begin to send data back and forth, we need to know either the
GKSession or the GKMatch that was created for our multiplayer game. To do this, we
create a new ivar in the GameCenterManager class. We name it matchOrSession and
set it to an ID type. We need to set this property before we begin a new multiplayer
game, after we have been returned either a new GKSession or GKMatch. Let's first take
a look at sending data to all peers. The new method is posted as follows. After you have
examined it, we will discuss it in further detail.

```
-(void)sendStringToAllPeers:(NSString *)dataString reliable:(BOOL)reliable
{

        if (self.matchOrSession == nil)
        {
                NSLog(@"Game Center Manager matchOrSession ivar was not set, this⏎
 needs to be set with  the GKMatch or GKSession before sending or receiving data");
                return;
        }

        NSData *dataToSend = [dataString dataUsingEncoding:NSUTF8StringEncoding];
        GKSendDataMode mode;
        if (reliable)
```

```
        {
                mode = GKSendDataReliable;
        }
        else
        {
                mode = GKSendDataUnreliable;
        }

        NSError *error = nil;
        if ([self.matchOrSession isKindOfClass: [GKSession class]])
        {
                [self.matchOrSession sendDataToAllPeers:dataToSend withDataMode:↵
mode error:&error];
        }

        else if ([self.matchOrSession isKindOfClass: [GKMatch class]])
        {
                [self.matchOrSession sendDataToAllPlayers:dataToSend withDataMode:↵
mode error:&error];
        }

        else
        {
                NSLog(@"Game Center Manager matchOrSession was not a GKMatch or↵
 a GKSession, we are unable to send data");
        }

        if (error != nil)
        {
                NSLog(@"An error occurred while sending data: %@", [error↵
 localizedDescription]);
        }
}
```

We need to make sure that we have properly set the matchOrSession property. If we haven't, we will not be able to continue, as we will be using this object to send data. After we have ensured that we have the proper information to continue, we then transform our NSString to an NSData object. This encodes the string into a format that is safe for sending over the network. We also need to set the reliability mode, as discussed in Chapter 7.

Now that we have everything in place to actually send data, we first detect whether we are working with a GKMatch from a Game Center type connection or a GKSession from a Peer Picker type connection. All that is left to do is send the data using the Game Kit APIs.

Now is a good time to look at how we will selectively send data only to certain peers. We can build off the example we already have for sending data to all peers. Let's take a look at our sendString method.

```
-(void)sendString:(NSString *)dataString toPeers:(id)peers reliable:(BOOL)reliable
{
        if (self.matchOrSession == nil)
        {
                NSLog(@"Game Center Manager matchOrSession ivar was not set, this↵
```

```
needs to be set with the GKMatch or GKSession before sending or receiving data");
                        return;
        }

        NSData *dataToSend = [dataString dataUsingEncoding:NSUTF8StringEncoding];
        GKSendDataMode mode;
        if (reliable)
        {
                mode = GKSendDataReliable;
        }
        else
        {
                mode = GKSendDataUnreliable;
        }

        NSError *error = nil;
        if ([self.matchOrSession isKindOfClass: [GKSession class]])
        {
                        if ([peers isKindOfClass:[NSArray class]])
                        {
                        [self.matchOrSession sendData:dataToSend toPeers:peers↵
withDataMode:mode error:&error];
                }

                else
                        {
                        NSLog(@"Game Kit requires peers be sent as an NSArray of Peer↵
ID Strings");

                        }
        }

        else if ([self.matchOrSession isKindOfClass: [GKMatch class]])
        {
                        if ([peers isKindOfClass:[NSArray class]])
                        {
                        [self.matchOrSession sendData:dataToSend toPlayers:peers↵
withDataMode:mode error:&error];
                        }

                        else
                        {
                        NSLog(@"Game Center requires peers be sent as an NSArray of↵
Peer ID Strings");
                        }

        }

        else
        {
                NSLog(@"Game Center Manager matchOrSession was not a GKMatch or↵
a GKSession, we are unable to send data");
        }

        if (error != nil)
        {
```

```
            NSLog(@"An error occurred while sending data: %@", [error↵
    localizedDescription]);
        }
    }
```

This method is very similar to the method for sending data to all peers. The main difference is that we use a new API call and feed in an array of peer IDs. You can, of course, change these methods to accept more than an NSString when sending data, but for the simplicity of our test game, a string is all we need.

This concludes everything you need to know about sending data between two or more iOS devices. In the next section, we will look at how to receive and parse the data we get from another peer.

Receiving Data

GKSession and GKMatch each have their own system for receiving delegate callbacks for incoming data. Both of these systems depend on a delegate. Game Center uses the same delegate that we used for our invitation handler in Chapter 5; Game Kit allows us to use a separate call, setDataReceiveHandler:withContext:, to specify the instance that will be in charge of handling incoming data from the network.

The first step in setting up our app to receive data is to set the receive data delegate for both systems to our GameCenterManager class. We will use the GameCenterManager class as a filter point for passing data back into our game. While you could easily receive data in your game controller itself, if we pipe everything throughout GameCenterManager, it makes it much easier to plug this class into future apps and we can direct both Game Kit and Game Center networking to the same protocols to make life easier later down the road.

Modify both matchmakerViewController and peerPickerController of UFOViewController.m to match the following.

```
- (void)matchmakerViewController:(GKMatchmakerViewController *)viewController↵
  didFindMatch:(GKMatch *)match
{
        [self dismissModalViewControllerAnimated:YES];
        gcManager.matchOrSession = match;
        //Set a new received data handler
        [gcManager setupInvitationHandler: gcManager];
        UFOGameViewController *gameVC = [[UFOGameViewController alloc] init];
        gameVC.gameIsMultiplayer = YES;
        gameVC.peerIDString = nil;
        gameVC.peerMatch = match;
        [self.navigationController pushViewController:gameVC animated:YES];
        [gameVC release];
}

- (void)peerPickerController:(GKPeerPickerController *)picker didConnectPeer:↵
(NSString *)peerID toSession:(GKSession *)session
{
        [picker dismiss];
        currentSession = session;
```

```
        gcManager.matchOrSession = session;

        //Set a new received data handler
        [session setDataReceiveHandler: gcManager  withContext: nil];
        UFOGameViewController *gameVC = [[UFOGameViewController alloc] init];
        gameVC.gameIsMultiplayer = YES;
        gameVC.peerIDString = peerID;
        gameVC.peerMatch = nil;
        [self.navigationController pushViewController:gameVC animated:YES];
        [gameVC release];
}
```

The important change to focus on in the two preceding methods is setting the delegate to handle the incoming data request to our GameCenterManager class. This allows us to handle all incoming data in one centralized place; from there, we can relay it out to the relevant sections of the app.

Next, you need to add the following two methods to your GameCenterManager class. The first handles incoming data from Game Kit and the second handles incoming data from Game Center. Both of these methods assume we will be working with only incoming strings, because that is the design we have chosen when dealing with sending data in our game. You can easily adapt these methods to handle receiving other types of objects. In addition, we need to add a new protocol method to handle sending the data back to our game classes. You can also further adapt this setup to use a more complex and intelligent system of data parsing, but it will be more than suitable for the needs of UFOs.

```
- (void)receiveData:(NSData *)data fromPeer:(NSString *)peer inSession: (GKSession↵
 *)session context:(void *)context;
{

        NSString *dataString = [[NSString alloc] initWithData:data↵
 encoding:NSUTF8StringEncoding];
        NSDictionary *dataDictionary = [NSDictionary dictionaryWithObjects:↵
[NSArray arrayWithObjects:dataString, peer, session, nil] forKeys:↵
[NSArray arrayWithObjects:@"data", @"peer", @"session, nil]];
        [dataString release];
        [self callDelegateOnMainThread: @selector(receivedData:) withArg:↵
 dataDictionary error: nil];
}

- (void)match:(GKMatch *)match didReceiveData:(NSData *)data fromPlayer:↵
(NSString *)playerID
{
        NSString *dataString = [[NSString alloc] initWithData:data↵
 encoding:NSUTF8StringEncoding];

        NSDictionary *dataDictionary = [NSDictionary dictionaryWithObjects:↵
[NSArray arrayWithObjects:dataString, playerID, match, nil] forKeys:↵
[NSArray arrayWithObjects:@"data", @"peer", @"session", nil]];
        [dataString release];
        [self callDelegateOnMainThread: @selector(receivedData:) withArg:↵
 dataDictionary error: nil];
}
```

> **TIP:** You can use the context property to pass any data to the received delegate method.

The new protocol method is named receivedData, and you can see how it fits into our existing list of available protocols, as follows.

```
@protocol GameCenterManagerDelegate <NSObject>
@optional
- (void)processGameCenterAuthentication:(NSError*)error;
- (void)friendsFinishedLoading:(NSArray *)friends error:(NSError *)error;
- (void)playerDataLoaded:(NSArray *)players error:(NSError *)error;
- (void)scoreReported: (NSError*) error;
- (void)leaderboardUpdated: (NSArray *)scores error:(NSError *)error;
- (void)mappedPlayerIDToPlayer:(GKPlayer *)player error:(NSError *)error;
- (void)mappedPlayerIDsToPlayers:(NSArray *)players error:(NSError *)error;
- (void)localPlayerScore:(GKScore *)score error:(NSError *)error;
- (void)achievementSubmitted:(GKAchievement *)achievement error:(NSError *)error;
- (void)achievementEarned:(GKAchievementDescription *)achievement;
- (void)achievementDescriptionsLoaded:(NSArray *)descriptions error:(NSError *)error;
- (void)playerActivity:(NSNumber *)activity error:(NSError *)error;
- (void)playerActivityForGroup:(NSDictionary *)activityDict error:(NSError *)error;
- (void)receivedData:(NSDictionary *)dataDictionary;
@end
```

All that is left now is to implement our received data protocol method. We need to add the following method to the UFOGameViewController implementation file.

```
- (void)receivedData:(NSDictionary *)dataDictionary;
{
        if ([[dataDictionary objectForKey: @"data"] doubleValue] == randomHostNumber)
        {
                NSLog(@"Host numbers are equal, we need to reroll them");
                [self generateAndSendHostNumber];
        }

        else if ([[dataDictionary objectForKey: @"data"] doubleValue] >↵
    randomHostNumber)
        {
                NSLog(@"We are the host");
                isHost = YES;
        }

        else if ([[dataDictionary objectForKey: @"data"] doubleValue] <↵
    randomHostNumber)
        {
                NSLog(@"They are the host");
                isHost = NO;
        }
}
```

If you run the game on two devices now, you can see that each log reflects whether the device has been designated a host or whether the other device is the host. The receivedData method is very flawed, though, because it only works with the host data message. In the next section, we will refine this method to accept not only the host message, but also input for player movements, cow movements, and other game actions.

You now have all the basic skills required to send data between two different iOS devices, as well as receive and parse that data and have your system react to it. If you want to experiment with working with these calls in practice, the next section will walk you through several examples of sending and receiving data in our UFOs game.

Putting Everything Together

In the last section, we learned how to receive the data that has been sent to a device. In this section, we walk through the exercise of actually using received data in a useful way for our game. We add a second player, allow movement information to be sent over the network, sync up state data across both devices (such as cow movement), track each player's score, and complete various other required overhead tasks associated with our particular game.

Selecting the Host

Let's start by improving the host selection logic that was implemented in the previous section. Right now, any data that we receive is assumed to be the host number. Because most of the data we receive will not be the host number, we need to find a way to filter that data to where we can parse it. Modify the generateAndSendHostNumber method to match the following code block.

```
-(void)generateAndSendHostNumber;
{
        randomHostNumber = arc4random();
        NSString *randomNumberString = [NSString stringWithFormat: @"$Host:%f",↵
 randomHostNumber];
        [self.gcManager sendStringToAllPeers:randomNumberString reliable: YES];
}
```

As you can see, we now add an identifier prefix to the message that we will send. I have chosen for this example the prefix of $Host:, but you can use whatever system you want. In addition, we need to modify the receivedData callback to support the new format.

```
- (void)receivedData:(NSDictionary *)dataDictionary;
{
        if ([[dataDictionary objectForKey: @"data"] hasPrefix:@"$Host:"])
        {
                    [self determineHost: dataDictionary];
        }
        else
        {
                    NSLog(@"Unable to determine type of message: %@",↵
 dataDictionary);
        }
}
```

If we determine that the message is a host message, we send it to a new helper method called determineHost to determine which device is the host. If we are unable to determine the type of message, we print a warning message to the console, which will help us debug later down the road. We need to move the old code from receivedData into determineHost. In addition to moving the code, we need to strip off the prefix. Although stripping off the prefix has a lot of overhead, it is the easiest way to accomplish this task. In more complex apps, you might need to design a more robust message system.

```
-(void)determineHost:(NSDictionary *)dataDictionary
{
        NSString *dataString = [[dataDictionary objectForKey: @"data"]↩
 stringByReplacingOccurrencesOfString:@"$Host:" withString:@""];
        if ([dataString doubleValue] == randomHostNumber)
        {
                        NSLog(@"Host numbers are equal, we need to reroll them");
                [self generateAndSendHostNumber];
        }

        else if ([dataString doubleValue] > randomHostNumber)
        {
                        NSLog(@"We are the host");
                        isHost = YES;
        }

        else if ([dataString doubleValue] < randomHostNumber)
        {
                        NSLog(@"They are the host");
                        isHost = NO;
        }
}
```

Now we can still determine who the host is, but we have opened the door to be able to process more than only this type of data.

The next step will be transmitting and displaying our peer's UFO into our game. In this chapter, I have added two new images to the project, EnemySaucer1.png and EnemySaucer2.png. These are the same as the originals, but with a different color scheme applied to them. We will use this new artwork to display the opponent's spacecraft.

Displaying the Enemy UFO

The first thing we need to do is detect whether we are a multiplayer game, and if so, we need to draw the enemy UFO in the viewDidLoad method of UFOGameViewController. You will notice this is the exact same code we use for drawing the player in single-player mode except we use a different graphic asset.

```
-(void)viewDidLoad
{
        if (self.gameIsMultiplayer)
        {
                        CGRect otherPlayerFrame = CGRectMake(100, 70, 80, 34);
```

```
                          otherPlayerImageView = [[UIImageView alloc] initWithFrame:↵
     otherPlayerFrame];
                          otherPlayerImageView.animationDuration = 0.75;
                          otherPlayerImageView.animationRepeatCount = 99999;
                 NSArray *imageArray = [NSArray arrayWithObjects: [UIImage imageNamed:↵
     @"EnemySaucer1.png"], [UIImage imageNamed: @"EnemySaucer2.png"], nil];
                          otherPlayerImageView.animationImages = imageArray;
                          [otherPlayerImageView startAnimating];
                          [self.view addSubview: otherPlayerImageView];
             }
     }
```

If we were to run the game on two devices and begin a new multiplayer game, we would now see a red enemy UFO that just sits in the sky. The next step is to send our movement data to our peer so that they can update where the enemy player is. To do so, we add a new code snippet to the end of our movePlayer method.

```
-(void) movePlayer:(float)vertical :(float)horizontal;
{

        //…

        if (self.gameIsMultiplayer)
        {
                NSString *positionString = [NSString stringWithFormat:↵
     @"$PlayerPosition: %f %f", playerFrame.origin.x, playerFrame.origin.y];
                        [self.gcManager sendStringToAllPeers:positionString reliable:↵
     NO];
        }
}
```

Here we send your player's x and y coordinates to the peer every time you move. We will be sending the data as unreliable, since if we fail, we can just use the next packet; the data will always be updating while the player is moving. This would be a great place to use predictive technology, as discussed in Chapter 7, but for simplicity's sake, we will be syncing every frame. In addition, there are better ways to send the x and y coordinates to another device, such as a dictionary or custom data format. However, encoding them into a string is the easiest to understand. As you develop your game or app, you can design this type of function to be more streamlined with less overhead.

> **TIP:** Using stringWithFormat carries with it a lot of overhead. In practice, you should use methods such as stringByAppendingString to further optimize this type of code.

We also need to update our receivedData method to handle the new type of data we are expecting. Modify that method to match the new one as follows. In addition, we add a new method to parse the incoming data. Also add a new method called drawEnemyShipWithData, as follows.

```
- (void)receivedData:(NSDictionary *)dataDictionary;
{
        if ([[dataDictionary objectForKey: @"data"] hasPrefix:@"$Host:"])
        {
```

```
                                    [self determineHost: dataDictionary];
           }

           else if ([[dataDictionary objectForKey: @"data"] hasPrefix:@"$PlayerPosition:"])
           {
                                    [self drawEnemyShipWithData: dataDictionary];
           }

           else
           {
                                    NSLog(@"Unable to determine type of message: %@",↩
    dataDictionary);
                }
    }


-(void)drawEnemyShipWithData:(NSDictionary *)dataDictionary
{
           NSArray *dataArray = [[dataDictionary objectForKey: @"data"]↩
    componentsSeparatedByString:@" "];
           float x = [[dataArray objectAtIndex: 1] floatValue];
           float y = [[dataArray objectAtIndex: 2] floatValue];
           otherPlayerImageView.frame = CGRectMake(x, y, 80, 34);
}
```

This method parses the incoming data from the network. We pull the x and y coordinates out of the string that we received and we update the enemy player's frame with the new position. This type of approach is syncing the two devices frame by frame and is very inefficient. Given more time, this method should be updated to use predictive technology to determine where the player is heading, and only update the feed if the player goes against the prediction. However, for the purposes of this demo, it suits our needs. For more information on predictive networking see Chapter 7.

If you were to run the game now and begin a new multiplayer game, you would see that each device reflects the movement of its partnered device. We still need to spawn the cows, add the tractor beam, and update the scores, but we have a functional (albeit dull, for the time being) multiplayer game, as shown in Figure 8–1.

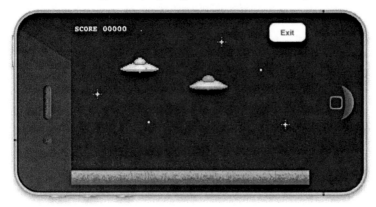

Figure 8–1. *Adding a second player to UFOs. Each player can move around independently and is kept in sync through the network.*

Spawning Cows

Because we want the cow movement to be synced between each device, we need to dedicate one device to handling the cow spawning and movement paths. We have already picked a host device, so we will let the host determine where the cows will be placed. We begin by modifying the determineHost method. As you can see in the following code, if we are the host, we begin our normal spawn cow process.

```
-(void)determineHost:(NSDictionary *)dataDictionary
{
        NSString *dataString = [[dataDictionary objectForKey: @"data"]↵
  stringByReplacingOccurrencesOfString:@"$Host:" withString:@""];
        if ([dataString doubleValue] == randomHostNumber)
        {
                NSLog(@"Host numbers are equal, we need to reroll them");
                    [self generateAndSendHostNumber];
        }

        else if ([dataString doubleValue] > randomHostNumber)
        {
                    isHost = YES;
                    for(int x = 0; x < 5; x++)
                    {
                            [self spawnCow];
                    }

                    [self updateCowPaths];
         }

        else if ([dataString doubleValue] < randomHostNumber)
        {
                    isHost = NO;
        }
}
```

We also need to modify our spawnCow method to support the new networking behavior. All we are doing here is determining whether we are a network game and whether we are the host, and then sending the data to our network handlers.

```
-(void)spawnCow;
{
        int x = arc4random()%480;
        UIImageView *cowImageView = [[UIImageView alloc] initWithFrame:CGRectMake(x,↵
  260, 64, 42)];
        cowImageView.image = [UIImage imageNamed: @"Cow1.png"];
        [self.view addSubview: cowImageView];
        [cowArray addObject: cowImageView];
        [cowImageView release];

        if (isHost && self.gameIsMultiplayer)
        {
                [gcManager sendStringToAllPeers:[NSString stringWithFormat:↵
  @"$spawnCow:%i", x] reliable:YES];
        }
}
```

Modify the receivedData method to support the new $spawnCow message type. We also want to extract the x axis origin from the message and pass it to a new method that will handle spawning a cow from the network. Both of these methods are shown next.

```
else if ([[dataDictionary objectForKey: @"data"] hasPrefix:@"$spawnCow:"])
{
        int x = [[[dataDictionary objectForKey: @"data"]↵
 stringByReplacingOccurrencesOfString:@"$spawnCow:" withString:@""] intValue];
        [self spawnCowFromNetwork: x];
}
-(void)spawnCowFromNetwork:(int)x
{
        UIImageView *cowImageView = [[UIImageView alloc] initWithFrame:CGRectMake(x,↵
 260, 64, 42)];
        cowImageView.image = [UIImage imageNamed: @"Cow1.png"];
        [self.view addSubview: cowImageView];
        [cowArray addObject: cowImageView];
        [cowImageView release];
}
```

> **TIP:** Our host doesn't need to pass the y axis coordinate for the cows because they are always spawned on the same y axis. If you can eliminate data from a packet, it is always beneficial.

If you were to run the game now, you would see that both devices spawn cows in the exact same location, but the host device is the only device that animates the cow movements.

The next step is to add the logic to share the animation control for the cows. Modify the existing updateCowPaths method to send the newX and array position of the cow we want to update. The following new code should be added to the end of the for loop.

```
if (self.gameIsMultiplayer)
{
        NSString *dataString = [NSString stringWithFormat:@"$cowMove:%i:%f", x, newX];
        [gcManager sendStringToAllPeers:dataString reliable:YES];
}
```

> **NOTE:** Because we set the data for the spawn cow call to reliable, it is guaranteed to be received in the order that it was sent. This means that we can be assured that the objects in our cowArray on both devices will be in the same order.

We also need to add a new data handler to our receivedData method. We pass the entire dictionary to our new updateCowPathsFromNetwork method.

```
else if ([[dataDictionary objectForKey: @"data"] hasPrefix:@"$cowMove:"])
{
        [self updateCowPathsFromNetwork: dataDictionary];
}


-(void)updateCowPathsFromNetwork:(NSDictionary *)dataDictionary;
```

```
{
        NSArray *dataArray = [[dataDictionary objectForKey: @"data"]↩
componentsSeparatedByString:@":"];
        int placeInArray = [[dataArray objectAtIndex: 1] intValue];
        UIImageView *tempCow = [cowArray objectAtIndex: placeInArray];
        float currentX = tempCow.frame.origin.x;
        [UIView beginAnimations:@"cowWalk" context:nil];
        [UIView setAnimationDuration: 3.0];
        [UIView setAnimationCurve:UIViewAnimationCurveLinear];
        float newX = [[dataArray objectAtIndex: 2] intValue];
        if (tempCow != currentAbductee)
        {
                        tempCow.frame = CGRectMake(newX, 260, 64, 42);
        }

        [UIView commitAnimations];
        tempCow.animationDuration = 0.75;
        tempCow.animationRepeatCount = 99999;

        //flip cow
        if (newX < currentX)
        {
                NSArray *flippedCowImageArray = [NSArray arrayWithObjects: [UIImage↩
imageNamed: @"Cow1Reversed.png"], [UIImage imageNamed: @"Cow2Reversed.png"], [UIImage↩
imageNamed: @"Cow3Reversed.png"], nil];
                        tempCow.animationImages = flippedCowImageArray;
        }

        else
        {
                NSArray *cowImageArray = [NSArray arrayWithObjects: [UIImage↩
imageNamed: @"Cow1.png"], [UIImage imageNamed: @"Cow2.png"], [UIImage imageNamed:↩
@"Cow3.png"], nil];
                        tempCow.animationImages = cowImageArray;
        }

        [tempCow startAnimating];
}
```

This method is very similar to our existing method for updating cow paths. The two differences are that we get our place in the array from the network, and we don't randomly generate a newX position. If you were to run the game again, you would see that both sets of cows are now in sync with each other. When a cow changes position, it is reflected exactly the same on both devices. Figure 8–2 shows the current state of the game.

Figure 8–2. *Syncing up the cow movements over the network between two iOS devices*

Each player can now abduct cows and increment their score. There are, however, still two remaining issues that need to be addressed. The first is that we don't share scores between devices, and the second is that we don't show the other player's tractor beams or animate the cows into the UFO during the abduction. Let's start off by adding in support for the score.

Sharing Scores

When we increment the score, we send that data to our peers. Add the following snippet of code to our finishAbducting method, right after we increment the score.

```
if (self.gameIsMultiplayer)
{
        [gcManager sendStringToAllPeers:[NSString stringWithFormat:@"$score:%f",
 score] reliable:YES];
}
```

We, again, need to modify our receivedData method to support the new $score message. I have chosen to increment the enemy score within the receivedData method. You can, of course, write a new method to handle this functionality. In addition, we need to add a new label for the enemy score. It will be placed directly below the local player's score. Figure 8–3 shows the scores in place.

```
else if ([[dataDictionary objectForKey: @"data"] hasPrefix:@"$score:"])
{
        float enemyScore = [[[dataDictionary objectForKey: @"data"]
 stringByReplacingOccurrencesOfString:@"$score:" withString:@""] floatValue];
                enemyScoreLabel.text = [NSString stringWithFormat: @"ENEMY %05.0f",
 enemyScore];
}
```

> **TIP:** Technically, you don't need to pass the score value in with the network call, because scores are always incremented by one; we can assume a new score message means increment the value by one.

Figure 8–3. *Adding the score for the networked player*

> **Exercise**   It would be very easy to add logic to declare a winner of the game when either player reaches a score of ten. Try to add this logic into the game.

Adding Network Abduction Code

The last thing that we need to handle is tying in network support for the abduction code. We need to properly remove and respawn cows as they are abducted, as well as show the enemy UFO using their tractor beam and animating a cow into the ship.

Let's begin by showing and hiding the tractor beam on each device. Because we start a tractor beam every time a user touches the screen, and end it when the user releases that touch, we can begin there. We have no values that need to be transmitted; the only thing we need to be aware of is starting and stopping the animation itself. Modify the touchesBegan and touchesEnd methods to send a message to the peer. The modified methods are shown as follows.

```
- (void)touchesBegan:(NSSet *)touches withEvent:(UIEvent *)event
{
        currentAbductee = nil;
        tractorBeamOn = YES;
        if (self.gameIsMultiplayer)
        {
                [gcManager sendStringToAllPeers:@"$beginTractorBeam"↩
 reliable:YES];
```

```
        }

        tractorBeamImageView.frame = CGRectMake(myPlayerImageView.frame.origin.x+25,↵
myPlayerImageView.frame.origin.y+10, 28, 318);
        tractorBeamImageView.animationDuration = 0.5;
        tractorBeamImageView.animationRepeatCount = 99999;
        NSArray *imageArray = [NSArray arrayWithObjects: [UIImage imageNamed:↵
@"Tractor1.png"], [UIImage imageNamed: @"Tractor2.png"], nil];
        tractorBeamImageView.animationImages = imageArray;
        [tractorBeamImageView startAnimating];
        [self.view insertSubview:tractorBeamImageView atIndex:4];
        UIImageView *cowImageView = [self hitTest];
        if (cowImageView)
        {
                currentAbductee = cowImageView;
                [self abductCow: cowImageView];
        }

}


-(void)endTractorFromNetwork
{
        [otherPlayerTractorBeamImageView removeFromSuperview];
}

- (void)touchesEnded:(NSSet *)touches withEvent:(UIEvent *)event
{
        tractorBeamOn = NO;
        if (self.gameIsMultiplayer)
        {
                        [gcManager sendStringToAllPeers:@"$endTractorBeam"↵
 reliable:YES];
        }

        [tractorBeamImageView removeFromSuperview];
        if (currentAbductee)
        {
                [UIView beginAnimations: @"dropCow" context:nil];
                [UIView setAnimationDuration: 1.0];
                [UIView setAnimationCurve:UIViewAnimationCurveEaseIn];
                [UIView setAnimationBeginsFromCurrentState: YES];
                CGRect frame = currentAbductee.frame;
                frame.origin.y = 260;
                frame.origin.x = myPlayerImageView.frame.origin.x +15;
                currentAbductee.frame = frame;
                [UIView commitAnimations];
        }

        currentAbductee = nil;
}
```

As you can see, we simply check to make sure that we have a network game, and then pass a message to begin or end the tractor beams. Next, we add a handler to our receivedData method to call two new methods that will display and animate the tractor beam on the peer's device. These two methods are modifications of our current tractor beam animation methods and are shown next for your convenience.

```
-(void)beginTractorFromNetwork
{
        otherPlayerTractorBeamImageView.frame =↵
CGRectMake(otherPlayerImageView.frame.origin.x+25,↵
otherPlayerImageView.frame.origin.y+10, 28, 318);
        otherPlayerTractorBeamImageView.animationDuration = 0.5;
        otherPlayerTractorBeamImageView.animationRepeatCount = 99999;
        NSArray *imageArray = [NSArray arrayWithObjects: [UIImage imageNamed:↵
@"Tractor1.png"], [UIImage imageNamed: @"Tractor2.png"], nil];
        otherPlayerTractorBeamImageView.animationImages = imageArray;
        [otherPlayerTractorBeamImageView startAnimating];
        [self.view insertSubview:otherPlayerTractorBeamImageView atIndex:4];
}


-(void)endTractorFromNetwork
{
        [otherPlayerTractorBeamImageView removeFromSuperview];
}
```

If you were to run the game now, you would see that when each user touches the screen, the tractor beam appears on both devices. We don't need to worry about locking the movement for the UFO while the tractor beam is on since this is handled for us in the single-player game, and movements are only transmitted to another device if they are acceptable on the single-player mode. Next, we need to add additional code to handle the hit test, so modify the hitTest method, as follows.

```
-(UIImageView *)hitTest
{
        if (!tractorBeamOn)
        {
                return nil;
        }

        for (int x = 0; x < [cowArray count]; x++)
        {
                UIImageView *tempCow = [cowArray objectAtIndex: x];
                CALayer *cowLayer= [[tempCow layer] presentationLayer];
                CGRect cowFrame = [cowLayer frame];
                if (CGRectIntersectsRect(cowFrame, tractorBeamImageView.frame))
                {
                        tempCow.frame = cowLayer.frame;
                        [tempCow.layer removeAllAnimations];
                                if (self.gameIsMultiplayer)
                                {
                                [gcManager sendStringToAllPeers:[NSString↵
 stringWithFormat: @"$abductCowAtIndex:%i", x] reliable:YES];
                                }

                        return tempCow;
                }
        }
}
```

```
        return nil;
}
```

Here we are using the same trick that we used earlier when we populated the cow array. Because we sent the data reliably to enter objects into our array, we know that the order of the array is always going to be the same. Because we know the order of the array, we can pass the index of the cow we want to modify. In addition to sending the data, we also need to write a new if statement to catch this message, as shown below. You can see this method is set up a lot like the score method in which we extract the value that we are interested in and call a new method using it.

```
else if ([[dataDictionary objectForKey: @"data"] hasPrefix:@"$abductCowAtIndex:"])
{

        int index = [[[dataDictionary objectForKey: @"data"]↵
 stringByReplacingOccurrencesOfString:@"$abductCowAtIndex:" withString:@""] intValue];
            [self abductCowFromNetworkAtIndex:index];
}
```

The following two methods handle the abduction animations that are received over the network. They are both very similar to the methods that we use to animate an abduction in the single-player mode. You could even modify your existing methods to handle the network behavior by calling them with a flag to indicate that they are coming from a remote device.

```
-(void)abductCowFromNetworkAtIndex:(int)x
{
        otherPlayerCurrentAbductee = [cowArray objectAtIndex: x];

        otherPlayerCurrentAbductee.frame = otherPlayerCurrentAbductee.frame;
        [otherPlayerCurrentAbductee.layer removeAllAnimations];
        [UIView beginAnimations: @"abductNetwork" context:nil];
        [UIView setAnimationDuration: 4.0];
        [UIView setAnimationCurve:UIViewAnimationCurveEaseIn];
        [UIView setAnimationDelegate: self];
        [UIView setAnimationDidStopSelector: @selector(finishAbductingFromNetwork)];
        [UIView setAnimationBeginsFromCurrentState: YES];
        CGRect frame = otherPlayerCurrentAbductee.frame;
        frame.origin.y = otherPlayerImageView.frame.origin.y;
        otherPlayerCurrentAbductee.frame = frame;
        [UIView commitAnimations];
}

-(void)finishAbductingFromNetwork;
{
        [cowArray removeObjectIdenticalTo:otherPlayerCurrentAbductee];
        [self endTractorFromNetwork];
        [otherPlayerCurrentAbductee.layer removeAllAnimations];
        [otherPlayerCurrentAbductee removeFromSuperview];
        otherPlayerCurrentAbductee = nil;
        if (isHost)
        {
                    [self spawnCow];
        }
}
```

We also need to do some overhead to make sure we don't generate any new bugs. For example, we add a new pointer to keep track of which cow the enemy is currently abducting, if any. If you recall, in the updateCowPaths method we don't want to update the path for the cow that is being abducted because it will break the animation that is being used for the abduction. We need to modify that method to also ignore whatever cow the enemy happens to be abducting. If you were to run the game again, you would now notice that we have a fully functional multiplayer game, as seen in Figure 8–4.

Figure 8–4. *A fully functional multiplayer UFO game being played by two people using a Bluetooth connection*

Disconnections

The last step that we need to take when working with multiplayer support is to add in logic to handle disconnections and other failures that are unrecoverable. Luckily for us, Apple's APIs handle most of the legwork. We do, however, want to add a more universal call to our GameCenterManager class to make things easier for us.

```
- (void)disconnect;
{
        if ([self.matchOrSession isKindOfClass: [GKSession class]])
        {
                [self.matchOrSession disconnectFromAllPeers];
        }

        else if ([self.matchOrSession isKindOfClass: [GKMatch class]])
        {
                [self.matchOrSession disconnect];
        }
}
```

This method should be called whenever you wish to end a multiplayer game. It will make sure that the peers are safely disconnected and prevent a number of issues that would be very hard to troubleshoot.

Summary

In this chapter, we covered a lot of information in a very condensed manner. You learned how to send and receive data between two or more iOS devices using both Game Kit networking and Game Center networking. In addition, you learned how to handle network state changes, such as disconnections. We put the principles learned in this chapter into use in our UFO game, creating a multiplayer iOS game from the ground up in less than eight chapters. In the next chapter, we will explore Game Center's turned-based gaming APIs, which were added with the release of iOS 5.

Chapter **9**

Turned-Based Gaming
with Game Center

Apple announced iOS 5 at its own World Wide Developers Conference (WWDC) in 2011. In addition to a number of smaller enhancements that this new SDK brought to Game Center, it included one very important new feature: turned-based gaming is the newest addition to the Game Center platform. With turn-based gaming, you can now provide your users with asynchronous gaming. Turned-based games are simply any game in which players take turns playing, such as in tic-tac-toe, chess, Battleship, and Monopoly.

Turned-based gaming on iOS has become very popular in the past few years, starting with Words with Friends. Words with Friends, shown in Figure 9–1, is an asynchronous word game similar to Scrabble. Each player receives a selection of letters that they must play, in turn, on a board to create a word. They are awarded points based on the difficulty of the word, as well as layout on the board. Turned-based gaming is traditionally done with a store and forward type platform; the server holds on to the game data until the next client logs in and retrieves it. Asynchronous games have traditionally been casual games and don't require all players to be present at all times.

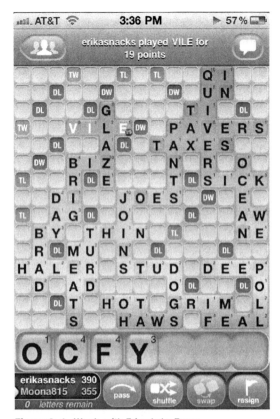

Figure 9–1. *Words with Friends by Zynga*

Before the introduction of iOS 5, Game Center had provided real-time gaming in which all the devices involved needed to be active and logged in continuously throughout the multiplayer experience. Turned-based gaming adds a more casual experience, letting people run up to 20 matches at a time and only playing when it is their turn in a particular match. Prior to the new Game Center enhancements, writing this type of game would have required you to write and deploy your own server to handle the game interaction. Now, you can add the networking component of turned-based gaming and be up and running in less than a day of work. In this chapter, we explore how to write a simple tic-tac-toe game using iOS 5 and Game Center's new turned-based gaming APIs.

A New Sample Project

Unfortunately, our existing UFOs sample game is not a suitable experience for testing turned-based gaming. It wouldn't make much sense to have each player make a move and then wait for the other player to catch up. Luckily, there is another very simple type of game that we can build a project around: tic-tac-toe. This classic children's game is something almost all of us have played, and we have experience with the rules and strategy.

We begin by creating a new navigation controller–based project. There are three views that we will be working with throughout the project.

- Main View: This view simply contains a button that launches the GKTurnedBasedMatchmakerViewController.

- GKTurnedBasedMatchmakerViewController: This is the view provided by Apple to create and resume turned-based games. You will not need to create this view yourself.

- Game View: This is the class that handles user input, determining winners and ties, and populating the game board at the start of each turn.

We begin by working with the main view. These files will be created for you when you create the new project. The very first thing we need to do is make sure to import the proper Game Kit frameworks and add our reusable GameCenterManager class that we have been working on throughout this book; you can include the existing one from Chapter 8. We also need to create a single button in the view to start a new game, as shown in Figure 9–2.

Figure 9–2. *The main view for our new tic-tac-toe game*

The header file for the new base view controller class should match the following code snippet. We need to adhere to the GameCenterManagerDelegate as well as the GKTurnedBasedMatchmakerViewController. As in previous chapters, we also need to create a class instance of GameCenterManager. The last thing that needs to be added is an IBAction method to begin a new game. Make sure to hook up the Start New Game button to the IBAction in Interface Builder.

```
#import <UIKit/UIKit.h>
#import <GameKit/GameKit.h>
#import "GameCenterManager.h"

@interface tictactoeViewController : UIViewController <GameCenterManagerDelegate,
GKTurnBasedMatchmakerViewControllerDelegate>
{
    GameCenterManager *gcManager;
}

-(IBAction)beginGame:(id)sender;
@end
```

We also need to modify the viewDidLoad method to check for and then authenticate our local user with Game Center. This is the same approach that we followed in Chapter 2.

```
- (void)viewDidLoad
{
    [super viewDidLoad];
    if ([GameCenterManager isGameCenterAvailable]) {
        [[NSNotificationCenter defaultCenter] addObserver:self
selector:@selector(localUserAuthenticationChanged:)
name:GKPlayerAuthenticationDidChangeNotificationName object:nil];
        gcManager = [[GameCenterManager alloc] init];
        [gcManager setDelegate: self];
        [gcManager authenticateLocalUser];
    }
}
```

We also need to implement two delegate methods to monitor for successful authentication and local user changes. We are using both of these methods to print some debugging output.

```
- (void)processGameCenterAuthentication:(NSError*)error;
{
    if (error != nil) {
        NSLog(@"An error occured during authentication: %@", [error
localizedDescription]);
    }
}

- (void)localUserAuthenticationChanged:(NSNotification*)notif;
{
    NSLog(@"Authenication Changed: %@", notif.object);
}
```

In the next section, we will see how to call the GKTurnedBasedMatchmakerViewController and how to handle the delegate methods that are required in order to handle errors and resuming or creating new matches.

GKTurnedBasedMatchmakerViewController

Apple provides a default class to present the GUI for creating a new turned-based match. For programmatically creating a match, see the later section "Programmatic Matches."

We begin by working with a new matchmaker object in the IBAction for the single button that we created in the previous section. The approach that we use here is very similar to iOS 4 Game Center matchmaking. We first alloc and init a copy of GKMatchRequest and set the minimum and maximum players. We then create a new GKTurnedBasedMatchmakerViewController and init it with the match object that we just created. Finally, we set the delegate to self and present the view modally to the user. The user will be presented with a view similar to the one shown in Figure 9–3.

```
- (IBAction)beginGame:(id)sender
{
    GKMatchRequest *match = [[GKMatchRequest alloc] init];
    [match setMaxPlayers:2];
    [match setMinPlayers:2];

    GKTurnBasedMatchmakerViewController *tmvc = nil;
    tmvc = [[GKTurnBasedMatchmakerViewController alloc] initWithMatchRequest:match];
    [tmvc setTurnBasedMatchmakerDelegate: self];
    [self presentModalViewController:tmvc animated:YES];
    [tmvc release];
    [match release];
}
```

> **NOTE:** You must first authenticate with Game Center before you can create a new turned-based game match.

There are four delegate methods that you need to implement to conform to the GKTurnedBasedMatchmakerViewControllerDelegate. The first handles the user canceling in the matchmaker. The only requirement here is to call dismissModalViewControllerAnimated. You may add additional logic, as required, for your app.

```
- (void)turnBasedMatchmakerViewControllerWasCancelled:
(GKTurnBasedMatchmakerViewController*)viewController
{
    [self dismissModalViewControllerAnimated:YES];
}
```

> **IMPORTANT:** The list of current games does not update until you close and reopen the GKTurnedBasedMatchmakerViewController.

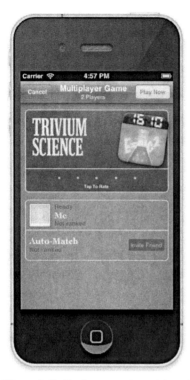

Figure 9–3. *Starting a new turned-based match*

We also need to implement a delegate method to catch any errors that occur during this phase. The following method is called whenever an error is encountered during the matchmaking process. For debugging purposes, we are printing the error to the console; however, you will want to inform the user that an error has occurred.

```
- (void)turnBasedMatchmakerViewController:
(GKTurnBasedMatchmakerViewController*)viewController didFailWithError:(NSError *)error
{
    NSLog(@"Turned Based Matchmaker Failed with Error: %@", [error
localizedDescription]);
}
```

The last delegate method that we discuss in this section handles the user quitting a match from the matchmaker screen. This is accomplished by swiping from right to left across a game and selecting the quit option. In the following method, we call participantQuitOutOfTurnWithOutcome on the match object that is passed to us as part of the method. We pass in the outcome of GKTurnBasedMatchOutcomeQuit. If you do not call the proper method here, you will be able to quit a game, but it will reappear within a few seconds.

```
- (void)turnBasedMatchmakerViewController:(GKTurnBasedMatchmakerViewController
*)viewController playerQuitForMatch:(GKTurnBasedMatch *)match
{
    [match participantQuitOutOfTurnWithOutcome:GKTurnBasedMatchOutcomeQuit
withCompletionHandler:^(NSError *error) {
```

```
        if (error) {
            NSLog(@"An error occurred ending match: %@", [error localizedDescription]);
        }
    }];
}
```

The final required method, didFindMatch, is discussed in the next section, "Starting a New Game."

> **NOTE:** A user can now rate your app from inside your app when using the GKTurnBasedMatchmakerViewController, shown previously in Figure 9–3.

Starting a New Game

Starting a new match with turned-based gaming is a very straightforward and simple process. To do so, you need to implement the following method. This new method dismisses the GKTurnBasedMatchmakerViewController, and then passes a copy of the match object to your game controller. The following code snippet is the procedure we follow for tic-tac-toe.

```
- (void)turnBasedMatchmakerViewController:(GKTurnBasedMatchmakerViewController
*)viewController didFindMatch:(GKTurnBasedMatch *)match
{
    [self dismissModalViewControllerAnimated: YES];
    tictactoeGameViewController *gameVC = [[tictactoeGameViewController alloc] init];
    gameVC.match = match;
    [[self navigationController] pushViewController:gameVC animated:YES];
    [gameVC release];
}
```

Let's now switch attention to the tictactoeGameViewController class. Starting with the header file, we create a new property to hold on to our match object, which we set in the previous method. We also create a new mutable dictionary to hold on to our game data, which will be discussed in more depth throughout the rest of this chapter.

```
#import <UIKit/UIKit.h>
#import <GameKit/GameKit.h>

@interface tictactoeGameViewController : UIViewController
@property(nonatomic, retain) NSMutableDictionary *gameDictionary;
@property(nonatomic, retain) GKTurnBasedMatch *match;
@end
```

> **IMPORTANT:** You are strictly limited to passing only 4k of data with each new turn. If you cannot limit your game data to less than 4k, you can use a URL to point to a server holding the complete data set. Alternatively, you could pass only the delta of the game state and store the existing data locally.

We need to pause here to configure the actual game view (tictactoeGameViewController). We need nine spots for the user to move in the tic-tac-toe game, as well as a forfeit option and a label to inform the players of whose turn it is.

We use simple UIButtons to handle user input. Modify the xib with a layout similar to that pictured in Figure 9–4. You need to create IBOutlets for each of the buttons and the label as well as new IBAction methods for both making a move and forfeiting. Connect all the board buttons to the makeMove method that you previously created. We also need to set tags on the UIButtons to help us locate them. Begin with tag 1 in the upper-left corner and move left to right, up to down, numbering them.

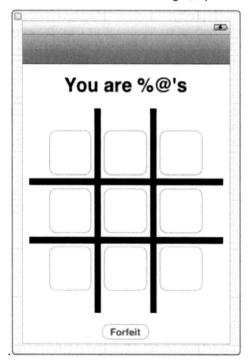

Figure 9–4. *A view of the game board, as seen from interface builder*

You now have two new methods in your game view controller, as well as nine button outlets and one label outlet. This covers how to begin a new turned-based gaming match. In the next section, we look at how to make a move and pass control to the next player.

Making the First Move

The first thing we need to do in a new match-based game, before we make a move, is determine who the player is representing. In our example game, there are two sides: X and O. We are going to set the first person to always be X, and the second to always be O. This means that X will always make the first move. With this setup, it becomes easy to determine who the player currently is representing using the following code snippet.

```
if (match.currentParticipant == [match.participants objectAtIndex:0]) {
    myPlayerCharacter = @"X";
    identifyTeamLabel.text = @"It is X's Turn";
} else {
    myPlayerCharacter = @"O";
    identifyTeamLabel.text = @"It is O's Turn";
}
```

After we have determined who the users are, then we can allow them to make a move. We will modify the code for the action to which the nine game buttons are connected. First, let's take a look at the method in its completed form. Then, we can break it down and look at each part in depth.

```
- (IBAction)makeMove:(id)sender
{
    [sender setTitle:myPlayerCharacter forState:UIControlStateNormal];
    NSString *buttonIndexString = [NSString stringWithFormat:@"%d", [sender tag]];
    [gameDictionary setObject:myPlayerCharacter forKey:buttonIndexString];
    NSData *data = [NSPropertyListSerialization dataFromPropertyList:gameDictionary
format:NSPropertyListXMLFormat_v1_0 errorDescription:nil];
    GKTurnBasedParticipant *nextPlayer;
    if (match.currentParticipant == [match.participants objectAtIndex:0]) {
        nextPlayer = [[match participants] lastObject];
    } else {
        nextPlayer = [[match participants] objectAtIndex:0];
    }

    if ([self checkWinner] != nil) {
        if ([[self checkWinner] isEqualToString:@"Tie"]) {
            UIAlertView *alert = [[UIAlertView alloc] initWithTitle:@"Game Over"
message:@"Its a draw" delegate:nil cancelButtonTitle:@"Dimiss" otherButtonTitles: nil];
            [alert show];
            [alert release];
        } else {
            UIAlertView *alert = [[UIAlertView alloc] initWithTitle:@"Game Over"
message:nil delegate:nil cancelButtonTitle:@"Dimiss" otherButtonTitles: nil];
            [alert show];
            [alert release];
        }

        [self.match participantQuitInTurnWithOutcome:GKTurnBasedMatchOutcomeWon
nextParticipant:nextPlayer matchData:data completionHandler:^(NSError *error) {
            if (error) {
                NSLog(@"An error occurred ending match: %@", [error
localizedDescription]);
            }
        }];
    } else {
        [self.match endTurnWithNextParticipant:nextPlayer matchData:data
completionHandler:^(NSError *error) {
            if (error) {
                NSLog(@"An error occurred updating turn: %@", [error
localizedDescription]);
            }

            [self.navigationController popViewControllerAnimated: YES];
        }];
    }
}
```

This method might appear complex at first glance, but after we have stepped through all the details, you will see it is fairly straightforward. The first thing we do is set the sender's (the game button) title to our player character, which we determined with the previous code snippet.

Next, we know that we will need to hold on to our game data to persist it throughout each turn, so we store the player's character into a dictionary using the button's tag for our key. This allows us to later iterate over the dictionary and repopulate previous moves (more about this in the next section "Continuing a Game in Progress").

We now need to prepare and send our game data to the next player. This requires several steps. Because we need to send our game data as NSData, we convert our existing game dictionary to NSData. We do this with the NSPropertyListSerialization methods. We can then send and later retrieve this data.

The next step is to determine who the next player will be. In a two-person game, this is fairly simple: we look at the array of our participants and determine which one isn't us, and then we set that one to the next player. When dealing with more players, you need to simply determine your current index in the match's participant array and call the next player; or, in the case that you are the last player, call the first.

> **NOTE:** The size and order of the participant's array is determined when the match first begins, and will be the same throughout the match and on each device.

> **TIP:** You might see that there are nil objects in the participant array; these are placeholders for unmatched players. Game Center will only match new players when it is their turn to move. This means that every time you are automatched, it will be your turn to move.

The next section of code deals with checking to see whether there is a winner of the match. We go over this in more detail in the "Ending a Match" section of this chapter.

The last thing that we will do at the end of each move is send the new game data to the next player. This player will, in turn, update the game state and send it to the next player (which happens to be the first player again). To do this, we call endTurnWithNextParticipant on our match object. We need to pass in the next player that we determined earlier in the method.

Continuing a Game in Progress

When you resume a game on your next turn, assuming it is not the first turn of a match, you will need to first restore the game state to its current position. To do this, we begin by modifying our viewDidLoad method to get the current match data. We need to call loadMatchDataWithCompletionHandler on our match object. This returns the data that we sent to the next player in the previous method. We then convert the NSData back into a dictionary and then add it to our gameDictionary.

```
- (void)viewDidLoad
{
    //Existing viewDidLoad code…
    [self.match loadMatchDataWithCompletionHandler:^(NSData *matchData, NSError *error)
{
        NSDictionary *myDict = [NSPropertyListSerialization
propertyListFromData:match.matchData mutabilityOption:NSPropertyListImmutable format:nil
errorDescription:nil];
        [gameDictionary addEntriesFromDictionary: myDict];
        [self populateExistingGameBoard];
        if (error) {
            NSLog(@"loadMatchData - %@", [error localizedDescription]);
        }
    }];
}
```

> **TIP:** If you persist the game state locally, you will only need to update the turns that have occurred since your last move. This approach will help you keep packet sizes under the 4k limit.

After populating the game data dictionary, we need to call a new convenience method to populate our game GUI from that dictionary. This method will loop through all the keys in our dictionary and populate the relevant game buttons with the player's character. We also set the enabled state of the button to NO, which prevents the player from moving on top of their opponent's location.

```
- (void)populateExistingGameBoard
{
    NSArray *dataArray = [gameDictionary allKeys];
    for (NSString *key in dataArray) {
        UIButton *button = (UIButton*)[self.view viewWithTag: [key intValue]];
        [button setTitle:[gameDictionary objectForKey:key]
forState:UIControlStateNormal];
        [button setEnabled: NO];
    }
}
```

With the code in place, you can now play through a complete round of tic-tac-toe using two Game Center accounts; however, the game will never detect a winner or a draw. In the next section, we look at the logic required to detect an end-of-game event. An example of a populated game is shown in Figure 9–5.

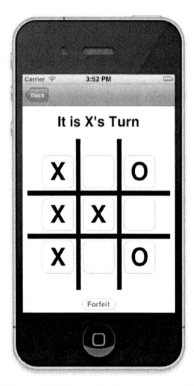

Figure 9–5. *Populating the game board through the match's data*

Ending a Match

In the section "Making the First Move," we saw a call to a method called checkWinner. In this section, we take a look at that method. For tic-tac-toe, we are using a brute force approach to see if we have a winner, by checking all the rows and columns for three repeating characters. We also need to check for a tie if there are no more places to move.

```
- (NSString*)checkWinner
{
    //top row
    if ([gameButton1.titleLabel.text isEqualToString:gameButton2.titleLabel.text] &&
[gameButton2.titleLabel.text isEqualToString:gameButton3.titleLabel.text])
        return gameButton1.titleLabel.text;
    //middle row
    if ([gameButton4.titleLabel.text isEqualToString:gameButton5.titleLabel.text] &&
[gameButton5.titleLabel.text isEqualToString:gameButton6.titleLabel.text])
        return gameButton4.titleLabel.text;
    //bottom row
    if ([gameButton7.titleLabel.text isEqualToString:gameButton8.titleLabel.text] &&
[gameButton8.titleLabel.text isEqualToString:gameButton9.titleLabel.text])
        return gameButton7.titleLabel.text;
    //first column
```

```
    if ([gameButton1.titleLabel.text isEqualToString:gameButton4.titleLabel.text] &&
[gameButton4.titleLabel.text isEqualToString:gameButton7.titleLabel.text])
        return gameButton1.titleLabel.text;
    //middle column
    if ([gameButton2.titleLabel.text isEqualToString:gameButton5.titleLabel.text] &&
[gameButton5.titleLabel.text isEqualToString:gameButton8.titleLabel.text])
        return gameButton2.titleLabel.text;
    //last column
    if ([gameButton3.titleLabel.text isEqualToString:gameButton6.titleLabel.text] &&
[gameButton6.titleLabel.text isEqualToString:gameButton9.titleLabel.text])
        return gameButton3.titleLabel.text;
    //diagonal
    if ([gameButton1.titleLabel.text isEqualToString:gameButton5.titleLabel.text] &&
[gameButton5.titleLabel.text isEqualToString:gameButton9.titleLabel.text])
        return gameButton1.titleLabel.text;
    if ([gameButton3.titleLabel.text isEqualToString:gameButton5.titleLabel.text] &&
[gameButton5.titleLabel.text isEqualToString:gameButton7.titleLabel.text])
        return gameButton3.titleLabel.text;

    if (gameButton1.titleLabel.text != nil && gameButton2.titleLabel.text != nil &&
gameButton3.titleLabel.text != nil && gameButton4.titleLabel.text != nil &&
gameButton5.titleLabel.text != nil && gameButton6.titleLabel.text != nil &&
gameButton7.titleLabel.text != nil && gameButton8.titleLabel.text != nil &&
gameButton9.titleLabel.text != nil) {
        return @"Tie";
    }

    return nil;
}
```

If you return your attention to the makeMove method from the previous section, you will see that if we determine the player has won, we make a new call. We need to call participantQuitInTurnWithOutcome to end the match. We pass in GKTurnBasedMatchOutcomeWon for the argument, but if we have a scenario in which the player has lost, we can also pass in GKTurnBasedMatchOutcomeLost.

```
[self.match participantQuitInTurnWithOutcome:GKTurnBasedMatchOutcomeWon
nextParticipant:nextPlayer matchData:data completionHandler:^(NSError *error)  {
    if (error) {
        NSLog(@"An error occurred ending match: %@", [error localizedDescription]);
    }
}];
```

Quitting and Forfeiting

A player can quit a match at any time by swiping across it from the matchmaker view controller. However, you might want to add a path for your users to forfeit or quit a match from inside of your game itself. To allow a player to forfeit a match, use the following code snippet.

```
- (IBAction)forfeit:(id)sender
{
    [self.match participantQuitOutOfTurnWithOutcome:GKTurnBasedMatchOutcomeQuit
withCompletionHandler:^(NSError *error) {
        if (error) {
            NSLog(@"An error occurred ending match: %@", [error localizedDescription]);
        }
    }];
}
```

Programmatic Matches

If you want to bypass the GKTurnBasedMatchmakerViewController and implement your own GUI, there is an option to do so. Using the following method will create a new match without having the user go through the matchmaker.

```
- (void)findMatch
{
    GKMatchRequest *match = [[GKMatchRequest alloc] init];
    [match setMaxPlayers:2];
    [match setMinPlayers:2];

    [GKTurnBasedMatch findMatchForRequest:match withCompletionHandler:^(GKTurnBasedMatch
*match, NSError *error) {
        if (error == nil) {
            //start new game with returned match
        } else {
            NSLog(@"An error occurred when finding a match: %@", [error
localizedDescription]);
        }
    }];
}
```

In addition to creating a game, you need to be able to load a list of existing games for your local user. You can do so with the following method.

```
- (void)loadMatches
{
    [GKTurnBasedMatch loadMatchesWithCompletionHandler:^(NSArray *matches, NSError
*error) {
        if (error == nil) {
            NSLog(@"Existing Matches: %@", matches);
        } else {
            NSLog(@"An error occurred while loading matches: %@", [error
localizedDescription]);
        }
    }];
}
```

> **NOTE:** Because both of these methods use background tasks in order to handle the request, code that you implement within the block needs to be thread safe.

GKTurnBasedEventHandler

The GKTurnedBasedEventHandler is a delegate protocol that is responsible for handling important messages related to turn-based games. To set a delegate for events, use the following code.

```
[[GKTurnBasedEventHandler sharedTurnBasedEventHandler] setDelegate: self];
```

The protocol has three optional methods.

- handleInviteFromGameCenter: When your delegate receives this method, it should populate a new GKMatchRequest with the playersToInvite that are passed in through the method. You then need to begin a new match or present the matchmaker GUI. This method is called when the user accepts a match invite from a friend.

- handleTurnEventForMatch: Your delegate receives this message when the user has accepted a push notification for an in-progress match. You need to end whatever task you are performing and display the game for the match that is passed in with this method.

- handleMatchEnded: When your delegate receives this message, it should display the match's results and game-over views to the player and allow the player the option of removing the match data from Game Center.

Summary

In this chapter, we learned about the new turn-based gaming additions to Game Center in iOS 5. We worked with our existing GameCenterManager class and wrote an entirely new sample game to work with the turn-based technology. You should now have a firm grasp on how to create a new turn-based game, as well as retain and send turn data between peers. With the skills learned in this chapter, you should now be able to easily get the networking component of turned-based gaming up and running in a few hours.

In the next chapter, will be looking at another exciting topic: voice chat. Apple has gone through tremendous lengths to make voice over IP easy to use in iOS apps, and we will explore how to quickly get VOIP up and running in your Game Center– or Game Kit–enabled apps.

Chapter 10

Voice Chat

Voice chat, more than any other service provided as part of Game Kit, is a true testament to Apple engineering. Apple has turned one of the most complicated features on other platforms into one of the easiest to implement on iOS. When working with Voice over Internet Protocol (VOIP) on other platforms, it is often the most complex and daunting task of an entire project. In this chapter, we will explore how to add voice chat services to UFOs or any iOS app. The shortness of this chapter is evidence of how much work Apple has put into this technology to bring it within the grasp of even the greenest of developers.

Unlike preceding chapters, we will be dealing with Game Kit Voice Chat and Game Center Voice Chat separately, as opposed to writing a shared class as done previously. While there are many similarities between the two services, they differ enough that it makes sense to handle each approach separately. In addition, we will apply the topics covered in this chapter as we implement voice chat into UFOs.

Voice Chat for Game Center

We begin by looking at voice chat for Game Center. Using a GKMatch to create a voice chat session has many advantages, such as ease of use, quickness to implement, and reduced required overhead compared to using Game Kit or having to implement your own system. A GKMatch voice chat can have multiple channels, each with an associated list of recipients. For example, you could have one channel for teammates in a first-person shooter game, and another channel for all players. This would allow you to talk about tactics for winning the match without giving away information to the other team.

> **NOTE:** Voice chat using a GKMatch is only available to participants who are connected to the Internet via Wi-Fi; voice chat does not support cellular networks.

Creating an Audio Session

Before you can begin to work with voice chat, you first need to create a new audio session. It is important to do this before you begin any chat services. If you create the audio session after you create the chat session, you will not be able to send or receive voice data. In the following example, we create a new audio session that allows our app to play and record audio, and then set it to active.

> **TIP:** Your app might already use an audio session for playing sound effects; if you have already created an audio session, you are not required to make a new one. If you are reusing an existing audio session, make sure that you set it to allow both play and record functionality.

```
NSError *error = nil;
AVAudioSession *audioSession = [AVAudioSession sharedInstance];
[audioSession setCategory:AVAudioSessionCategoryPlayAndRecord error:&error];
[audioSession setActive: YES error: &error];
if (error)
{
    NSLog(@"An error occurred while starting audio session: %@", [error↵
localizedDescription]);
}
```

Creating New Voice Channels

You can have as many voice chat channels as you want in your app, and each peer can register to be part of as many channels as they want. Channels are created and organized by a name string. This is how we will determine what channels we want the user to join. When two or more peers join a channel with the same name, they are connected to the same chat.

The code snippet that follows shows an example of how to create three different channels. Take note that the channels are created with the GKMatch object that is returned to us when we begin a new Game Center–based networking game.

```
GKVoiceChat *allChannel = [[match voiceChatWithName:@"allPlayers"] retain];
GKVoiceChat *teamChannel = [[match voiceChatWithName:@"blueTeam"] retain];
GKVoiceChat *squadChannel = [[match voiceChatWithName:@"BlueTeamSquad2"] retain];
```

In this example, we have a channel for communicating with all players, a channel for communicating with our entire team, and a third channel that is used to talk with our squad. Just because channels have been created doesn't mean that they are automatically turned on. In the next section, we will look at how to start and stop communication on a specific channel.

Starting and Stopping Voice Chat

In the previous section, we created three new voice channels for use with Game Center–type voice chat. When you want to transmit and receive voice on those channels, you need to first tell the API that you want to begin using that channel. After you are connected to a channel, you are able to send and receive data from that channel. If you want to connect to a channel and do not want to transmit any voice audio, see the following section on muting the microphone.

To begin using a voice channel, you need to call the start method on the GKVoiceChat object that was created in the previous section.

```
[allChannel start];
[teamChannel start];
```

When you want to leave a channel, you simply call the stop method. This is a better approach than simply muting all participants in the channel because the app will not be required to receive additional network data. A stopped channel can be restarted at any time.

```
[allChannel stop];
[teamChannel stop];
```

> **TIP:** It is highly recommended that you provide both a visual and audio indicator when you are transmitting voice data, such as a red light and a click sound. This reduces the chance that a user will accidentally transmit voice data when they don't intend to. Always remember that a user's microphone and transmitted voice should be treated as sensitive data.

Chat Volume and Muting

The voice chat volume is set on a per-channel basis. Each channel has an associated property that can be used to lower the overall volume of that chat. You cannot raise the volume past what the user has selected as the device's current volume. To modify a channel's volume, add the following line of code.

```
allChannel.volume = 0.5; //half of max volume
```

In addition, you can mute individual players in a channel by referencing their playerID. Players can be muted and unmuted using the following two lines of code.

```
[teamChannel setMute:YES forPlayer: playerID];
[teamChannel setMute:NO forPlayer:playerID];
```

There might also be circumstances in which you do not want to transmit the user's voice at all times. By default, a user starts a chat in the muted state. You will need to unmute a user before he can begin to transmit voice data.

```
squadChannel.active = YES;
```

> **NOTE:** A user can only transmit voice on one channel at a time; if you unmute a channel, the API will automatically mute all other channels.

This is all that is required in order to completely enable voice chat in your Game Center–based networking app. Everything else, including sending and receiving the data, is handled for you by the APIs.

Monitoring Player State

I mentioned earlier in this chapter that it is important to let the user know that they are currently transmitting data. Letting the player see who is speaking is also an important step. By monitoring player state changes, you can determine which users are currently transmitting voice and highlight them in a player list or perform some other kind of indication of which player is speaking. The following block is easy to set up when you begin your chat, and saves you from performing polling or delegate callbacks.

```
allChannel.playerStateUpdateHandler = ^(NSString *playerID, GKVoiceChatPlayerState↩
  state)
{
       switch (state)
               {
                        case GKVoiceChatPlayerSpeaking:
                               [self showSpeakingPlayer: playerID];
                         break;
                        case GKVoiceChatPlayerSilent:
                               [self stopShowingSpeakingPlayer: playerID];
                               break;
               }
     };
```

> **NOTE:** Player state updates are handled per channel. You will need to configure one for each channel that you wish to watch for changes on.

Voice Chat for Game Kit

When working with Game Kit Voice Chat, we will focus on the GKVoiceChatService object. The fundamentals of Game Kit Voice Chat are very similar to Game Center Voice Chat. A good starting point for implementing this system is after you are returned a GKSession object, when you connect to another player using the Peer Picker system. It is important to note that GKVoiceChatService is designed to send data to only one peer at a time. Although this isn't a limitation as of yet, as Game Kit only supports two peers, it is important to keep in mind should the API ever be expanded.

> **NOTE:** Don't forget to check [GKVoiceChatService isVolPAllowed] to make sure you are able to support voice chat before you continue. Some devices, such as the first generation iPod touch, are unable to support voice chat.

Creating an Audio Session

As with Game Center, we can begin to work with Game Kit Voice Chat by first creating a new AVAudioSession. It is important to make sure that you create the session prior to beginning any chat service calls.

```
NSError *error = nil;
AVAudioSession *audioSession = [AVAudioSession sharedInstance];
 [audioSession setCategory:AVAudioSessionCategoryPlayAndRecord error:&error];
 [audioSession setActive: YES error: &error];
 if (error)
 {
     NSLog(@"An error occurred while starting audio session: %@", [error
localizedDescription]);
 }
```

Required Overhead

Unlike the Game Center approach, Game Kit requires a bit more overhead to get things up and running. The first thing you need to do is implement a few required methods. The following first method posted returns the peerID for the player that you wish to communicate with. This value is easily retrieved from your current GKSession object.

```
- (NSString *)participantID
{
    return session.peerID;
}
```

You also need to implement a method to send the actual voice data to the connected peer, and another that will handle receiving the data; both of these methods are available in the following code snippets. Together, these two methods will handle the sending and receiving of voice data for your app.

```
-(void)voiceChatService:(GKVoiceChatService *)voiceChatService sendData:
(NSData *)data     toParticipantID:(NSString *)participantID
 {
             [session sendData: data toPeers:[NSArray arrayWithObject: participantID]
        withDataMode: GKSendDataReliable error: nil];
 }

 - (void) receiveData:(NSData *)data fromPeer:(NSString *)peer inSession:
 (GKSession *)session context:(void *)context;
 {
     [[GKVoiceChatService defaultVoiceChatService] receivedData:data
     fromParticipantID:peer];
 }
```

Getting Things Running

In addition to the three new methods that we discussed in the previous section, you will need to complete some additional steps to get everything up and running. First, you need to initialize a new instance of GKVoiceChatClient, which should be a custom subclass of GKVoiceChatClient that you create. For more information on this step, see the next section, "Putting It Together."

```
    GKVoiceChatClient *voiceChatClient = [[GKVoiceChatClient alloc] initWithSession:↵
session];
    [GKVoiceChatService defaultVoiceChatService].client = voiceChatClient;
```

After you have created a new instance of GKVoiceChatClient, you need to connect your peer to it. The following code demonstrates how to accomplish this.

```
[[GKVoiceChatService defaultVoiceChatService] startVoiceChatWithParticipantID:↵
[self    participantID] error: &error];
```

To end the voice chat session, you need to call a similar method, as follows.

```
[[GKVoiceChatService defaultVoiceChatService] stopVoiceChatWithParticipantID:↵
[self    participantID]];
```

After you have established a connection to the other peer, you will begin to receive voice chat data. If you want to send data, all that you need to do is unmute the microphone using the following code snippet.

```
    [GKVoiceChatService defaultVoiceChatService].microphoneMuted = NO;
```

These are all the steps that are required to get Game Kit Voice Chat up and running. Although it is slightly more work than Game Center Voice Chat, it is still significantly easier than implementing your own VOIP system.

Putting It Together

In this chapter, we modify our existing code base from Chapter 8. Begin there by creating a new audio session for your voice chat service. Add the following block of code to the UFOGameViewController.m viewDidLoad: method. In addition, you need to add the AVFoundation.framework to your project. Modify the relevant section of the viewDidLoad method to match the following.

```
if (self.gameIsMultiplayer == NO)
{
    for (int x = 0; x < 5; x++)
    {
        [self spawnCow];
    }

    [self updateCowPaths];
}

else
{
```

```
    [self generateAndSendHostNumber];
    NSError *error = nil;
    AVAudioSession *audioSession = [AVAudioSession sharedInstance];
    [audioSession setCategory:AVAudioSessionCategoryPlayAndRecord error:&error];
    [audioSession setActive: YES error: &error];
    if (error)
    {
        NSLog(@"An error occurred while starting audio session: %@", [error↵
localizedDescription]);
    }

    [self setupVoiceChat];
}
```

> **CAUTION:** Make sure the device you are building against has both a speaker and a microphone
> available for use.

You also need to add a new method called setupVoiceChat. This method will handle the
basic configuration for both Game Center and Game Kit.

```
-(void)setupVoiceChat
{
    //GameKit
    if (self.peerIDString)
    {
        NSError *error = nil;
        UFOVoiceChatClient *voiceChatClient = [[UFOVoiceChatClient alloc] init];
        voiceChatClient.session = self.gcManager.matchOrSession;
        [GKVoiceChatService defaultVoiceChatService].client = voiceChatClient;
        [[GKVoiceChatService defaultVoiceChatService]↵
startVoiceChatWithParticipantID:self.peerIDString error:&error];

        [GKVoiceChatService defaultVoiceChatService].microphoneMuted = YES;
        if (error)
        {
            NSLog(@"An error occurred when setting up voice chat: %@",↵
[error localizedDescription]);

        }
    }

    //Game Center
    else
    {
        mainChannel = [[self.peerMatch voiceChatWithName:@"main"] retain];
        [mainChannel start];
        mainChannel.volume = 1.0;
        mainChannel.active = NO;
    }
}
```

You might have noticed that we have a new class type called UFOVoiceChatClient in the
preceding code snippet. This is the class that we will use to handle the incoming and

outgoing data for voice, as well as other methods used to watch status and errors. The implementation for that class is posted next.

```objc
@implementation UFOVoiceChatClient
@synthesize session;
-(NSString *)participantID
{
    return self.session.peerID;
}

- (void)voiceChatService:(GKVoiceChatService *)voiceChatService sendData:↵
(NSData *)data toParticipantID:(NSString *)participantID
{
    [self.session sendData:data toPeers:[NSArray arrayWithObject: participantID]
withDataMode:GKSendDataReliable error:nil];
}

- (void)receivedData:(NSData *)arbitraryData fromParticipantID:(NSString *)participantID
{
    [[GKVoiceChatService defaultVoiceChatService] receivedData:arbitraryData↵
 fromParticipantID:participantID];
}

- (void)voiceChatService:(GKVoiceChatService *)voiceChatService↵
 didReceiveInvitationFromParticipantID:(NSString *)participantID↵
 callID:(NSInteger)callID
{
    NSLog(@"Did Recieve Invitation");
}

- (void)voiceChatService:(GKVoiceChatService *)voiceChatService↵
 didNotStartWithParticipantID:(NSString *)participantID error:↵
(NSError *)error
{
    NSLog(@"Did Not Start Invitation");
}

- (void)voiceChatService:(GKVoiceChatService *)voiceChatService↵
 didStartWithParticipantID:(NSString *)participantID
{
    NSLog(@"Did Start Invitation");
}

@end
```

NOTE: Make sure your voiceChatClient conforms to the GKVoiceChatClient protocol.

You also need to make some slight modifications to the GameCenterManager to handle incoming voice data. Modify the existing receiveData:fromPeer:inSession:Context: method to match the following.

```objc
- (void)receiveData:(NSData *)data fromPeer:(NSString *)peer inSession: (GKSession↵
 *)session context:(void *)context;
{
```

```
    NSString *dataString = [[NSString alloc] initWithData:data↵
encoding:NSUTF8StringEncoding];
    if (dataString == nil)
    {
        [[GKVoiceChatService defaultVoiceChatService] receivedData:data↵
fromParticipantID:peer];
        [dataString release];
        return;
    }

    NSDictionary *dataDictionary = [NSDictionary dictionaryWithObjects:[NSArray↵
arrayWithObjects:dataString, peer, session,  nil] forKeys:[NSArray arrayWithObjects:↵
@"data", @"peer", @"session",  nil]];

    [dataString release];
    [self callDelegateOnMainThread: @selector(receivedData:) withArg: dataDictionary↵
error: nil];
}
```

Notice that we added another block of code that handles passing the data to our defaultVoiceChatService client. We determine whether data is voice data if we cannot decode a string from the NSData. Your app may be more complex and require a prefix or other type of designator to determine whether the data is voice, but this is very suitable for a simple game like UFOs.

The last thing we need to do is hook up an action to turn our microphone on and off. I have decided to go with a simple toggle button for UFOs, but you may feel the need to implement a different approach. Add a new button, as shown in Figure 10–1, and hook up the new action posted next.

Figure 10–1. *Adding a microphone button to our UFO game demo*

```
-(IBAction)startVoice:(id)sender;
{
        micOn = !micOn;
        if (micOn)
        {
                        [micButton setTitle:@"Mic On" forState:UIControlStateNormal];
                        //GameKit
```

```
                          if (self.peerIDString)
                          {
                          [GKVoiceChatService defaultVoiceChatService].microphoneMuted =↵
    NO;
                          }

                          //Game Center
                          else
                          {
                                  mainChannel.active = YES;
                          }
                  }

          else
          {
                  [micButton setTitle:@"Mic Off" forState:UIControlStateNormal];
                  //GameKit
                  if (self.peerIDString)
                  {
                  [GKVoiceChatService defaultVoiceChatService].microphoneMuted =↵
    YES;
                  }

                  //Game Center
                  else
                  {
                          mainChannel.active = NO;
                  }
          }
    }
```

This method determines the current state of the microphone (on/off) and toggles it to the new state. When that happens, we update the button title and turn the microphone on or off for the type of network that we are using.

These are all the required steps to add voice chat into our UFO example project. If you run the game on two devices, you will be able to communicate with voice back and forth.

Summary

In this chapter, we learned how to incorporate a traditionally very complex technology into our iOS app with very little work. We explored the differences with using voice chat on both Game Kit and Game Center, as well as implemented examples of both systems into our UFO demo game. You now have the skills required to add full-featured VOIP technology to any iPhone or iPad app. If you have been following the book along from the beginning, you now have all the skills needed to implement all aspects of Game Kit and Game Center into your apps.

In the next chapter, we will take a look at another important technology when writing games or apps for iOS—StoreKit. Using StoreKit technology, we will learn how to sell additional features and add-ons to your product.

Chapter 11

In-App Purchase with StoreKit

Throughout this book, we have been working with both Game Center and Game Kit to add rich social networking into your apps. However, there is another important feature slowly becoming more popular in modern software: in-app purchases. Allowing your users to purchase upgrades or additional content for your app, from directly within your app, opens up a potentially significant new revenue stream. Over the past few years, a new business model has emerged called Freemium. Freemium is a new type of game or product that is offered to your users for free, but is monetized through selling add-ons.

We will be taking a look at We Rule by ngmoco:) as an example. The game is initially offered for free for both iPhone and iPad players. Each user is in control of a virtual kingdom, in which they are responsible for constructing buildings and growing crops. The user generates "mojo" over time and can use that in-app currency to create new structures and farms. However, some users want to construct faster than is normally allowed due the restrictive nature of mojo, which slowly accumulates. These power-users can visit the in-app store to purchase more mojo in bulk. Shown in Figure 11–1 is We Rule's built-in store. As you can see, it offers a number of purchases ranging from very affordable to shockingly expensive. It is important to cater to both types of users when working with sellable add-ons. Some of your users will be interested in spending one or two dollars occasionally, while some will be power-users who want to spend one hundred dollars, or more, at a time.

Figure 11–1. *The in-app purchase store, as seen in We Rule by ngmoco:)*

Freemium has become such a strong business model that ngmoco:) has stopped working on games that do not fit into the Freemium model, going so far as to even cancel Rolando 3 in mid-development because it couldn't be adapted to the model. The model appears to be paying off well for ngmoco:). As shown in Figure 11–2, the current highest selling item in the We Rule store is a $9.99 item. This one in-app purchase is retailing for more than most stand-alone iOS games, and the reason it was able to get that customer is that it hooked them with a free game first.

Not all games or apps supported by in-app purchase need to be free. In fact, until recently, you were not allowed to implement in-app purchase in free apps. You can easily add additional features or unlocks in a paid game, such as the Mighty Eagle in Angry Birds. In-app purchase is also not only just for games. Almost any software can benefit from it, whether you are unlocking pro-level features or charging users a subscription for push notification support. As we dive into this chapter, we will explore how to add a full-featured in-app store to your iOS software.

Top In-App Purch...

1	Bottle of 75 Mojo	$9.99
2	Flask of 30 Mojo	$4.99
3	Carafe of 165 ...	$19.99
4	Decorative Item	$0.99
5	Decorative Item	$0.99
6	Case of 300 Mojo	$29.99
7	Decorative Item	$0.99
8	Vintage 800 Mojo	$49.99
9	Decorative Item	$1.99
10	Decorative Item	$0.99

Figure 11–2. *Current listing of the best-selling in-app purchases for We Rule by ngmoco:)*

Setting Up Your App in iTunes Connect

As with Game Center, we need to begin working with in-app purchases in iTunes Connect.

1. Log in to iTunes Connect (`http://itunesconnect.apple.com`), as discussed in Chapter 2. You will need an existing project to work on. If you don't have a project created in iTunes Connect yet, go ahead and create one.

2. Select the project you want to add in-app purchase support to. Then, click the button called Manage In-App Purchases, as shown in Figure 11–3.

> **IMPORTANT:** You have 90 days from creating an app to upload a binary for review. Make sure to save the in-app purchase configuration until you are within 90 days of finishing your project.

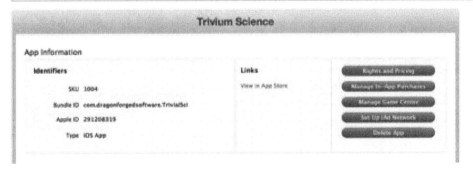

Figure 11–3. *App listing in iTunes Connect showing Manage In-App Purchases button*

3. Selecting the Manage In-App Purchases button will bring you to a screen for setting up a new product, as shown in Figure 11–4. Once there, click the Create New button in the upper left corner of the window.

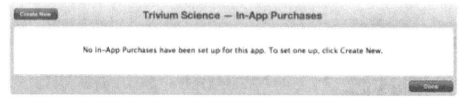

Figure 11–4. *Setting up your first in-app purchase in iTunes Connect*

There are several types of in-app purchase products that you can configure. They are detailed here for your convenience.

 ▪ Consumable: A consumable in-app purchase must be purchased every time the user downloads it. These include in-game currency, as we saw in the We Rule example in the previous section. Figure 11–5 shows the consumable purchase setup screen.

Figure 11–5. *Setup screen for both consumable and non-consumable purchases in iTunes Connect*

 ▪ Non-Consumables: A non-consumable purchase needs to be purchased only once by each user, and is often used for unlockable features. Examples of non-consumable purchases include additional levels, reusable power-ups, or additional content.

- Auto-Renewable Subscriptions: An auto-renewable subscription allows the user to purchase in-app content for a set duration of time. At the end of that time frame, the subscription will automatically renew and charge the customer unless they opt out. Magazines and newspapers follow this model, delivering a new issue every week or month until the user opts out. Figure 11–6 shows the auto-renewable purchase setup screen.

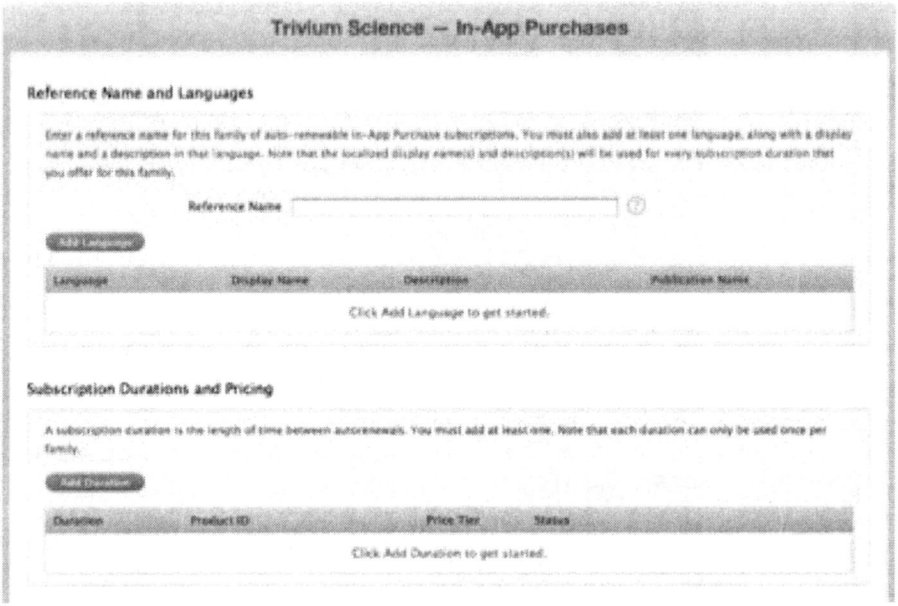

Figure 11–6. *Setup screen for auto-renewable purchases in iTunes Connect*

- Non-Renewing Subscriptions: For the most part, renewable subscriptions have done away the need for this model. A non-renewing subscription functions the same as an auto-renewable subscription, except that a user is required to renew it every time it is set to expire.

NOTE: Auto-renewable subscriptions will be sent to all devices associated with the user's Apple ID.

We will begin by adding a non-consumable purchase. We will be using this item in our sample UFO game.

The first item we want to add is a paid upgrade to your current ship; name the item com.dragonforged.ufo.newShip1. I used the same title for both the product ID and the reference name. The reference name is for reference only when searching in iTunes Connect, whereas the product ID is what will be used in your code base to identify this item.

After you have created a new item, you need to add at least one localized description and title, as shown in Figure 11–7. The last thing that you need to do is select a pricing tier for this item. You might have also noticed that there is a section for uploading a screenshot; we discuss this in the later section "Submitting a Purchase GUI Screenshot."

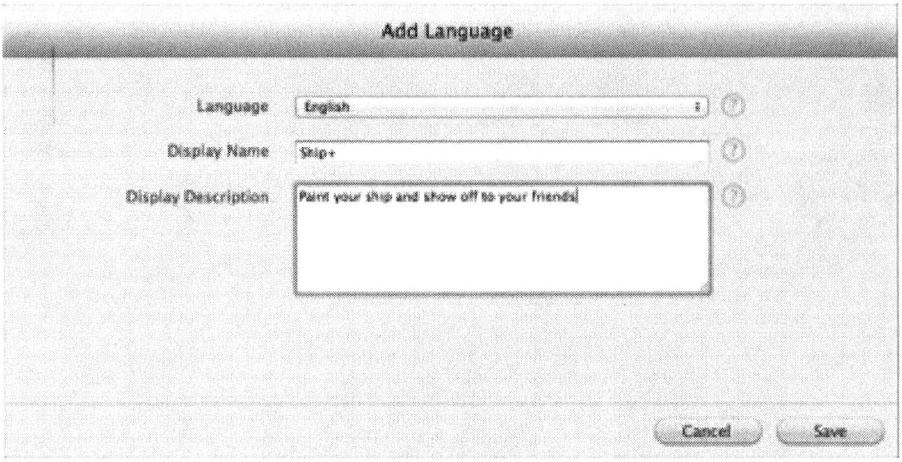

Figure 11–7. *Adding a localized description to a product in iTunes Connect*

Adding a consumable product follows the same procedure as adding a non-consumable product. If you want to add a subscription-based product, there are a few new fields that you need to be aware of, as shown in Figure 11–8. When configuring a subscription, you need to define a duration. iTunes Connect allows you to set any of the following: one week, one month, two months, three months, six months, or one year. You also have the ability to offer a free subscription if the user agrees to a marketing campaign, such as providing you with their e-mail address.

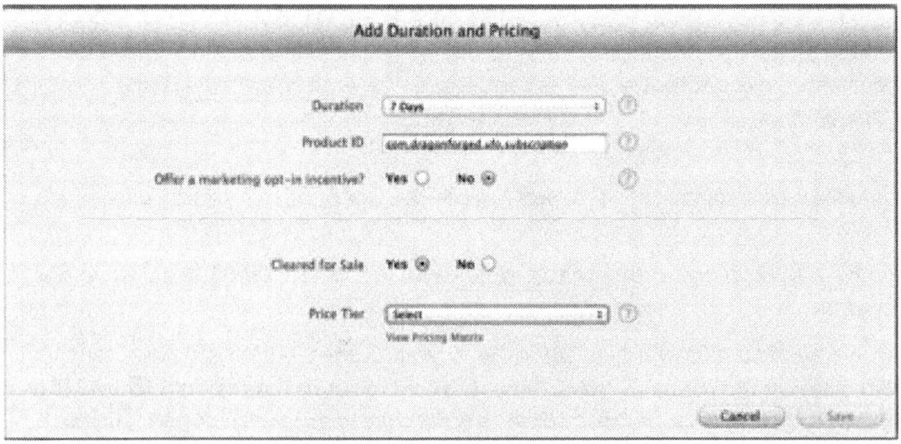

Figure 11–8. *Configuring subscription duration in iTunes Connect*

You should now have at least one product configured for in-app purchase. Your screen in iTunes Connect should look similar to the one shown in Figure 11–9. This concludes the initial configuration that we need to do in iTunes Connect to get in-app purchases working. In the next section, we begin to work with the code required to complete a purchase on a device.

> **NOTE:** Don't worry about the "Waiting for Screenshot" error yet; this will be handled later in the process. You will still be able to test your purchases while waiting to upload a screenshot.

Figure 11–9. *Products set up and ready for use in our app*

Adding Products to Your App

Unlike with Game Center, Apple does not offer a predesigned GUI for in-app purchases. You, as the developer, are required to design a storefront for your user. In this section, we learn how to get products that you add in iTunes Connect to show up for sale in your app.

> **NOTE:** It can take several hours for new purchases and changes to be reflected. If you double-check everything and are still not seeing products, wait a few hours and try again.

App IDs and In-App Purchase

When working with in-app purchases, Apple requires that your App ID does not include a wildcard, such as 76P4G6KX56.*. You are required to have a unique App ID, such as 76P4G6KX56.com.dragonforged.ufo. If you do not have a unique App ID, you need to create one. Use the following steps to create a new unique App ID.

1. Navigate to http://developer.apple.com/iPhone in your web browser and select the iPhone Developer Program Portal from the list on the right.

2. Select App ID from the column on the left, and select the New App ID button in the upper right.

3. Fill in the required information about your app.

4. Click Submit.

5. Click Configure next to the listing, and make sure In-App Purchase is turned on (it should be on by default).

Setting Up

We begin by requesting a list of products from our app. First, add the StoreKit framework to your project. We will be modifying our existing UFO project from the previous chapter; you can follow along in your own project if that is more convenient.

> **IMPORTANT:** In-App Purchase does not work on the simulator; all testing needs to be done on a device.

Create a new class called UFOStoreViewController. We will use this class to display a store to the user. Set up the header to match the following.

```
#import <UIKit/UIKit.h>
#import <StoreKit/StoreKit.h>

@interface UFOStoreViewController : UIViewController <SKProductsRequestDelegate>
{
    SKProductsRequest *productsRequest;
}

@end
```

As you can see, we imported the StoreKit headers. Set up the SKProductsRequestDelegate, and create a new object to hold on to the product request. We need to create a way for the user to access the store, so go ahead and add a button to the main screen and relevant code to present the new view controller.

Retrieving the Product List

Modify the viewDidLoad and viewDidUnload methods of our new store view controller to begin a new store request using the product identifiers that we set up in iTunes Connect. You might need to modify your product identifiers to match the ones that you set up in the previous section.

```
- (void)viewDidLoad
{
    [super viewDidLoad];
    NSSet *productIdentifiers = [NSSet setWithObjects:↵
@"com.dragonforged.ufo.newShip1", @"com.dragonforged.ufo.subscription", nil];
    productsRequest = [[SKProductsRequest alloc]↵
 initWithProductIdentifiers:productIdentifiers];
    productsRequest.delegate = self;
    [productsRequest start];
}

- (void)viewDidUnload
{
    productsRequest.delegate = nil;
}
```

The product request is released in the delegate callback, shown next. Right now, this method just prints your product information to the console and logs any invalid products.

```
- (void)productsRequest:(SKProductsRequest *)request↵
 didReceiveResponse:(SKProductsResponse *)response
{
    NSArray *productArray = [response products];
    for (SKProduct *product in productArray) {
    NSLog(@"Product title: %@" , product.localizedTitle);
    NSLog(@"Product description: %@" , product.localizedDescription);
    NSLog(@"Product price: %@" , product.price);
    NSLog(@"Product id: %@\n\n" , product.productIdentifier);
    }

    for (NSString *invalidProduct in response.invalidProductIdentifiers)
    {
    NSLog(@"Invalid: %@" , invalidProduct);
    }

    [request release];
}
```

> **NOTE:** Although you can retrieve a list of invalid product identifiers using the code in this section, there are no associated errors to determine why a product is being flagged as invalid. Under most occurrences, the product ID is mistyped or not enough time has passed for the product to be distributed to the servers.

If you were to run the game now and navigate to the store, you should get output similar to the following.

```
2011-08-19 17:31:23.970 UFOs[3580:707] Product title: Ship+
2011-08-19 17:31:23.973 UFOs[3580:707] Product description: Paint your ship and show
off to your friends
2011-08-19 17:31:23.975 UFOs[3580:707] Product price: 8.99
2011-08-19 17:31:23.977 UFOs[3580:707] Product id: com.dragonforged.ufo.newShip1
2011-08-19 17:31:23.979 UFOs[3580:707] Product title: Subscription
2011-08-19 17:31:23.981 UFOs[3580:707] Product description: A subscription service
2011-08-19 17:31:23.983 UFOs[3580:707] Product price: 1.99
2011-08-19 17:31:23.987 UFOs[3580:707] Product id: com.dragonforged.ufo.subscription
```

> **NOTE:** It can take several seconds to get a response from the product request. Best practices dictate that you should present your user with some sort of loading indicator.

These are all the steps required to retrieve your products from Apple's servers. In the next section we present this data to the user using a standard table view.

Presenting Your Products to the User

We begin by adding a table view to our store view controller. Don't forget to hook up the data source and delegates, as required. We also add a new property to our class to hold on to the products. Create a new class array named productArray and set the product results to it in the productsRequest method.

Add the two required table view delegate and data source methods to your class, as shown in the following code snippets.

```
- (NSInteger)tableView:(UITableView *)tableView numberOfRowsInSection:(NSInteger)section
{
    return [productArray count];
}

- (UITableViewCell *)tableView:(UITableView *)tableView⤸
 cellForRowAtIndexPath:(NSIndexPath *)indexPath
{

    static NSString *CellIdentifier = @"Cell";
    UITableViewCell *cell = [tableView⤸
dequeueReusableCellWithIdentifier:CellIdentifier];
    if (cell == nil) {
        cell = [[[UITableViewCell alloc] initWithStyle:⤸
UITableViewCellStyleSubtitle reuseIdentifier:CellIdentifier] autorelease];
        cell.selectionStyle = UITableViewCellSelectionStyleNone;
    }

    SKProduct *product = [self.productArray objectAtIndex: [indexPath row]];
    cell.textLabel.text = [NSString stringWithFormat:@"%@ - $%@",⤸
product.localizedTitle, product.price];
    cell.detailTextLabel.text = product.localizedDescription;
    return cell;

}
```

The first method simply returns the number of products that we retrieved from Apple's servers for the number of rows in the table. When we display them as a cel,l we use the built-in UITableViewCellStyleSubtitle. We set the main label to the product title and price, and use the detail label to display the description. All that is left is to add a reload table method to the end of the productsRequest method. Upon running the game again, your output should look similar to that shown in Figure 11–10.

> **NOTE:** Although the API returns a localized title and description, it doesn't localize the price. You
> need to take this extra step yourself in international apps.

Figure 11–10. *Displaying a list of products in a standard table view*

Purchasing a Product

In the previous section, we learned how to add products to your app. Without the ability to purchase these products, our implementation is only partially complete. In this section, we look at how to handle purchasing products directly through your app.

Purchasing Code

The first thing that we need to do is make our store's view controller class conform to the SKPaymentTransactionObserver protocol. After that is done, we modify our existing viewDidLoad method. We add ourselves as a new transaction observer. Additionally, we perform a test to make sure that we can make payments on this device, and if not, display a UIAlert to inform the user.

```
- (void)viewDidLoad
{
    [super viewDidLoad];
    [[SKPaymentQueue defaultQueue] addTransactionObserver:self];
    if ([SKPaymentQueue canMakePayments]) {
        NSSet *productIdentifiers = [NSSet setWithObjects:↵
@"com.dragonforged.ufo.newShip1", @"com.dragonforged.ufo.subscription", nil];
        productsRequest = [[SKProductsRequest alloc]↵
 initWithProductIdentifiers:productIdentifiers];
        productsRequest.delegate = self;
        [productsRequest start];
    }
    else {
        UIAlertView *alert = [[UIAlertView alloc] initWithTitle:nil message:↵
@"Unable to make purchases with this device." delegate:nil cancelButtonTitle:@"Dimiss"↵
 otherButtonTitles: nil];
        [alert show];
        [alert release];
    }
}
```

Next, we need to add a didSelectRowAtIndexPath method to register selection events in our table view.

```
- (void)tableView:(UITableView *)tableView didSelectRowAtIndexPath:↵
(NSIndexPath *)indexPath
{
    SKProduct *product = [self.productArray objectAtIndex: [indexPath row]];
    SKPayment *payment = [SKPayment paymentWithProductIdentifier:↵
product.productIdentifier];
    [[SKPaymentQueue defaultQueue] addPayment:payment];
}
```

If you were to run the app now and select a table row, you would get a confirmation alert, as shown in Figure 11–11. However, we have not yet written any code to process this transaction, nor have you set up a test user, so this is as far as you can currently get.

Figure 11–11. *Confirming a purchase in the Sandbox*

Purchasing Multiple Items

Apple has made it easy to allow your users to purchase multiple items at a time. The following code snippet can be used to bulk purchase multiple quantities of an item at one time, such as a user purchasing five packs of 100 gold.

```
SKMutablePayment *payment = [SKMutablePayment paymentWithProductIdentifier:↵
  com.dragonforged.rpg.100gold];
payment.quantity = 5;
[[SKPaymentQueue defaultQueue] addPayment: payment];
```

Processing a Transaction

After your user has requested a purchase, there are several steps that you need to take in order to ensure that their purchase is completed successfully. First, we implement the required method from the SKPaymentTransactionObserver. As you can see in the following code example, we test the current transaction state, and then call some new methods, depending on whether the transaction succeeded, failed, or restored.

```objc
- (void)paymentQueue:(SKPaymentQueue *)queue updatedTransactions:(NSArray *)transactions
{
    for (SKPaymentTransaction *transaction in transactions) {
        if ([transaction transactionState] == SKPaymentTransactionStatePurchased) {
        [self transactionDidComplete:transaction];
        }

        else if ([transaction transactionState] == SKPaymentTransactionStateFailed) {
            [self transactionDidFail:transaction];
        }

        else if ([transaction transactionState] == SKPaymentTransactionStateRestored) {
            [self transactionDidRestore:transaction];
        }

        else {
            NSLog(@"Unhandled case: %@", transaction);
        }
    }
}
```

We need to implement some convenience methods to help streamline the process. If a transaction completed successfully or is restored, we need to record the transaction event, unlock the content that the user purchased, and perform some cleanup. If the transaction failed or was cancelled, we just need to perform the cleanup and probably notify the user that something went wrong.

```objc
- (void)transactionDidComplete:(SKPaymentTransaction *)transaction
{
    [self recordTransactionData:transaction];
    [self unlockContent:[[transaction payment] productIdentifier]];
    [self finishTransaction:transaction withSuccess:YES];
}

- (void)transactionDidRestore:(SKPaymentTransaction *)transaction
{
    [self recordTransactionData:transaction.originalTransaction];
    [self unlockContent:[[[transaction originalTransaction] payment]↵
productIdentifier]];
    [self finishTransaction:transaction withSuccess:YES];
}

- (void)transactionDidFail:(SKPaymentTransaction *)transaction
{
    if ([[transaction error] code] != SKErrorPaymentCancelled) {
        [self finishTransaction:transaction withSuccess:NO];
    }
    //SKErrorPaymentCancelled
    else
    {
        [[SKPaymentQueue defaultQueue] finishTransaction:transaction];
    }
}
```

Now let's take a look at each of the methods that we are calling in a more broken-down fashion, starting with the recordTransactionData method. The main purpose of this method is to keep a virtual paper trail for our purchases. We are using NSUserDefaults to hold on to an array of all completed transactions, which allows us to check transaction data at any point in the future.

```
- (void)recordTransactionData:(SKPaymentTransaction *)transaction
{
    NSArray *transactions = [[NSUserDefaults standardUserDefaults]↵
objectForKey:@"transactions"];
    NSMutableArray *transactionArray = [transactions mutableCopy];
    [transactionArray addObject:[transaction transactionReceipt]];
    [[NSUserDefaults standardUserDefaults] setObject:transactionArray↵
forKey:@"transactions"];
    [transactionArray release];
}
```

Next, we take a look at the unlockContent method. This is where things could differ in your actual app. In this example, we set a flag in the NSUserDefaults that we can check against to see whether the user has purchased a feature. Depending on how your app is structured, you might want to take a different approach, but no matter what approach you take, remember that you need to preserve the unlocked content through app restarts. See the section "Tying Everything Together in UFOs" for a sample on how to implement this approach.

```
- (void)unlockContent:(NSString *)productId
{
    if ([productId isEqualToString:@"com.dragonforged.ufo.newShip1"]) {
        [[NSUserDefaults standardUserDefaults] setBool:YES forKey:↵
@"shipPlusAvailable" ];
    }

    if ([productId isEqualToString:@"com.dragonforged.ufo.subscription"]) {
        [[NSUserDefaults standardUserDefaults] setBool:YES↵
forKey:@"subscriptionAvailable" ];
    }
}
```

The last step that we take for both successful and nonsuccessful purchases is to perform a bit of cleanup on our transaction. The most important step in the following method is to call the finishTransaction method. We also log the results of the transaction for debugging purposes. Until you have called finishTransaction, the transaction remains open and in the system.

```
- (void)finishTransaction:(SKPaymentTransaction *)transaction withSuccess:(BOOL)success
{
    [[SKPaymentQueue defaultQueue] finishTransaction:transaction];
    NSDictionary *transactionDictionary = [NSDictionary↵
dictionaryWithObjectsAndKeys:transaction, @"transaction" , nil];
    if (success) {
        NSLog(@"Transaction was successful: %@", transactionDictionary);
    }
    else {
        NSLog(@"Transaction was unsuccessful: %@", transactionDictionary);
    }
}
```

Restoring Previously Completed Transactions

Often, your users will need to restore purchases that they have previously made. This could happen if they have reinstalled your app or have begun using it on a different device. It is important to always add a path for your user to download all of their content again. Luckily, Apple has planned ahead for this scenario and has provided a simple method for restoring the user's purchases.

```
[[SKPaymentQueue defaultQueue] restoreCompletedTransactions];
```

This will repurchase all of your content as if the user had selected it from your store. You will receive appropriate callbacks to the paymentQueue:updatedTransactions method and can use your existing code to unlock content.

Test Accounts and Testing Purchases

If you were to try and purchase one of your items in the Sandbox now, you would receive an account error. You need to first create a new test account in order to be able to test purchases without being charged for them. To set up a new test user, you need to log in to iTunes Connect (http://iTunesConnect.apple.com). Select the Manage User section from the main screen of iTunes Connect; from here, select the option for a new Test User.

Test users do not need to use a real e-mail address, and you will want to select something quick to type and easy to remember, such as abc@def.com. Although you do need to enter a date of birth and other identifying information, there is no reason you cannot fabricate this data. Make sure to select the iTunes Store as the one to test your localization against. You can make a new account for each region that you will test with.

Signing in with a Test Account

You cannot simply sign in with your test account in the Settings App. Doing so would result in you being forced to agree to the standard user agreement and being prompted to enter a credit card number. In order to resolve this issue, you need to use the Settings App to log out of your existing iTunes account. After you are logged out of an account, you will be prompted to log in or create a new account during a purchase attempt. This is where you will enter your test account credentials.

> **NOTE:** If you are testing on your primary device, don't forget to revisit the Settings App to log out of your test account before making real purchases or downloading updates.

Submitting a Purchase GUI Screenshot

We talked briefly about this step in the earlier sections of this chapter. Apple requires that you submit a screenshot of your in-app purchase before it will clear it for sale. There is some confusion about what Apple is specifically looking for in this screenshot. Apple is looking, in the simplest terms, for a screen capture proving that your in-app purchase is working as intended. For unlockable content, this would be a screenshot of the item being used, such as the user playing a purchased level or using a purchased item. However, sometimes your product might not be visible while being used. In cases such as these, Apple has accepted a screenshot of the store showing that the item has been purchased, an example of which is shown in Figure 11–12.

> **NOTE:** You will not be required to submit a screenshot until you have finished writing and debugging your app and are ready to submit it for review.

Figure 11–12. *An example of an acceptable screenshot for in-app purchase when there isn't an item to capture*

Developer Approval

The last step that you need to take before your in-app purchase is ready to go is developer approval. Return to iTunes Connect in your web browser and navigate to the Manage In-App Purchase section of your app review page. There will be a new green button in the upper right-hand corner of the screen.

You will be prompted on how to submit your product. The following two options are available.

- Submit with Binary: This option will turn on in-app purchase with your next binary upload.

- Submit Now: This will allow you to submit a new product to an existing app.

> **NOTE:** If you see the option to Submit with a New Binary, it could be because the last version of your App was uploaded before in-app purchasing was available in 3.0.

Receipts

When you successfully complete a transaction, you are provided with a receipt as part of the competed transaction object. The following is a sample receipt from one of the purchases in UFOs demo project.

```
{
        "signature" =
"AnQ+nzB6oK5Lc6pI6zh8bptEO+GSGUJ+xT5DSef2p66H8gz/P/D13mBqf96ciJoLesI64fohhZTNb9NrCEkZMVy
eqkJed2t38509XpckLWeLJCDYUJqUS1t+fsoy7fwSUOv8TUBzF3Eua1h83GszxlPyylo3mRDssrG+QcgrHwFOAAA
DVzCCA1MwggI7oAMCAQICCGUUkU3ZWAS1MAOGCSqGSIb3DQEBBQUAMH8xCzAJBgNVBAYTAlVTMRMwEQYDVQQKDAp
BcHBsZSBJbmMuMSYwJAYDVQQLDB1BcHBsZSBDZXJ0aWZpY2F0aW9uIEF1dGhvcml0eTEzMDEGA1UEAwwqQXBwbGU
gaVR1bmVzIFNob3JlIENlcnRpZmljYXRpb24gQXVOaG9yaXR5MB4XDTA5MDYxNTIyMDU1NloXDTEOMDYxNDIyMDU
1NlowZDEjMCEGA1UEAwwaUHVyY2hhc2VSZWN1aXB0Q2VydGlmaWNhdGUxGzAZBgNVBAsMEkFwcGxlIGlUdW5lcyB
TdG9yZTETMBEGA1UECgwKQXBwbGUgSW5jLjELMAkGA1UEBhMCVVMwgZ8wDQYJKoZIhvcNAQEBBQADgYOAMIGJAoG
BAMrRjF2ct4IrSdiTChaIOg8pwv/cmHs8p/RwV/rt/91XKVhNl4XIBimKjQQNfgHsDs6yju++DrKJE7uKsphMddK
YfFE5rGXsAdBEjBwRIxexTevx3HLEFGAt1moKx5o9dhxtiIdDgJv2YaVs49BOuJvNdy6SMqNNLHsDLzDS9oZHAgm
BAAGjcjBwMAwGA1UdEwEB/wQCMAAwHwYDVR0jBBgwFoAUNh3o4p2COgEYtTJrDtdDC5FYQzowDgYDVR0PAQH/BAQ
DAgeAMBOGA1UdDgQWBBSpg4PyGUjFPhJXCBTMzaN+mV8k9TAQBgoqhkiG92NkBgUBBAIFADANBgkqhkiG9w0BAQU
FAAOCAQEAEaSbPjtmN4C/IB3QEpK32RxacCDXdVXAeVReS5FaZxc+t88pQP93BiAxvdW/3eTSMGY5FbeAYL3etqP
5gm8wrFojXOikyVRStQ+/AQOKEjtqBO7kLs9QUe8czR8UGfdM1EumV/UgvDd4NwNYxLQMg4WTQfgkQQVy8GXZwVH
gbE/UC6Y7053pGXBk51NPM3woxhd3gSRLvXj+loHsStcTEqe9pBDpmG5+sk4tw+GK3GMeEN5/+e1QT9np/Kl1nj+
aBw7COxsyObFnaAd1cSS6xdory/CUvM6gtKsmnOOdqTesbpObs8sn6WqsOC9dgcxRHuOMZ2tm8npLUm7argOSzQ=
=";
        "purchase-info" =
"ewoJIml0ZWotaWQiIDOgIjQ1ODk4NjQ4NCI7Cgkib3JpZ2luYWwtdHJhbnNhY3Rpb24taWQiIDOgIjEwMDAwMDA
wMDU4NDM1MzgiOwoJInB1cmNoYXNlLWRhdGUiIDOgIjIwMTEtMDgtMjEgMjI6Mzk6NTIgRXRjLORVCI7CgkicHJ
vZHVjdC1pZCIgPSAiY29tLmRyYWdvbmZvcmdlLn51Zm8ubmV3U2hpcDIiOwoJInRyYW5zYWN0aW9uLWlkIiA9ICI
xMDAwMDAwMDAzODQzNTM4IjsKCSJxdWFudGl0eSIgPSAiMSI7Cgkib3JpZ2luYWwtcHVyY2hhc2UtZGF0ZSIgPSA
iMjAxMSowOCoyMSAyMjozOTo1MiBFdGMvR01UIjsKCSJiaWQiIDOgImNvbS5kcmFnb25mb3JnZS51Zm8iOwoJInZ
lcmlzaWFsU2NpIjsKCSJidnJzIiA9ICIxLjAiOwp9";
        "environment" = "Sandbox";
        "pod" = "100";
        "signing-status" = "0";
}
```

Apple urges developers to check this receipt for validity. Although this step remains optional, checking it adds an extra layer of security and prevents users from activating your in-app purchases without having to pay for the content. Apple provides two servers for you to validate reciepts against: one for Sandbox enviroments, and one for shipping software, as described in Table 11–1.

Table 11–1. *Server Addresses for Verifying Receipts with Apple*

Enviroment	Server Address
Sandbox	sandbox.itunes.apple.com
Production	buy.itunes.apple.com

Joe D'Andrea posted two methods to help your checking for valid receipts on Stack Overflow (http://stackoverflow.com/questions/1298998). His approach is streamlined and efficient with no outside dependencies, so I have included it here for your convenience.

```
-(BOOL)verifyReceipt:(SKPaymentTransaction *)transaction
{
    NSString *jsonObjectString = [self encode:(uint8_t *)↵
transaction.transactionReceipt.bytes length:transaction.transactionReceipt.length];
    NSString *completeString = [NSString stringWithFormat:↵
@"http://url-for-your-php?receipt=%@", jsonObjectString];
    NSURL *urlForValidation = [NSURL URLWithString:completeString];
    NSMutableURLRequest *validationRequest = [[NSMutableURLRequest alloc]↵
 initWithURL:urlForValidation];
    [validationRequest setHTTPMethod:@"GET"];
    NSData *responseData = [NSURLConnection sendSynchronousRequest:↵
validationRequest returningResponse:nil error:nil];
    [validationRequest release];
    NSString *responseString = [[NSString alloc] initWithData:responseData↵
 encoding: NSUTF8StringEncoding];
    NSInteger response = [responseString integerValue];
    [responseString release];
    return (response == 0);
}

- (NSString *)encode:(const uint8_t *)input length:(NSInteger)length
{
    static char table[] =↵
"ABCDEFGHIJKLMNOPQRSTUVWXYZabcdefghijklmnopqrstuvwxyz0123456789+/=";
    NSMutableData *data = [NSMutableData dataWithLength:((length + 2) / 3) * 4];
    uint8_t *output = (uint8_t *)data.mutableBytes;
    for (NSInteger i = 0; i < length; i += 3) {
        NSInteger value = 0;
        for (NSInteger j = i; j < (i + 3); j++) {
            value <<= 8;
            if (j < length) {
                value |= (0xFF & input[j]);
            }
        }

        NSInteger index = (i / 3) * 4;
        output[index + 0] =                     table[(value >> 18) & 0x3F];
        output[index + 1] =                     table[(value >> 12) & 0x3F];
        output[index + 2] = (i + 1) < length ? table[(value >> 6)  & 0x3F] : '=';
```

```
        output[index + 3] = (i + 2) < length ? table[(value >> 0)  & 0x3F] : '=';
    }

    return [[[NSString alloc] initWithData:data encoding:NSASCIIStringEncoding]↩
autorelease];
}
```

After you have added these two methods to your project, you simply need to call verifyReceipt with the transaction that was returned to you, and then perform a boolean test to see whether it is valid. This concludes all the steps that you need to take to check a receipt for authenticity.

This method of verifying receipts requires you to host an intermediate server, attached is a very stripped-down PHP script to validate receipts.

```
$receipt = json_encode(array("receipt-data" => $_GET["receipt"]));
// NOTE: use "buy" vs "sandbox" in production.
$url = "https://sandbox.itunes.apple.com/verifyReceipt";
$response_json = call-your-http-post-here($url, $receipt);
$response = json_decode($response_json);
// Save the data here!
print $response->{'status'};
```

Tying Everything Together in UFOs

Depending on the complexity of your in-app purchase, it could be very easy or very difficult to integrate it into your code. In UFOs, we have a very simple product, in which paying a one-time fee unlocks a different colored ship. When the user purchases the product, we store a key in our user defaults to reflect that. To unlock this purchase in code, we simply check for that key, and then perform the required steps. To do this, we need to add some new art assets to the project. These have already been included in the Chapter 11 sample code (available at the Apress web site).

After this is done, we need to modify our viewDidLoad method to change the ship's image. The following code snippet shows those changes.

```
-(void)viewDidLoad
{
    purchasedUpgrade = [[NSUserDefaults standardUserDefaults]↩
boolForKey:@"shipPlusAvailable"];
    CGRect playerFrame = CGRectMake(100, 70, 80, 34);
    myPlayerImageView = [[UIImageView alloc] initWithFrame: playerFrame];
    myPlayerImageView.animationDuration = 0.75;
    myPlayerImageView.animationRepeatCount = 99999;
    NSArray *imageArray;

    if (purchasedUpgrade) {
        imageArray = [NSArray arrayWithObjects: [UIImage imageNamed:↩
@"Ship1.png"], [UIImage imageNamed: @"Ship2.png"], nil];
    } else {
        imageArray = [NSArray arrayWithObjects: [UIImage imageNamed:↩
@"Saucer1.png"], [UIImage imageNamed: @"Saucer2.png"], nil];
    }
```

```
    myPlayerImageView.animationImages = imageArray;
    [myPlayerImageView startAnimating];
    [self.view addSubview: myPlayerImageView];
}
```

Summary

In this chapter, we covered StoreKit and in-app purchases. By leveraging StoreKit, you gain a number of new ways to monetize your app, from expandable content to special upgrades for your users. You should now feel confident adding a variety of products to your own in-app store. Although StoreKit isn't directly a part of Game Center or Game Kit, you will undoubtedly find an in-app store an invaluable addition to your iOS software.

We spent some time talking about ngmoco:) and its experiments and successes with the Freemium model. You should now feel confident with iTunes Connect and all the actions that are required to fully set up an in-app purchase product, as well as the required code to get that purchase to display.

We looked at how to handle failures with purchasing and also the path of a success. We also explored some of the advanced topics, such as validating receipts and multiple purchases at once. Lastly, we saw how we integrated the entire experience into our UFOs demo app.

Index

CPSIA information can be obtained at www.ICGtesting.com
Printed in the USA
LVOW050852061111

253690LV00003B/59/P